Desire and the Devil

American University Studies

Series II
Romance Languages and Literature
Vol. 159

PETER LANG
New York · San Francisco · Bern
Frankfurt am Main · Paris · London

Carlo Testa

Desire and the Devil

Demonic Contracts in French and European Literature

PETER LANG
New York · San Francisco · Bern
Frankfurt am Main · Paris · London

Library of Congress Cataloging-in-Publication Data

Testa, Carlo.
    Desire and the devil : demonic contracts in French and European literature / Carlo Testa.
        p. cm. — (American university studies. Series II, Romance languages and literature ; vol. 159)
        Includes bibliographical references.
        1. Devil in literature. 2. European literature—History and criticism. 3. French literature—History and criticism. 4. Desire in literature. I. Title. II. Series.
PN57.D4T4   1991   809'.93382—dc20   90-28412
ISBN 0-8204-1439-5   CIP
ISSN 0740-9257

© Peter Lang Publishing, Inc., New York 1991

All rights reserved.
Reprint or reproduction, even partially, in all forms such as microfilm, xerography, microfiche, microcard, offset strictly prohibited.

Printed in the United States of America.

Se livrer à Satan, qu'est-ce que c'est?
[No answer].

Baudelaire, *Fusées* XIV

De la vaporisation et de la centralisation du *Moi*.
Tout est là.

Baudelaire, *Mon cœur mis à nu*, I, 1

Acknowledgements

This book is entirely labor-donated; it has received no institutional support—financial or otherwise. To all the Offices solicited, whether located (as Heine would have put it) at the estuary of the Sacramento, on the banks of the Potomac, or somewhere near the Seine, I would like to express here my sincere gratitude: they have offered me a unique opportunity to be less embarrassed by the evident shortcomings of the present work and to feel a stronger sense of property toward its accomplishments—however minuscule these may be.

The same applies to the few individuals who found my research project, even in its embryonal stage, significant enough to justify their resolutely opposing it.

In recognition of the trust and esteem which my father has always shown toward my studies over the past many years, I would like to express to him here my most sincere appreciation. Without his work, my work would have never been possible.

I am deeply grateful to Profs. Bersani, Gasparov and Isaac, who, directly or indirectly, stimulated and inspired many conceptual notions essential to my project. Without their teaching, guidance and patient advice the latter would have never seen the light.

A further, special word of gratitude goes to those—my Mentors in other departments and universities, relatives, friends in Europe and North America, acquaintances, or simply Others—who, in the course of my long labor, have shared with me the pangs it entailed, without, for many reasons, being able to discern its advantages.

Sections of the Balzac and Bulgakov chapters have appeared in earlier versions respectively in *The Comparatist* (Vol. 14, May 1990) and *Canadian-American Slavic Studies / Revue Canadienne Américaine d'Études Slaves* (vol. 24:3, Fall 1990). I wish to thank both journals for their kind permission to revise my articles and publish them here in book form.

I am also indebted to the Museum "Het Rembrandthuis" in Amsterdam for its generous permission to reproduce Rembrandt's "Dr. Faustus" etching (ca. 1652).

Quotes from French texts are in the original. Quotes from other languages are translated. Unless otherwise indicated, all translations are mine. So are, of course, all errors.

Contents

Preliminary Notes

    I. Desire, Devil, The Other: The Uses of Demonic Literature   p.   1

    II. The Devil-Pact As Foregrounding Device: Gautier de Coinci, Rutebeuf, Spieß   p.   9

    III. Goethe's *Faust* and the Quest For the Lost Desire   p. 15

1. *Balzac's Laicized Demonism*

    I. Devil-Contracts In *La Comédie humaine*: Between Money and Mandarins   p. 31

    II. *La peau de chagrin* and the Dialectic of Energy   p. 36

    III. Vautrin and Utopia   p. 68

2. *Disrupting the Canon, Pulverizing the Self: Flaubert*

    I. Desire In Textual Wilderness   p. 77

    II. *La Tentation de Saint Antoine*: The Book About Everything   p. 84

    III. Flaubert and the Evacuation of Utopia   p. 121

3. *Bulgakov: The "Evil One" and the "evil ones"*

    I. The Diffraction of Evil   p. 129

    II. *The Master and Margarita*: Utopia In Times of Anguish   p. 136

    III. *Bêtise* and Others   p. 155

Appendix. *Gérard de Nerval: The "Beautiful Idiot"*   p. 161

Works Cited   p. 181

Index   p. 189

Desire and the Devil

Preliminary Notes

I

Desire, Devil, The Other: The Uses of Demonic Literature

There seems to be something intrinsically frustrating in attempting to define desire in general and in abstract. In all likelihood, its essence can ultimately be defined only by a tautology: desire is any *production of preference* leading to a choice that *appeals to the self*. As J. Bem effectively puts it, "le désir [...] n'a jamais parlé dans un langage articulé qui aurait été travesti ensuite. Du désir on ne connaîtra jamais le fond, seulement le texte qu'il travaille" (Bem 1979, 227).

An inquiry into the ontological status of desire seems to be doomed to inconclusiveness by an inevitable begging of the question. What is admissible, however, is the problematization of a plurality of concrete forms, a multitude of aspects of desire. While desire may well be a sort of twentieth-century companion to the Kantian notion of the abstractly unknowable thing-in-itself, the "obscure" (if empirically useful) notion called desire can successfully bring under a common denominator psychic processes which it would otherwise be impossible to synthesize and literary phenomena that could not otherwise be put to work to produce sense in a common direction.[1]

*

We do, of course, know from Lacan that desire is always desire for the Other—for an Other which is outside the self, separated from it by mutual absence. Absence is the empty space, the gap in reality, in which desire and the Other coexist, but in which, similar in this to Ulysses and the Sirens (to apply here the metaphor used by Blanchot in *Le livre à venir*), they are never allowed to make contact with each other, or halt, "fix" their floating (Blanchot 1959, 9-11). There is no desire without Other; and the unfathomability of the ultimate definition of desire is really the specular image of the impossibility to define the Other univocally.

The Other is not a fixed notion—a name, or a modifier of one; it is a shifter, in the full sense of the word. The concept "Other" functions like a pronoun, indicating different individuals or entities as it is applied to different contexts. Indeed, it could be argued that it is a perverse pronoun, designating, as it does, always "something else", "someone else" than those it purports to be naming each time. "The Other" is the pronoun of absence, the non-pronoun; it is the materialization of emptiness. The Other is a *liquid* notion—mobility itself. It does not obey the law of non-contradiction. And equally capable of self-contradiction is the desire which the Other activates.

But why are "the Sirens" of Otherness a threat? Why has desire been perceived as a danger? These are the theoretical questions to which I would indirectly like to contribute through my analysis of the demonic genre.

Fascination, enslavement, destruction of the self are notions which, in literature, have structured the history of desire—and of the demonic. My goal is to examine at a few significant, critical points the curve traced in the history of Western literature by the theme of the pact with the devil, in order to analyze and interpret some of the most important phases which it has undergone. The present work could be defined as an historico-cultural inquiry ultimately wishing to help elucidate the supra-temporal dilemma represented by the dual status of the Other.

*

Desire as fascinating, enslaving, destroying the self—what would best qualify it to be considered for definition as *demonic*? Not unlike desire, the devil, too, is the locus of opposite poles: fulfillment and danger, plenitude and punishment. Not unlike desire, the devil, too, is an oxymoron: its essence promises satisfaction, but the ugliness of its outward appearance reminds of an element of repulsiveness contained in it.

The literature centered on the demonic is, *par excellence*, the literature centered around the notion of desire. The Other in which desire circulates is but the de-anthropomorphized formulation of what pre-modern times described by a tangible image—the enticing threat proposed by the devil. In Slavic fairytales, in Russian Romantic literature, in folklore, and, to this day, by and large in popular belief as well, one of the recurrent names used to designate the Unnameable, the unspeakable paradox of the devil, is, not by chance, its Other Name: *Drugoy*—The Other.[2]

As Merezhkovsky put it in an illuminating text devoted to Gogol's art, Otherness is the ultimate "demonic" weapon:

> The greatest power the devil possesses is his capacity to look like something he is not. Though a median, he looks like one of the two extremes [...]
> Though a creature, he seems like a creator; though dark, he seems like the dayspring; though inert, he seems winged; though laughable, he seems to be laughing.
>
> (Merezhkovsky 1974, 59)

The devil can then be seen as a multiple entity capable of self-contradictorily assuming opposite meanings. Its physical Protean attitudes are well-known to the traditional repertoire of literature; these qualities are but an external trace of a moral condition. In literature, the Shifter / *Drugoy* / the Other can work in any number of ways with respect to human desire: it can materialize it, catalyze it, give it new power—or, by contrast, stifle it, advance treacherous propositions, betray the human. How? and why?

*

If we consider the devil-pact literature of modern Europe, we can point out a number of important formal facts which can be useful starting points for an analysis of the complex role of the demonic.

Firstly, the devil in the literary text is at best an ambiguous Mentor. Generally, what is readily acknowledged of the literary devil is its role of a more or less subservient "procurer of pleasures" for a hedonistic human being. Such a description is, of course, at times accurate, but it is far from exhausting the gamut of possibilities. Typically, this kind of devil is active in texts that emphasize a religious message: the Theophilus legend, for example, or Spieß's Faustbook, to name but the most famous in the group. In post-Klingerian times, roughly after the beginning of the nineteenth century, the situation has become extremely diversified, at least in literature "proper". In its ambivalence, Klinger's *Faust* marks a pivotal point—the transition between a receding hedonism and a developing decarnalization of desire. Goethe's "tragedy" will turn the devil's inadequacy into nothing less than its own supporting theme.

Sometimes the devil even appears as an outright enemy of the self. This is particularly true of Gérard de Nerval. For Balzac, the demonic offers satisfaction of desire, but does so by swindling the human out of something which to the hedonist is of much greater value than the soul: namely, life itself. As for Flaubert, the devil is for him so removed from being a procurer that it does not even manage to secure its own existence—it commits suicide by hyperbolic doubt before Saint Antony's very eyes.

Bulgakov's *The Master and Margarita* is the one work in which, to my knowledge, he who was traditionally called "the enemy of mankind" actually delivers satisfaction to the protagonists' desire. This, however, is only allowed to happen because the two lovers of Bulgakov's novel live in an almost fairytale-like distopic world which segregates and persecutes them: there, the devil can exceptionally accomplish the miraculous *tour de force* of protecting the honest, persecuting a wicked or stupid humanity, and satisfying the commands of a just God—all in one and the same stroke.

Human desire is far from concurring *tout court* with the "unclean spirit". There are moments and situations when the two seem to cooperate, but the opposite is more often true. This happens, of course, in Goethe's *Faust*, in which Mephisto's goal is to stifle, freeze, castrate the unbridled movement of Faust's polymorphous desire; and it applies, for example, to Nerval's Faustian fragments, as well as *L'imagier de Harlem*, whose Satan is an ally of the money-maker capitalist fathers and intends to frustrate the various inventors' efforts to enlighten humanity. In short, the devil's role in the history of the demonic genre has varied enormously; indeed, the history of the literature of the demonic can be described as the history of the mutations undergone by the textual functions of the supernatural partner in the pact.

Whether the devil is a mediator, a facilitator toward hedonism; or an enemy; or whether it oscillates between the two extremes—in all cases, the devil is the trace of an ongoing struggle between desire and an interdiction. Whichever side the devil takes in the plot of each given text is a function of the authors' personal world views and of the free play of their subconscious associations. The essential fact remains that the devil's deformed traits represent visually the self-portrait of the human in whom interdiction and desire are at war with each other (the self becoming then schizophrenically estranged from itself). The devil is, among other things, the displaced trace of an internal battle.

In the wake of Freud's *Interpretation Of Dreams*, Jones develops this notion in the context of the oneiric activity. The nightmare—the *incubus*—is for Jones the self's camouflaged way to formulate an inacceptable desire. In literature, experimenting with the devil figure has the same meaning: regardless of whose side the devil may take in the plot, it expresses the intention to bypass an interdiction. And, while the devil is not always an indispensable figure to express such transgressivity, it is by all means a convenient shortcut—an effective *device*—in order to implement it in and by the text.

*

What are the uses of the demonic contract? What appeal does the pact with the devil have for the writer of fiction who envisages to create "a story"? Or, in more formal terms: what does the devil-as-device *foreground*?

The answers to this question can be as different from one another as the authors themselves, and the epochs and civilizations in which they wrote. Yet the hypothesis can be advanced that not just the demonic in general, but the specific notion of a contract with the demonic (whatever its forms) offers the writer the best frame for a number of different effects: e.g., for the depiction of diverse and extreme forms of desire; or, alternatively, for the illustration of the threat implicit in the fulfillment of forbidden drives (a price, incidentally, often happily paid as a cover for the portrayal of that which is censored in direct representation). Authors of all times have been enticed by the convenience of a flexible experimentation with the hermeneutical availability of the devil figure in a wide range of identifications-projections.

Last but not least, the theme of the pact with the devil lends itself to a particularly intense, dramatic treatment of the subject matter by offering full use of a royal path to the *supernatural*. Especially in epochs and societies in which the supernatural has experienced a loss of epistemological value (although by no means only in those), the literary theme of the pact with the devil remains as perhaps the only viable *intellectual laboratory* in which it is somehow still licit and permissible to bracket out the "intermediate cases" recommended by an aesthetic of representational realism, and to experiment with the extremes instead. *What if ... ?*: such is the intellectual gesture presiding over the thought not resigned to accept the fact that "ifs" cannot be tested in reality.

These circumstances explain why there is a strong tendency toward universalization in literary works that treat the theme of the demonic contract. Such works tend to broach ultimate, universal questions about the meaning of the cosmos. One could justifiably describe them as philosophical, or perhaps more accurately—since every work of literature implies a philosophical stand, whether the author foregrounds it or not—as *explicitly* philosophical. A possible equivalent definition would be to categorize them as (tendentially) metalinguistic vis-à-vis the universe.

Whatever the wording, the pact with the devil clearly proves to be an ideal literary device for the author to consciously experiment with different ways of totalizing the world.

It is probable that, well beyond the persistence of the actual religious belief in God and devil, the authors' temptation to have recourse to the literary demonic contract as a device will regularly return, so long as they will consciously intend to sketch the model of a *system* explaining—or judging, or illustrating—the mechanisms of the world as a whole. If this should happen in total abstraction from the reality of transcendental entities, then the notion of the demonic will complete the transition from the ontological to the symbolic, and will be permanently anchored in the latter. This indeed is the path taken by the contemporary tendency toward an historico-materialistic reassessment of the notion of evil and by its ironic stylization in denouncing, for example, the effects of contemporary world imperialism.[3]

In sum, the name of the Other is truly the model-case of the Montaignean "salad", which "remains a salad" no matter what is tossed into it: "Quelque diversité d'herbes qu'il y ait, tout s'enveloppe sous le nom de salade" (Montaigne, *Essais*, Bk. I, Ch. XLVI). Similarly, the Other remains (or *becomes*) the Other not in spite of but precisely *by virtue of* the diversity of successive additions, accretions, contradictions. The devil is the Other—the "salad"—standing for the world of subconscious, repressed desire.

The devil can best be read as the eternal *Drugoy* of folklore—Other than God, Other than man, Other than desire, and also ever-varied, ever Other-than-itself. The plurality of the relationships which the Other entertains with the self is paralleled only by (because identical with) the infinite plurality of the relations that tie the human self to the ceaseless variability of its own desire.

*

Just as, in religious contexts, the devil represents the Other-than-God, on the psychological plane desire represents the threatening Other-than-Man. Man's desire, however, is an Other which is at the same time the Same, the same one psychological reality divided unto itself, allowing the self to exist positively only by virtue of its negation and limitation in "opaque", contingent matter.

Desire, the "alienating" Other-than-the-Self, is the condition without which the self cannot exist; it is the finite enunciation in which the enouncer comes to being. The self begins to exist only when its transparent indetermination is "obscured", "materialized" by a specific investment through the Other. *Non-desiring is signifying nothing*: a self without desire is a self that does not produce meaning—it is, strictly speaking, a non-existent, undefinable "non-self".

Limitation and "opacity" being the preconditions for the self's existing / signifying-in-the-world, the complex cosmological definition which Goethe's Mephisto gives of his own fragmentariness, inchoateness, partial-ness can equally be applied to the partial-ness of human desire—indeed of man *tout court*, anchored and revealed in language only as a projection of an otherwise unknowable noumenal Being:

> While man, this tiny world of fools, is droll
> Enough to think himself a whole,
> I am part of the part that once was everything,
> Part of the darkness which gave birth to light,
> That haughty light which envies mother night
> Her ancient rank and place and would be king—
> Yet it does not succeed: however it contend,
> It sticks to bodies in the end.
> It streams from bodies, it lends bodies beauty,
> A body won't let it progress;
> So it will not take long, I guess,
> And with the bodies it will perish, too.
> (Goethe, *Faust*, vv. 1347-58; transl. Kaufmann 1961, 161)[4]

Pure light, not *alienated* in a body, is invisible.

By contrast, desire, created by the self as the self's own "obstacle", is the self's only possible signifier, trace-in-being, call to being—*and* its fatal call to death. My diachronic scanning of the metamorphoses undergone by this synchronic paradox attempts to turn an absence into a presence: I am consciously endeavoring to nest my work precisely in that gap—in the space *opened* by the epistemological difficulty consisting in the ultimate unspeakability of desire.

II
The Devil-Pact As Foregrounding Device: Gautier de Coinci, Rutebeuf, Spieß

The theme of the pact with the devil is one of the most pervasive ones in Western literature and can be traced back to the most remote antiquity. From Biblical times until the Romantic era, and well into the twentieth century with Bulgakov and Mann, each epoch has re-evaluated and re-interpreted the pact theme by stressing its different aspects, and by *foregrounding*—i.e., emphasizing narratively—in each case the features that are most closely connected with its own existential quest.[5]

The sources, early history, and pre-modern developments of the theme of the pact with the devil are highlighted in DiAmico's "The Diabolical Pact In Literature". A series of definite cycles can be detected in the evolution of the pact theme:

> [A] simple seed born out of the Biblical tradition germinated into a rich literary motif. The period encompassing the III through the IX centuries is basically dominated by the early Greek legends and it could be distinguished as the first cycle in the motif's evolution. The period starting with the X century and ending with the XV, constituted by Latin reelaborations of the Greek legends and by a long series of medieval devil-pact stories, represents the second cycle. Both cycles have one thing in common: practically always, they relegate the "pact" to the function of an *exemplum*, thereby stifling its artistic evolution.
> By the end of the XIV century, the motif appears almost dead of exhaustion. During the XV century, however, it reappears, full of vigor and ready to start its third and most important literary cycle. By the XVI century, the motif becomes a source of inspiration to poets of great genius and finally begins its ascent towards truly great artistic heights.
> Two very important literary traditions characterize the evolution of this third cycle—one Latin and Catholic, the other basically Germanic and Protestant, both of which finally culminate in [...] Goethe's *Faust*.
> (DiAmico 1979, 160-61)

The filiation between the "first cycle" and the subsequent stages of the pact theme constitutes a historical and philological question with which DiAmico himself and other authors deal extensively: from the early Greek stories of Cyprian and Justina, Protherius, Anthemius, and above all Theophilus, there develop the medieval legends centered around Gerbert d'Aurillac and Militarius, the later dramas of the Spanish *Siglo de Oro*, and the *corpus faustianum*, which represents perhaps more than a cycle in itself (Rudwin, 1931; Dédéyan, 1954-1967; DiAmico, 1979).[6]

As for the nineteenth and twentieth centuries, no works written after Faust's *Tragödie* could ignore Goethe's work (and those who did, did so as a deliberate choice contesting Goethe's philosophical premises). Since the appearance of Goethe's philosophical poem the domains of the devil-compact theme and that of Faust have been pulled together more than ever, and their boundaries have been made to coincide more and more closely—arbitrarily perhaps, but understandably, given the immense echo of Goethe's work.[7] The Faust theme being only one of the innumerable possible variations on the theme of the demonic compact, I will not privilege here the analysis of Goethe's masterpiece; it is in fact more fruitful to emphasize instead the differences in the ways in which, in historical perspective, successive works highlight different relations between the self and desire.

The salient feature of the works belonging to the pre-Goethean tradition—the lineage which DiAmico calls the "three cycles" in the history of the genre— is that they all have a canonic, orthodox view of the pact with the devil. They are all *texts foregrounding a message*. Their message is simple: eternal damnation is no joking matter—*on ne badine pas avec le diable*. They show no particular questioning of the interaction between desire and the self: texts of religious orthodoxy tend to assume spontaneity and simplicity of the desiring process. The elements stressed are, by contrast, difficulty of fulfillment, dangerous moral or practical consequences (whether in this world or in the next).

The first devil-pact text relevant for our purposes is the legend of Theophilus, in the form which it received in Gautier de Coinci's and Rutebeuf's works (resp., ed. Koenig 1955; Kreßner 1885). At this early stage in the cycle, the main interest of the two poets is completely absorbed in the Christian world view. Theophilus's desire is seen in a polarized, black-and-white form; desire is here as simple as an instinct—it is truly *appetitus naturalis*. Having been deprived of worldly honor and power, Theophilus merely wants to win them back.

Gautier has the devil tempt Theophilus:

> Li decevans qui seit maint tor
> Jor et nuit tant tornoie entor
> Et tant l'asaut et tant le tente
> Et tant durement le tormente
> Et tant l'esprent d'ardeur et d'ire
> Ne seit que faire ne que dire.
>
> (Gautier, vv. 127-32)

Theophilus quickly succumbs and recurs to the services of "un gïu [...] / Qui tant d'engien et d'art savoit, / [...] / Que devant lui apertement / Faisoit venir a parlement / Les anemis et les dyables" (vv. 159-65). When the magician appears,

> Theophilus, qu'avait espris
> Vainne gloire trop durement,
> As piez li chiet isnelement.
>
> (Gautier, vv. 188-91)

Theophilus's psychology is here reduced to an embodiment of *vana gloria*, and for Gautier de Coinci the form and origin of his pride are non-problematic—an irrelevant factor.[8] The Biblical model of Adam and Eve's fall is here decisive: Theophilus's fall is abrupt and complete. The possible interior debate within the main character is externalized, theatricalized in an actual dialogue between the protagonist's own centralized self and the equally centralized, real self of the Other, which tempts him from the outside. (Such a splitting of roles is, of course, precisely the principle that allows the poet to endow the devil with anthropomorphic consistence). Clearly, in Gautier de Coinci's text the transcendental existence of the Evil One is taken for granted, and nothing is more possible and "natural" than Theophilus's collapse. For the author, foregrounding the process of Theophilus's fall would be tantamount to opening a debate on the dogma of man's original sin—in his perspective, an obvious absurdity.

Theophilus's wishes being instinctive and direct, he expresses them to the "Jewish magician" with perfect spontaneity. His speech typifies simplicity and naïvety of desire:

> — Sire, fait il, por Dieu, merci!
> Tant ai le cuer taint et noirci
> Por un petit je ne part d'ire.
> Mes evesques, mes noviaus sire,
> Qui Diex destruie, ensi l'assol,
> Bouté m'a jus de delassol
> Et mis en aré en espace.
> Si sui dolens ne sai que face.
> Tolue m'a ma seignorie:
> S'en ai tel duel et tele envie
> Por un petit d'ire ne crief.
> Se je par vos n'en vien a chief
> Et je par vos ne rai m'oneur,
> Morir m'estuet a desoneur.
>
> (Gautier, vv. 191-204)

Human nature being, in Christian perspective, tainted by original sin, it is only logical that Theophilus's desire to win back power and worldly glory should be an unproblematic factor in Gautier de Coinci's text. All the tension in the plot lies—here as in most literature of the demonic written in the mode of the religious *exemplum*—on the consequences of desire (repentance or eternal damnation) rather than on its genesis and aporias. For Gautier, desire is centered on the polarity *oneur-desoneur*: desiring *oneur* is natural, instinctive—and sinful; desiring *desoneur* is not quite as natural—*but* it is Christian. The element foregrounded in Gautier de Coinci's text is the conflict which the true Christian has to face between the "corrupt naturality" of worldly desires, on one hand, and on the other hand the necessary, but supremely difficult sacrifice of freely assuming upon oneself that crushing weight of humility which the early Christian apologists had provokingly come to describe as "the shame of the Cross".

In a dialogized version, Rutebeuf's Theophilus proposes essentially the same drama of the conflict between the world's apparent wisdom and God's true wisdom, which appears as folly to men. Shortly before the end, the text offers us a useful summary of a paradigmatic demonic pact as it gives us once more, in a dense structure *en abyme*, an instinctive, spontaneous illustration of worldly desire:

> [...] Theophiles ot a l'evesque rancune,
> Ne li lessa l'evesque seignorie nesune.
> Il fu desesperez quant l'en li fist l'outrage;
> A Salatin s'en vint qui ot el cors la rage,
> Et dist qu'il li feroit molt volentiers homage,
> Se rendre li pooit s'onor et son domage.
>   (Rutebeuf, vv. 642-47)

The devil's own words condense in a nutshell the simple logic of the events:

> [...] lors me fist homage, si r'ot sa seignorie.
>   (Rutebeuf, v. 651)

But instinctiveness of desire obviously does not mean theological innocence. The Christian problematization of the pact with the devil lodges precisely in this contradiction—in the existential "absurdity" of human *guilty spontaneity*, and in the difficulty of coming to terms with it.

When Theophilus complains to Salatins: "Qu'on m'apeloit seignor et mestre / De cest pais, ce ses tu bien; / Or ne me lesse on nule rien!" (vv. 48-50); when he specifies the very concrete object of his desire: "Por quoi je peusse r'avoir / M'onor, ma baillie et ma grace" (vv. 78-79); when Salatins, in an equally telling way, promises: "Quanques tes sires t'a mesfet / T'amendera, / Et plus forment t'onorera, / Et plus grant seignor te fera / Qu'onques ne fus" (vv. 207-11), we realize how compact and intuitive the notion of secular desire is in Rutebeuf's feudal-Christian medieval universe. Accordingly, the problematizing of the desiring process must of necessity be shifted outside desire proper and inscribed into the realm of the conflict between the worldly and the spiritual order of things.

The climax of Rutebeuf's drama is thus to be found in Theophilus's anguished *confusion of different orders*:

> Diex m'a grevé, jel greverai;
> James jor ne le servirai,
>   Je li ennui.
> Riches serai se povres sui;
> Se il me het, je harrai lui.
>
> (Rutebeuf, vv. 133-37)

Rather than questioning desire, Theophilus's mistake points to the difficulty experienced by the Christian soul in struggling its way to understanding the incompatibility of two conflicting entities: the world of feudal fidelity to a human lord, and the Other-worldly realm of Grace, where fidelity to the divine Lord can no longer be conceived in the strictly human terms of chivalric virtue. One step beyond Theophilus, medieval literature finds the ultimate expression of this conflict in Wolfram's *Parzival* and in its conscious foregrounding of the dishomogeneity and discontinuity existing between the human and the religious levels (or "cycles") of education.

Spieß's Protestant *Faustbuch* of 1587, however different it may be in its theological and historical significance from other legends of devil compacts rooted in Catholicism, does have an aspect in common with its predecessors: it, too, "automatizes" (in Mukarovsky's terms) the notion of desire and presents it as an instinctive fact. The center of gravity in this particular type of pact is shifted toward the threat of the eternal punishment.[9] As Mayer writes,

> Dr. Faust's chapbook [...] was Protestant literature of warning. Do not let yourself be seduced. The pitiful end of the *archmagician* ["Erzzauberer"] was depicted with pleasure. "This is what happens to one who ... " [...]
> Protestant orthodoxy did not seem to be ready to give divine Grace a chance when dealing with a man who had signed the demonic contract with his blood.
> (Mayer 1979, 21)

Indeed, in the perspective of a critical evaluation of the relationship between the self and desire, the most problematic aspect of Spieß's book can perhaps be located in the disproportionately gruesome, hair-raising punishment incurred by Faust, which condemns without return what is after all a joyous and "innocent" attitude toward life. Faust's tricks are often no more evil than many of the student pranks narrated in the most widely circulated late Medieval collections of novellas and short stories (the chapbook of Eulenspiegel, Pauli's *Schimpf und Ernst*, etc.), and they represent part of a childlike, bulimic *joie de vivre* directed toward the whole of the universe.

Desire is as natural to Spieß's Dr. Faust as eating is natural to Gargantua and Pantagruel—and for exactly the same reasons: *curiositas* toward the cosmos in the spirit of the Renaissance, world-immanent orientation of the spirit, and rejection of medieval theological fixed systems.[10] Here, the pitiless, shocking form of Faust's end has the effect of foregrounding the irrevocable incompatibility of the two orders in conflict: secular desire and religious faith. In Spieß's book the two remain mutually independent factors, each of which can be either totally accepted or totally rejected, but not analyzed within itself.

These and similar situations, in which desire is unproblematic, and in which the conflict with an opposed force is problematized instead, partake of what I will refer to as a "traditional" notion of desire—i.e., a tradition established by centuries of religious orthodoxy. Needless to say, in literature a series of variations all moving in the same direction may also, in turn, dialectically establish a new canon. In the due course of time, this is precisely what occurred in the Goethean and post-Goethean demonic tradition, more and more resolutely drifting away from the "orthodox" distribution of emphasis on the respective components of the text.

III

Goethe's *Faust* and the Quest For the Lost Desire

With increasing frequency, the first half of the nineteenth century ceased to use desire as a means to narrate stories of the devil; rather, the reverse became more and more visibly true, and the devil was used as a device for the purpose of asking, in the most general way, *what desire is*. In other words, in the epoch in question the devil was transformed into an instrument for a series of aesthetic inquiries into an ultimately philosophical problem. Such a radical problematization of desire was among the most genuinely innovative notions in the general reaccentuation of literary themes that took place in Europe in the Romantic period.

In this context, it simply would not be conceivable to neglect Goethe's *Faust*, which is probably the single most impressive—and most widely known—literary text written on the subject: among all other things, *Faust* also arguably is the most explicit one on the theme of desire. While recognizing that its vastness cannot be reduced to the mere foregrounding of the notions which interest us here, I am claiming that it "carries" its other meanings *through* the narrative device of such problematization. My reading of *Faust* leaves philological questions in the background and moves in the direction of a text-immanent quest for a coherent authorial *prise de position* on the subject.

Faust is the man of *desire beyond desire*. His dissatisfaction with life, as we witness it since his first appearance in the cabinet, is a dissatisfaction with the concrete forms of fulfillment which hold for the masses. His desire is desire for infinity; novelty is for him but a means toward that end. The crucial point, however, is that his quest is *not* a striving toward the accumulation of new forms: for Faust, whether new or old, forms are always by definition stillborn. The fantastic heaps of objects cluttering his cabinet are eloquent enough signs that the accumulation of *les formes et les êtres*, be they physical or intellectual, is for him the most poisonous possibility of desire. Against fixation, Faust propounds life, action; in the forms, Faust yearns to see the Formless—the Universe. What he seeks is the immediate intuition of the Macrocosm. Such is the meaning of the three main points which Goethe reaccentuates in his innovating upon the traditional legend, namely:

—Faust as a man already at the apex of his earthly career;
—the evocation of the Spirit of the Earth, and the latter's rejection of Faust's plea;

—the meditation on the New Testament words: "In the beginning was *the Act*" (v. 1237; transl. Kaufmann 1961, 153).

The pursuit of *desire beyond forms* is the structural theme of Faust's *Streben*. The rejection of traditional science, Faust's desire to flee out into the world and into the open air, his pride in confronting the Spirit of the Earth, his desire to (literally) *reinvent tradition* moment by moment, are all factors that eloquently testify to this mobile condition:

> What from your fathers you received as heir,
> Acquire if you would possess it.
> What is not used is but a load to bear;
> But if today creates it, we can use and bless it.
> (vv. 682-85; Kaufmann, 115)

Faust insists on the notion of his dissatisfaction with concrete, immanent desires. In his second meeting with Mephistopheles in the study, he laments the disproportion existing between the totality of the expectation, and the accidentality and pettiness of its concrete fulfillment:

> Frightened I wake to the dismal dawn,
> Wish I had tears to drown the sun
> And check the day that soon will scorn
> My every wish—fulfill not one.
> If I but think of any pleasure,
> Bright critic day is sure to chide it,
> And if my heart creates itself a treasure,
> A thousand mocking masks deride it [...]
>
> The god that dwells within my heart
> Can stir my depths, I cannot hide—
> Rules all my powers with relentless art,
> But cannot move the world outside;
> And thus existence is for me a weight,
> Death is desirable, and life I hate.
> (vv. 1554-61, 1566-71; Kaufmann, 175)

Faust's desire is so strongly oriented toward infinity and the absolute, and at the same time so frustratingly insatiable, that he comes to the point of envying the men of concrete desires: he is tempted to wish for himself the peace of mind of those who can be content with glory or social pleasures (vv. 1573-76). However, although anguished by his own insatiable thirst for transcendental satisfaction, he explicitly condemns all contingent satisfaction of "fixed", i.e. concretely definable desires.

The passage deserves being quoted in some detail, as it specifies both Faust's rejection of the inanity of desire, and (somewhat contradictorily) his despair at no longer being capable to love concrete, contingent forms:

> I now curse all that would enamor
> The human soul with lures and lies,
> Enticing it with flattering glamour
> To live on in this cave of sighs.
> Cursed above all our high esteem,
> The spirit's smug self-confidence,
> Cursed be illusion, fraud, and dream
> That flatter our guileless sense!
> Cursed be the pleasing make-believe
> Of fame and long posthumous life!
> Cursed be possessions that deceive,
> As slave and plough, and child and wife!
> Cursed, too, be Mammon when with treasures
> He spurs us on to daring feats,
> Or lures us into slothful pleasures
> With sumptuous cushions and smooth sheets!
> A curse on wine that mocks our thirst!
> A curse on love's last consummation!
> A curse on hope! Faith, too, be cursed!
> And cursed above all else be patience!
>
> (vv. 1587-1606; Kaufmann, 177-79)

With an only partial simplification of Goethe's thought, one could state that Faust's pact with the devil is necessarily contracted in order to *win back* at least some form of desire.

As is well known, the peculiarity of Faust's pact is that it takes the conditional form of a wager:

> If ever I recline, calmed, on a bed of sloth,
> You may destroy me then and there.
> If ever flattering you should wile me
> That in myself I find delight,
> If with enjoyment you beguile me,
> Then break on me, eternal night!
> This bet I offer.
>
> (vv. 1692-98; Kaufmann, 183)

Reduced to its crudest form, the devil's bet could be reformulated as follows: "I bet that I will be able to imprison you, as all other humans, in the death of a contingent desire". Faust's answer is: "I bet that I will not be content with any of the dead hypostases of desire; I will only be content with desire *in its abstract form*" (which, granted, is an oxymoron and a logical impossibility).

In this respect, Faust's formulation of the pact in his address to Mephistopheles cannot be quoted too often:

> If to the moment I should say:
> Abide, you are so fair—
> Put me in fetters on that day,
> *I wish* to perish then, I swear.
> Then let the death bell ever toll,
> Your service done, you shall be free,
> The clock may stop, the hand may fall,
> As time comes to an end for me.
>
> (vv. 1699-1706; Kaufmann, 185; emphasis in the original)

Fulfilled desire is here called by Faust the equivalent of death.

Relatively less famous, but just as important in showing Faust's rejection of concrete, limited desires, is the incisive passage that follows. In it, Faust operates a complete reversal of the traditional pact-motif purposes. Far from being impelled by hedonism, Faust sees in gain and pleasure the worst enemies of his free-flowing drive:

> *Do you not hear, I have no thought of joy!*
> The reeling whirl I seek, the most painful excess,
> Enamored hate and quickening distress.
> Cured from the craving to know all, my mind

> Shall not henceforth be closed to any pain,
> And what is portioned out to all mankind,
> I shall enjoy deep in my self, contain
> Within my spirit summit and abyss,
> Pile on my breast their agony and bliss,
> And thus let my own self grow into theirs, unfettered,
> Till as they are, at least I, too, am shattered.
>   (vv. 1765-75; Kaufmann, 189; emphasis added)

The devil interprets well the situation: his snare is precisely the fallacious promise of desires which may arrest man's striving. Mephistopheles's function in Goethe is thus radically new, in that he not only and not so much promises to satisfy specific wishes—as had always been the case in the devil-pact tradition—but above all promises to "normalize" desire: to provide man with *satisfactory desires* in the first place. He not only explicitly promises the means for *jouissance* (for example, the famous six steeds of vv. 1824-25, which attracted Karl Marx's attention for a fundamental passage of his economico-philosophical manuscripts of 1844) but above all implicitly promises the very desire for enjoyment—which is precisely what Faust lacks, and what causes his despair.

In a sense, then, it could be argued that in their pact the two partners bet past each other. But Mephistopheles is well aware of the situation and simply intends to corrupt Faust into pleasure as they go. From his point of view, his plan is sensible: to the radical skeptic, to the man of movement Faust, standstill can only be proposed surreptitiously. One thus understands the logic of the strategy voiced by Mephistopheles:

> The spirit which he has received from fate
> Sweeps ever onward with unbridled might,
> Its hasty striving ["übereiltes Streben"] is so great
> It leaps over the earth's delights.
> Through life I'll drag him at a rate,
> Through shallow triviality,
> That he shall writhe and suffocate;
> And his insatiability,
> With greedy lips, shall see the choicest plate
> And ask in vain for all that he would cherish—
> And were he not the devil's mate

And had not signed, he still must perish.
(vv. 1856-67; Kaufmann, 195)

However, before we examine the outcome of the struggle between Faust, the spirit of infinite desire, and Mephistopheles, the spirit of partial, dead desires (a struggle which Goethe tellingly shows as being overseen by the paternal, protective eye of the Lord), we need to examine how Faust's desiring beyond and against fixed forms sharply conflicts with his assistant Wagner's scholarship.

Wagner, the *famulus*, has a contrastive role; his function in the poem is to give impressive relief to the novelty of Faust's endless striving. He marks the exact antipode to the master's infinite quest: a true Homais *ante litteram*, he illustrates in an exemplary way the notion of a scientific career all oriented toward worldly success and fame, blinded by a strictly immanent interpretation of science and knowledge. With a comic *skaz* he declaims:

> Oh God, art is forever,
> And our life is brief.
> I fear that with my critical endeavor
> My head and heart may come to grief.
> How hard the scholars' means are to array
> With which one works up to the source;
> Before we have traversed but half the course,
> We wretched devils pass away.
(vv. 558-65; Kaufmann, 107)

Goethe accentuates this effect by having Mephistopheles casually echo the same notion (v. 1787; Kaufmann, 189): "Time is too brief, though art's forever". The implication of the ironic quote is that Mephistopheles's best partner for the pact would be Wagner, rather than Faust. Only Wagner would be lowly enough to be content with the devil's help—whereas Faust's problematic quest soars above the pettiness of his ambitious adjutant's desires.

The affinity in narrowness of spirit explains the other main point of convergence between Wagner and Mephistopheles: the predilection they share for the fixity of the written word. Wagner craves to ingest the contents of the texts written down on the "smoky paper" (v. 405; Kaufmann, 97) of tradition. Similarly, the devil insists on putting on paper his contract with Faust—which elicits the latter's brusque reply: "You pedant need it black on white?" ("Auch was Geschriebnes forderst du Pedant?", v. 1716; Kaufmann, 185). Wagner is a pedant, and the devil is his true ideal sponsor. All the subsequent developments in *Faust* could, in a sense, be described as the story of a colossal mistake—the story of the wrong choice of a partner on Mephistopheles's part.

As in the best and most canonic of all possible *Bildungsromane*, Faust's desire for the infinite is opposed to Wagner's desire for finitude. One of the clearest expressions of this state of affairs is to be found in the dialogue which the two exchange outdoors at the moment of twilight:

> *Faust.* Oh, happy who still hopes to rise
> Out of this sea of errors and false views!
> What one does *not* know, one could utilize,
> And what one knows one cannot use [...]
>
> See how, touched by the sunset's parting power,
> The huts are glowing in the green.
> The sun moves on [...]
>
> Oh, that no wings lift me above the ground
> To strive and strive in his pursuit!
> ["Ihr nach und immer nach zu streben!"] [...]
>
> The spirit's wings will not change our shape:
> Our body grows no wings and cannot fly.
> Yet it is innate in our race
> That our feelings surge in us and long
> When over us, lost in the azure space
> The lark trills out her glorious song;
> When over crags where fir trees quake
> In icy winds, the eagle soars,
> And over plains and over lakes
> The crane returns to homeward shores.
>   (vv. 1064-67, 1070-75, 1090-99; Kaufmann, 141-43)

To which Wagner's exhilarating response is:

> I, too, have spells of eccentricity,

> But such unrest has never come to me.
> One soon grows sick of forest, field, and brook,
> And I shall never envy birds their wings.
> Far greater are the joys the spirit brings—
> From page to page, from book to book.
> Thus winter nights grow fair and warm the soul;
> Yes, blissful life suffuses every limb,
> And when one opens up an ancient parchment scroll,
> The very heavens will descend on him.
>   (vv. 1100-09; Kaufmann, 143)

Wagner, the man of the dead letter, the man of *Logos as Word*, is here perfectly contrasted with Faust, the man of *Logos as Act*. The man of "science" and "knowledge" as immobilization and death is perfectly contrasted with the man of science and knowledge as life. Mephistopheles himself calls Faust "one who thinks the word so beggarly, / Who holds what seems in disrepute, / And craves only [the depths of] reality" (vv. 1328-30; Kaufmann, 159).

Faust opposes his own "craving truth" (v. 667; Kaufmann, 115) to Wagner's "critical endeavor" (v. 560; Kaufmann, 107). To Faust, the parchments which Wagner so highly prizes are indissolubly connected with "skulls and skeletons and death" (v. 417; Kaufmann, 97); and for him, inherited knowledge is pitiful indeed:

> Should I read in a thousand books, maybe,
> That men have alway suffered everywhere,
> [that] now and then some man lived happily?
>   (vv. 661-63; Kaufmann, 115)

The opposition between the two characters clarifies sufficiently that it would be incorrect to state, as is sometimes done, that Faust's desire is channeled in the direction of scientific knowledge. Wagner's comic craving for more of the same, as well as his creation (in Part II, Act II, "Laboratorium") of the artificial man, Homunkulus, are in Goethe's text the true paradigms of an instinct which desires finitude—but Faust's striving always remains on a quite different plane.

Wagner's, and not Faust's, ultimate descendants will be at work on the nuclear research projects of Dürrenmatt's *The Physicists*. It is only by a gross misunderstanding of Faust's infinite desire that the contradictions of contemporary science and technology can be attributed to an allegedly "Faustian" spirit. Faust has nothing to do with technology; he is not a scientist—above all, he is not a producer. Faust is a man who *consumes* himself in striving for the unknown. Wagner is a "critic", i.e. a man of positive accretion of letter over letter; Faust is the effacement of the text, permanent abolition of the text that has been accumulated over time. His existence is an existence in acting and not in knowing; more precisely, his knowing is functional to his acting. And even his acting is mobile: far from being goal-conscious, it creates itself on the way. It is pure becoming. Faust's desire resists defining its own forms—it refuses to annihilate them in fulfillment.

At the representational level, taking Goethe's poem as the very model of the novel of education which, after all, it is, one must then inevitably contrast Faust's metaphysical *Streben* with Wagner as a petty *Streber* ("social climber"): the transcendental quest of the searcher being diametrically opposed to the lowly (albeit successful) *arrivisme* of the "dreary creeper" (v. 521; Kaufmann, 105). At the theoretical level, however, one must oppose the two in an even more essential, radical way. Whereas, in the process of desiring, Wagner augments his self by successive superpositions, Faust squanders his own, thoughtlessly. From the psychological standpont, Wagner is a miser; Faust is a prodigal spirit. Wagner is an accumulator; Faust, a dissipator. The psychological contrast of the two existential opposites of Goethe's *Faust* prepares the reader well to seize the meaning of the hero's salvation in the second part of the poem: Goethe breaks with all previous Christian tradition, both Catholic and Protestant, and redeems Faust, because his world view contemplates a valorizing image of the existential expenditure of man. For Goethe, loss is real—but precisely that loss proves and guarantees human dignity.

Saving from "Hell" a man who has compromised himself with evil and demonic forces (cf. Faust's avowal shortly before his death, vv. 11,403-19; Kaufmann, 457) implies that Goethe's supreme values are mobility and fluidity of desire; and that on grounds of perpetual mobility and fluidity alone can the desiring self be narratively "saved" (i.e., philosophically justified). Indeed, the moment of Faust's most intense humanity is perhaps the one in which the old man, blind and nearing his death, regrets having consumed his youth in the flame of desire, and repents having striven for infinity, instead of quietly following his way, from one moment to the next, always equally ... unhappy with each of them.

> Through all the world I only raced:
> Whatever I might crave, I laid my hand on,
> What would not do, I would abandon,
> And what escaped, I would let go.
> I only would desire and attain,
> And wish for more, and thus with might and main
> I stormed through life; first powerful and great,
> But now with calmer wisdom, and sedate.
> The earthly sphere I know sufficiently,
> But into the beyond we cannot see;
> A fool, that squints and tries to pierce those shrouds,
> And would invent his life above the clouds!
> Let him survey this life, be resolute,
> For to the able this world is not mute.
> Why fly into eternities?
> What man perceives, that he can seize.
> ["Was braucht er in die Ewigkeit zu schweifen!
> Was er erkennt, läßt sich ergreifen"].
> Thus he may wander through his earthly day;
> Heedless of ghosts, let him pusue his way,
> In his progression agony and joy,
> At every moment still dissatisfied[!]
> ["Im Weiterschreiten find' er Qual und Glück,
> Er, unbefriedigt jeden Augenblick!"]
>   (vv. 11,433-52; Kaufmann, 459)

Faust's apparent repentance turns out to be the most Faustian statement that could be made—further reinforcing the intentions expressed in Part I, before and during the pact-episode. The moment of disavowal is thus the very moment of Faust's supreme Faustism. Satisfaction is here the agony of being ever-dissatisfied: the refusal to "fix" desire, to limit it to a single object, to administer it in an economic way, is more than ever upheld.

Little wonder, then, that the fulfillment of the pact's clause, which is meant to determine the moment of Faust's death, can only happen in the well-known hypothetical form:

> *Then*, to the moment I *might* say:
> Abide, you are so fair! [...]
>
> As I presage a happiness so high,
> I now enjoy the highest moment.
>
> (vv. 11,581-86; Kaufmann, 469)

At this point, Faust's life is consumed; consumption *is* the only redeeming value which it can claim. Even though the pact has formally been respected, Goethe lets a superior philosophical order prevail, when the angels proclaim the Lord's supreme principle that whoever, ever-striving, does one's utmost, can be redeemed ("Wer immer strebend sich bemüht, den können wir erlösen", vv. 11,936-37; Kaufmann, 493). Adorno insightfully calls this phrase "a maxim of world-immanent asceticism" (Adorno 1974, II, 134).

Adorno's own formulation best summarizes the meaning of Faust's salvation:

> The bet is lost [...]
> If Faust had been meant to win the bet, then it would [...] have been absurd to put in his mouth, at the moment of his death, precisely the verses which, in accordance with the pact, hand him over to the devil. Far from that, Law ["Recht"] itself is here suspended. A superior instance halts the course of the perennial equality of credit and debit ["Eine höhere Instanz gebietet der Immergleichheit von Credit und Debet Einhalt"]. It is Grace [...] taking precedence over Law [...] that shatters ["zerbricht"] the cycle of cause and effect [...]
> The metaphysics of *Faust* is [...] the vanishing ["das Verschwinden"] of the order of the Natural into another one.
>
> (Adorno 1974, II, 136-37)

The other, superior order into which the economic order of the devil pact is subsumed, is clearly the supra-individual one at whose level the notion of specific guilt loses its meaning. In Goethe's world view, the guilt incurred by Faust in and through his compromise with the demonic is more than compensated for by the "self-less" (or, in Baudelaire's terms: self-vaporizing) *élan* with which the hero has absorbed all desires. Because he was never immobilized in any one of them, because he eventually consumes his whole energy for no "self-ish" purpose, and because he dies through *consumption by desire*, Faust eventually achieves justification and salvation.

In a brilliant page, Abrams formulates the essential philosophical frame of the superior intellectual order which saves Faust:

> *Faust* [...] adopts, but in order radically to reinterpret, the Christian supernatural itself. Goethe employs the traditional frame [...] only as a narrative *donnée* to express an entirely secular scheme of salvation [...]
> Mephistopheles "excites and works and must create, in his very nature as devil", in a cosmic irony, as Mephistopheles himself ruefully acknowledges, that makes him the unwilling agent of theodicy [...]
> Faust arises as a secular new Adam, to resume his unwitting pilgrimage toward a redemption in this life [...] His triumph consists simply in the experience of sustaining a desire which never relaxes into the stasis of a finite satisfaction.
> (Abrams 1971, 244-45)

Accordingly, Goethe substitutes the traditional foregrounding of faith with a radical foregrounding of desire:

> Goethe adopts the concept of salvation as a triumph of aspiration toward an infinite God, but alters it in a fashion that shears away Christian supernaturalism and transvalues Christian morality. The final ascension of Faust does not signify his rejection of the possibilities of this world [...], but his success in maintaining a desire for a totality of experience that is infinitely beyond the possibilities of the world to satisfy, in an errorful and suffering striving which is its own reward, by making him that which he becomes and could not have been without it.
> (Abrams 1971, 245)

One could hardly express more effectively Goethe's acceptance of the existential expenditure of man, grounded in his view of another dimension, a superior hierarchy of values, which guarantees "on High" the meaning of a loss of self apparently not compensated for by tangible results on earth. Goethe's own bet against the "Spirit that ever denies" is that precisely in this loss mankind finds the ultimate foundation of humanity; and that *owning* and *spending* the capital of one's being-in-the-world cannot be defined independently of each other. Owning and spending life can only occur through one another and constitute one and the same process. Stasis is here death, movement is life; and both life and death can only be seized in the passage. The *passage of desire*, its mobility, is for Goethe the ultimate locus in which the self invests its energy—and inevitably consumes it.

*

Such an extreme problematization of the relationship between self and desire is what makes Goethe's *Faust* so uniquely meaningful in the perspective of the modern revival of traditional demonic themes. Unfortunately, the break with conventions proposed by Goethe's text was long misconstrued in France; and in French literature we do not find a work of a comparable originality treating the theme of the pact with demonic forces until the appearance of Balzac's *La peau de chagrin*—which poses the problem of the expenditure of desire and energy in a way not dissimilar from Goethe's, although in the frame of a much more somber and pessimistic world view.[11]

It was not until the publication of Nerval's translation that the French-speaking public could form an at least approximate notion of *Faust*; even then, Gérard himself was more than hesitant to recommend some difficult passages to the attention of his readers. Very few works of the epoch are grafted directly onto the vital core of Faust's preoccupations; only much later was Flaubert to reformulate the dilemma of man disintegrated by the power of desire in *La Tentation de Saint Antoine*. And only the twentieth century, with its radical epistemological break from the Romantic centripetal view of the world, could then reaccentuate the Goethean pact with "that force which would / Do evil evermore, and yet creates the good" (vv. 1335-36; Kaufmann, 159) to the limiting point of what could be termed Bulgakov's revolutionary traditionalism in *The Master and Margarita*.

Notes

[1] For a survey of the notion of desire in philosophy and psychology, cf. the articles: "Désir", in Lalande 1947; "Désir", in Laplanche-Pontalis 1967; "Begehren, *appetitus naturalis*", by Friedrich, "Begehren, Begierde", by Schönpflug, both in Ritter 1971; "Desiderio", by Gomila, in Gomila 1978 (all with bibliography); and the historical introduction and "The Concept of Libido" in *Symbols of Transformation* [of Libido], Jung 1976. For the notion of desire in Lacan, cf. Lacan 1966, 804-5, 814.

[2] It may be impossible to compile a complete list of the names taken by the devil in Slavic folklore: Others will always slip out through the cracks of "comprehensive" definitions. For an extensive one (some 40 items), see Maksimov n.d. [1908-1913], 4n.

[3] On the subject, cf. e.g. "El imperio del Mal / El Mal del imperialismo ... " (Rodríguez-Hernández, 1987).

[4] In Mephisto's original words: "Wenn sich der Mensch, die kleine Narrenwelt, / Gewöhnlich für ein Ganzes hält / Ich bin ein Teil des Teils, der anfangs alles war, / Ein Teil der Finsternis, die sich das Licht gebar, / Das stolze Licht, das nun der Mutter Nacht / Den alten Rang, den Raum ihr streitig macht, / Und doch gelingt's ihm nicht, da es, so viel es strebt, / Verhaftet an den Körpern klebt. / Von Körpern strömt's, die Körper macht es schön, / Ein Körper hemmt's auf seinem Gange, / So, hoff' ich, dauert es nicht lange, / Und mit den Körpern wird's zugrunde gehn".

[5] The notion of *foregrounding* has been originally developed in linguistics, and I will use it here in a similar sense—at the level of narrative macrostructures. With "foregrounding" I indicate the procedure by which a particular element of the plot, or a particular aspect of the composition, has received a special stress so as to render it the prominent, central feature of the work of art, to which the author intends to attract the reader's attention. By contrast, those features on which the author's interest concentrates at degree zero can be described as "automatized". Automatization is the opposite of foregrounding. Thus, "the component highest in the hierarchy becomes the dominant. All other components, foregrounded or not, as well as their interrelationships, are evaluated from the standpoint of the dominant" (Mukarovsky 1964, 20). As Mukarovsky's article "Standard Language and Poetic Language" stresses, the original authorial foregrounding may, in a different cultural-historical context, be replaced by new criteria, which in and by the act of reading foreground other aspects of the original text. (This, usually diachronic, "reshaping of the foregrounded component" I define with the Bakhtinian term of *reaccentuation*—v. *infra*).

[6] The borderlines between traditions are often hard to draw with absolute precision. So, for example, Dédéyan includes Mary Shelley's *Frankenstein*, Lewis's *The Monk*, Hugo's *Notre-Dame de Paris*, George Sand's *Les sept cordes de la lyre*, etc., in his multi-volume work on the Faust-theme.

Perhaps the best analysis of how Protestant and Catholic versions / interpretations / "cycles" of the theme of the devil-compact contrast and are opposed to each other has been offered by H. Mayer in his *Doktor Faust und Don Juan*: whereas the Catholic versions, derived from the Theophilus tradition, insist on the notion of intercession from above, the fortune of the Faust legend in Protestant lands can be explained with the abolition precisely of all mediation between earth and heaven (Mayer 1979, 16-19, 21-24) and the human self's anguished exposedness to the difficulty of independent thought ("grenzenlose Selbstverantwortung") (Mayer 1979, 17).

[7]M. Butler and C. Dédéyan have explored in great detail the metamorphoses of the theme of Faustian or para-Faustian pacts, both before and after Goethe.

[8]On *vana gloria* and its role in medieval Christian world view, cf. Hempel 1970, 20.

[9]On the opposition between the two traditions, see Mayer 1979, 21-22.

[10]Cf. DiAmico 1979, 108-11.

[11]Indeed, certain objections to Faustian and para-Faustian themes were virtually commonplace among the cultivated readers of the epoch. Stendhal's dismissal of Faust's donjuanesque striving is typical: "Goethe [...] a donné le diable pour ami au docteur Faust, et avec un si puissant auxiliaire, Faust fait ce que nous avons tous fait à vingt ans, il séduit une modiste", quot. in Baldensperger 1904, 42. At a much later date, Nietzsche's view of *Faust*—for obviously very different reasons—did not substantially diverge from Stendhal's; cf. Nietzsche, *Human, All-Too-Human*, Bk. II, Sect. II, # 124. Parallel considerations on the "banality" of demonism in life and literature can be found in Leopardi's philosophical *Dialogo di Malambruno e Farfarello* (1827) in his *Operette Morali* (Leopardi 1982, 97).

As for the inverse proportionality existing in society between honors and honesty, it clearly is a favorite target of Balzac's *enthusiastic cynicism*. In *La peau de chagrin* the desperate, suicidal Raphaël exchanges the following dialogue with the antique dealer: "Votre père vous a-t-il trop vivement reproché d'être venu au monde, ou bien êtes-vous déshonoré?" — "Si je voulais me déshonorer, je vivrais" (Balzac 1979, X, 81).

1

Balzac's Laicized Demonism

I
Devil-Contracts In *La Comédie humaine*: Between Money and Mandarins

In his *Le diable dans la littérature française de Cazotte à Baudelaire*, Max Milner justly points to the technical difficulties which await the writer trying to extend to the long form of the novel the liberties permitted in shorter or more experimental forms. Milner observes that the extended narrative time of the novel lends itself poorly to taking the reader by surprise and hardly allows the narrator to develop "des données fantastiques dont les implications deviennent vite absurdes pour peu que l'on descende aux conséquences" (Milner 1960, II, 7). Accordingly, the devil's place is at the same time very limited and extremely important in Balzac's novels written after 1830: limited if the notion is taken in a literal sense, but all-pervasive if one considers Satan as an archetype, as a myth, on which the author molds the traits of many characters of *La Comédie humaine* and which serves as an interpretive key to promptly identify their function in the plot (Milner 1960, II, 8,12).

Some critics, on the other hand, take the opposite view of completely devaluing the notion of the demonic in Balzac. In the context of *Illusions Perdues,* Moretti writes that

> Balzac's extraordinary invention was to show that a young man's life could be exciting without his having to get shipwrecked on a desert island, sign a pact with the devil, or create homicidal life-size dolls. It is sufficient to write a theatrical review, lose one's heart to a light-headed actress, and lack an iron will [...]
>
> With Balzac the "prose of the world" ceases to be boring. It is precisely the very prosaic social relationships of incipient capitalism that constitute his plots and confer on them their gripping syntagmatic-temporal features.
>
> (Moretti 1983, 115)

While the merit of Moretti's remark lies in its illuminating perception of the value of the innovations diachronically introduced by Balzac with the *Comédie humaine,* it is doubtful whether one can deny the *lato sensu* "demonic" dimension of the series of murky deals which, in his works, are incurred left and right by his characters—and not by the evil ones alone. In Balzac, the demonic is nowhere; but also, in a broader sense of the word, everywhere. The devil, the *Other* of Slavic folk tradition, does not have a single, definite locus, invariable through cultures and centuries: if Spieß's Faust sells his soul, more modestly (or perhaps more ambitiously) Lucien Chardon offers the only incorporeal resource available in the Paris of 1830—his *esprit.* The devil of literature being a device designed to materialize a part of man himself, a convenient narrative *shortcut* which sends back to man the presence of his own conflicts, it is little wonder that Balzac's Parisian Other of 1830 does not dress, think, "exist" in the same way as his equivalents of other epochs or nations.

The two critical positions stress complementary and equally important features of *La Comédie humaine*: the former in describing the nature of its diffuse demonic atmosphere, the latter in emphasizing Balzac's corageous choice of discarding traditional signatures traced with blood. This can happen because Balzac takes up the devil-pact and the notion of "selling one's soul" in their essence rather than in their form, re-elaborating the theme according to his own historical universe and personal mythology. He presents it in a secularized, *laicized* version. It would have been pedantic to demand that he do otherwise—pedantism being, after all, precisely the accusation which Goethe's Faust levelled at Mephistopheles when asked to sign a document as proof of their contract.[1]

Balzac specifically concentrates on the demonic-obsessional side of a particular category of human beings. Such characters are the main protagonists of a number of his novels, and are in general the ones endowed with the most (positively or negatively) powerful personalities. Balzac calls them "hommes à passion", and the whole of the *Comédie humaine* is, in a sense, but a stage for their exploits. Vautrin describes them in *Le père Goriot:*

> Ils chaussent une idée et ils n'en démordent pas. Ils n'ont soif que d'une certaine eau prise à une certaine fontaine, et souvent croupie; pour en boire, ils vendraient leurs femmes, leurs enfants; ils vendraient leur âme au diable. Pour les uns, cette fontaine est le jeu, la Bourse, une collection de tableaux ou d'insectes, la musique; pour d'autres, c'est une femme qui sait leur cuisiner des friandises.
>
> (Balzac 1951, II, 885)

The equivalence between desire and the demonic is here obvious; the conditional mode implies that the "pact" is already contracted in the spirit, and that desire—whatever its nature—has already taken over the self. Candidates for this role are cousin Bette and Valérie Marneffe, old Goriot, old Grandet, and virtually all the various hoarders of the *Comédie humaine*. The same would apply, symmetrically, to the squanderers of all denominations: Balthasar Claës in *La recherche de l'absolu*, Raphaël de Valentin in *La peau de chagrin*—and many others. The subservience to the demonism of passion (ambition, lust, hatred, scientific curiosity, covetousness, prodigality, etc.) is in Balzac a phenomenon peculiarly crossing all barriers of gender, age and social status. All these compulsive beings disarticulate the traditional notion of the demonic, in the sense that by the very act of their being prey to desire, they have already "sold their soul": they have alienated it because they no longer possess themselves. *Alienation in desire* replaces for them the "alienation" (intended in the legal sense: sale, transfer of property) of the soul in a pact.

The theme is so all-pervasive that it constantly surfaces at the major moral bifurcations which the protagonists have to confront as they advance. A typical example can be found in the dialogue between the inexperienced Rastignac and his friend Bianchon in *Le père Goriot*:

> — Je suis tourmenté par de mauvaises idées.
> — En quel genre? Ça se guérit, les idées.
> — [...] As-tu lu Rousseau?
> — Oui.
> — Te souviens-tu de ce passage où il demande à son lecteur ce qu'il ferait au cas où il pourrait s'enrichir en tuant à la Chine par sa seule volonté un vieux mandarin, sans bouger de Paris.
> — Oui.
> — Eh bien?
> — Bah! J'en suis à mon trente-troisième mandarin.
> — Ne plaisante pas. Allons, s'il t'était prouvé que la chose est possible et qu'il te suffit d'un signe de tête, le ferais-tu?
> — Est-il bien vieux, le mandarin? Mais, bah! jeune ou vieux, paralytique ou bien portant, ma foi ... Diantre! Eh bien, non.
> — Tu es un brave garçon, Bianchon. Mais si tu avais une femme à te mettre pour elle l'âme à l'envers, et qu'il lui fallait de l'argent [...]
> (Balzac 1951, II, 960)

The proairetic choice is here clearly between the two opposite poles of lack of scruples and human pity—or, as the text vividly illustrates them: between money and mandarins.

The same metaphor runs through Balzac's novels with obsessive clarity: one is to choose either "pact" and power, i.e. compromise with an immoral (or rather: a-moral) political establishment, or purity; and along with purity, impending doom. It would be an almost endless task to pursue the theme exhaustively throughout the *Comédie humaine*; few episodes of the entire cycle would *not* qualify for consideration. At the core of the colossal opus, however, Lucien de Rubempré's and Coralie's story exemplarily illustrates Balzac's view of the inescapable opposition: purity and poetry, with poverty; *or* money through journalism—with moral prostitution.

Illusions perdues is a particularly apt example of the continuity between everyday bourgeois perversion and demonic perversion: if the pact with the publishing industry eventually leads to suffering, solitude and suicide, how much worse could the pact with the demonic Vautrin be? On the verge of suicide, Lucien has nothing to lose but his chains; and he has just learned from society that morally speaking (as Isaac aptly puts it) "tous les refrains sont bons" (Isaac 1983, 73). There would then be no point in his refusing to sing the "human devil"'s refrain. *Illusions perdues* is a *Bildungsroman* teaching Lucien the fatal necessity of singing the song of the employer whose bread one eats: far from declaring moral bankruptcy, in renting himself out to Vautrin he arguably shows that he has at long last learned not merely something about, but indeed the very essence of, the mechanisms of capitalistic society.2

A not much more comforting world view is illustrated by Balzac through Rastignac in *Le père Goriot*. Even though Rastignac apparently refuses to "kill his mandarin", i.e., refuses to marry Victorine Taillefer over her brother's dead body, he resorts to a more elegant but morally equivalent solution: he shares his mistress with her banker husband. While turning down an obvious "demonic" pact, he has recourse to a hidden one: he leaves it up to a convenient spouse to "kill mandarins" for him. Rastignac's pact with the devil is merely disguised—or rather, subcontracted to someone else. Vautrin, the omniscient character, the destroyer of moral idols, had already unmasked the true essence of the young man's self-complacent hypocrisy when he had predicted—if not as devil, certainly as devil's advocate—the future development of the dandy's career:

> Vous ferez pis quelque jour. Vous irez coqueter chez quelque jolie femme et vous recevrez de l'argent. Vous y avez pensé! ... car, comment réussirez-vous, si vous n'escomptez pas votre amour? La vertu, mon cher étudiant, ne se scinde pas: elle est ou n'est pas.
> (Balzac 1951, II, 941)

As Moretti implied, society is here already too debased for that irreducible rest of tragedy which is intrinsic to the concept of a full-fledged demonic contract. In *Illusions perdues* tragedy is dead; journalism appears as the moral surrogate of demonic evil—and thereby transforms it, in parodic form, into a grotesque-monstrous pettiness which perhaps only finds a parallel in the most somber pages of Gogol's *Dead Souls*.

Balzac reinforces the same statement when he has Lucien share Esther with the other banker Nucingen in *Splendeurs et misères des courtisanes*. And the same predicament can be read again, only *e contrario*, when in *Illusions perdues* Coralie's death comes about as a consequence of her generous, but by all worldly standards suicidal refusal to belong to both Lucien and the merchant Camusot. Her choice of integrity over money turns out to be one of integrity over life. In this part of Balzac's novelistic world, the refusal to sign the pact with evil—in Rastignac's terms, the refusal to "kill one's mandarin"—can be evaluated, depending on the point of view, as either sublime or foolish. Only truly superior beings (Mme de Beauséant, Daniel d'Arthez) can stand up to such an option. The structure of *Illusions perdues*, however, does not seem to reward them with a close focus on their destinies: they remain tangential with respect to the main action. Morally strong characters remain pure, ideal—and marginalized. The internal forum where the questions for the "normal" human being are asked and debated is clearly Lucien.

While no univocal Mephisto-figure appears among the innumerable characters of the *Comédie humaine* (Vautrin will deserve a separate detailed treatment), the idea of the pact is ever-present; it is, indeed, the founding notion of the whole cycle. All such characters are possessed by their own form of desire, in a sort of multifarious capitalistic *Inferno* which (consciously, after all) borrows the principles of obsessive multiplicity from the circles of Dante's *Divine Comedy*.

II

La peau de chagrin and the Dialectic of Energy

La peau de chagrin represents in the most extreme form the insolubility of the aporias which, in *La Comédie humaine*, only Vautrin can attempt to resolve. *La peau de chagrin* is Balzac's ultimate statement about the dilemma of energy with respect to those of his characters who happen to be neither Gods nor devils—nor Vautrin.

Balzac classified *La peau de chagrin* among his *Études philosophiques*. This is his way of expressing the fact that, in the novel, narration is pulled in two opposite directions: the realist and the supernatural. The challenge was obviously immense. On the side of realism, the novel safeguarded the traditionally accepted postulate of *vraisemblance* as far as social setting was concerned. In it we see the Parisian society of 1830, portrayed with a high degree of historical and internal logical references. "Realism" in general (whatever the complexity and even the contradictoriness of this notion) was at the same time upheld and rendered flexible by attributing to the "wild ass's skin"—a concrete, but mysterious object—what could today be termed the special effects of the story. On the opposite side of the supernatural and the fantastic (which in 1830, in the wake of the success of Hoffman's tales, were in extreme favor), the novel maintains the principle of a demonic pact—but in a somewhat modified form: it transposes the traditionally transcendent, qualitative notion of the soul's eternal damnation into the immanent, quantitative dimension of the progressive exhaustion of vital force. These modifications were inevitable if one hoped to render the pact theme not only "acceptable" but even, in the first place, understandable to the Parisian public of the July monarchy. The reception allotted to Goethe's *Faust I* (and Balzac's very opinion of it) witness to the fact that in those times the standards for the intelligibility of philosophical stories about pacts with the devil varied enormously from one cultural situation to another.

La peau de chagrin could be described as the novel of a delicate thematic balance. It is equally distant, on one hand, from the totally fantastic amounts of money, power and knowledge bestowed upon Castanier in *Melmoth réconcilié* (and which Balzac viewed as destructive in their own right), as it is, on the other, from the totally real, all-too-real and anguishing hesitations about "money and mandarins" haunting Rastignac in *Le père Goriot*. In its faithfulness to the dynamics of social life as well as in its parallel focalization on the problem of desire, *La peau de chagrin* condenses and compacts into the wild ass's skin themes from both the realistic and the visionary faces of the *Comédie humaine*.

Within the genre of the literature of the demonic, *La peau de chagrin*'s main novelty consists in the fact that it breaks with the old notion of a pact rigid in duration and open as to the amount of power supplied. Both these notions are replaced in the novel by a single finite factor—the amount of energy which supernatural forces make available to Raphaël de Valentin. The notion of time, which traditionally was an independent function, becomes a dependent one; and the notion of total expenditure becomes foregrounded, while it had previously been irrelevant. Time is here subsumed into matter: the magic skin, which shrinks with its owner's every new desire, is at the same time an indicator of the amount of energy left and of the decreasing period for which it will be available. The hide is a new element in the demonic genre: spatial and temporal at the same time, it carries within itself the imminence of its own abolition. The novel's talisman is the *reification of desire* obtained through a demonic pact.

From the standpoint of the demonic genre the *peau* has an uncanny liminal status: it is "natural", in that it condenses, in a symbolic form, the finite amount of all of Raphaël's natural desires and vital force; it is also, however, "supernatural" because it guarantees that (within the set frame of a fixed energetic budget) *any* desire can be fulfilled. The first function is not, properly speaking, demonic; only the second one is. Yet the two are obviously each the obverse of the other: natural vital force diminishes because desire is supernaturally fulfilled; conversely, supernatural fulfillment is rooted in the consumption of a natural (i.e., finite) resource.[3] By inscribing the pact into (and—with the magic inscription—onto) a tangible object, with a legerdemain Balzac profoundly rearranges the data of the demonic pact as we had seen them firmly established in some of the earlier traditional time-limited, energy-unlimited contracts.

The fundamental novelties introduced by Balzac's "energy-only" pact can be condensed as follows. First of all, since in *La peau de chagrin* time is no longer an abstract factor, the notion of "end" of the period of the demonic contract (Faust's twelve or twenty-four years, for example) loses its meaning. Secondly, given the fact that abstractions take here anthropomorphic shape, the traditional notion of punishment (or divine pardon) is also discarded. Because in *La peau de chagrin* the end of the contract is the exhaustion of energy, retribution must turn from an extrinsic into an intrinsic concept (the consumption of vital force). Finally, since energy is no longer furnished by the devil in unlimited amounts, a definite narrative reaccentuation occurs. The interest of the plot is no longer dispersed on the adventitious *couleur locale* of the multifarious episodes in which the devil's partners use their power; rather, it is concentrated on analyzing why each specific usage consumes it. From a traditional equivalence and interchangeability of the episodes we are thus led to a reflection on their progression and on the logical chain that connects them and leads them toward the end. Balzac's *étude philosophique* can best be described as a novel whose main merit is that of replacing the received curiosity for a number of different-indifferent adventures, all performed thanks to the devil's infinite energy, with the typically Balzacian interest in exploring the gap that separates the infinity of desire from the finitude of vital force. This explains why *La peau de chagrin* must, first and foremost, be a novel preoccupied with the problematization of the notion of energy; and why the demonic in it has as its peculiar key terms the concepts of accumulation, thesaurization, dissipation, and expense.

*

The narration of *La peau de chagrin* opens when the story has already long been active. The reader witnesses a young man visiting a casino of the Parisian Palais-Royal, losing his last coin in the game, and desperately meditating a decisive plunge into the Seine. The reader is thus, in turn, directly plunged into the movement of the events; the technique of narrative transposition, which only in the central part of the novel will unveil the preceding events, efficiently demonstrates the relevance of the theme of dynamism. The monetary flow of a casino and the hydraulic flow of a river are here devices of a performative discourse that consciously strives to materialize the "flow" of narration; they aptly open a novel whose main focus lies in the transformations of different forms of energy.

Thematically, stopping at the casino is for the young Raphaël de Valentin the equivalent of the compromise with demonic forces. The narrator spares no means to stress this: he repeatedly calls the act of gambling "un contrat infernal", "le démon du jeu" (Balzac 1979, X, 57, 59; henceforward *Peau*). Raphaël's desire is already available for the stipulation of a pact; however, because fortune does not favor him at this time, such a pact is temporarily postponed. Since the last resource left to Raphaël after the loss of his last coin is suicide, i.e. the final dispersal of the energy left to him, the text inscribes Raphaël from the very beginning under the sign of gambling and the consumption of forces.[4]

A revealing episode, however, had taken place earlier, during Raphaël's years of apprenticeship—showing how Raphaël's father embodies an economic retentive principle that is opposed to the son's dispersive one and systematically intends to repress it. In it we see that, while Raphaël is given to complete subservience toward what could be called "demonic desire" (i.e., the pleasure principle), the father embodies the repression of both: the parallelism of the two gambling episodes and the structural opposition between characters unequivocally define Raphaël's attitude toward desire. In the autobiographical narration, Raphaël recounts to his friend Emile how his father used to deny him both money and the pleasures which money embodies: " [...] jusqu'à l'âge de vingt ans, il ne laissa pas dix francs à ma disposition, dix coquins, dix libertins de francs" (*Peau*, 121). Raphaël thereupon subtracted two coins from the purse his father had entrusted to him and went to gamble. By a mere coincidence, his father happened to pass by and see him; thus, guilt feelings and pleasure conflicted in giving Raphaël what he calls "l'une des plus terribles joies de ma vie" (*Peau*, 122).

The opposition between the two principles—pleasure and dispersion in the son, repression and thesaurization it the father—is exasperated when the latter paradoxically has to admit the abstract possibility of gambling and spending, provided that this be done for *practical* purposes. The father lectures:

> — Mais [...] il n'y aurait eu rien d'extraordinaire à ce que vous eussiez été forcé par amour-propre à mettre quelque argent sur le tapis. Aux yeux des gens du monde, vous paraissez assez âgé pour avoir le droit de commettre des sottises. Aussi vous excuserais-je, Raphaël, si vous vous étiez servi de ma bourse ...
>
> (*Peau*, 124)

In the same spirit, he allots a pension to his son, allegedly for him to dispose of as he pleases, but in reality for a less than hedonistic purpose:

> Mon fils, vous avez bientôt vingt ans. Je suis content de vous. Il vous faut une pension, *ne fût-ce que pour vous apprendre à économiser*, à connaître les choses de la vie. Dès ce soir, je vous donnerai cent francs par mois.
>
> (*Peau*, 125; emphasis added)

For Raphaël, devil-desire is the wish to spend "une journée entière plongé dans les crimes de mon âge" (*Peau*, 123); for his father, even spending turns out to be but a means of learning how to save. The novel could not oppose more clearly the father's utilitarianism and Raphaël's unproductive notion of pleasure.[5]

A text which Bataille published in 1933, *La notion de dépense*, opposes the same two principles in order to criticize the utilitarianism of modern bourgeois society. Bataille's text is a comprehensive, articulated argument in favor of the notion that pleasure cannot, by definition, be "useful", but must on the contrary be strictly unproductive. The formulations of *La notion de dépense* can be applied so closely to *La peau de chagrin* that they would almost seem to have been conceived on the basis of Balzac's text:

> l'utilité prétendue matérielle [...] a théoriquement pour but le plaisir—mais seulement sous une forme tempérée, le plaisir violent étant donné comme *pathologique*—et elle se laisse limiter à l'acquisition (pratiquement à la production) et à la conservation des biens d'une part—à la reproduction et à la conservation des vies humaines d'autre part [...]
> Le plaisir, qu'il s'agisse d'art, de débauche admise ou de jeu, est réduit en définitive, dans les représentations intellectuelles *qui ont cours*, à une concession, c'est-à-dire à un délassement dont le rôle serait subsidiaire. La part la plus appréciable de la vie est donnée comme la condition—parfois même comme la condition regrettable—de l'activité sociale productive.
>
> (Bataille 1967, 23-24; emphasis in the original)

In this view, Raphaël's demonic attraction for gambling is but one form of the intrinsic destructivity of pleasure—of the *natural* tendency of desire toward dispersion and loss. The theme of gambling at the beginning of *La peau de chagrin* merely anticipates *en abyme* the notion, to be developed in the rest of the novel, of the magic demonic hide which kills in and while satisfying desire.

Raphaël, who "spends himself" in desire, is then

> [...] incapable de justifier *utilitairement* sa conduite, et l'idée ne lui vient pas qu'une société humaine puisse avoir, comme lui, *intérêt* à des pertes considérables, à des catastrophes qui provoquent, *conformément à des besoins définis*, des dépressions tumultueuses, des crises d'angoisse et, en dernière analyse, un certain état orgiaque.
> (Bataille 1967, 24; emphasis in the original)

Bataille explicitly dwells on the symbolic role taken by gambling in the identification of desire with loss and expenditure of the self:

> Dans les divers jeux de compétition [...] [d]es sommes d'argent considérables sont dépensées pour l'entretien des locaux, des animaux, des engins ou des hommes. L'énergie est prodiguée autant que possible, de façon à provoquer un sentiment de stupéfaction, en tout cas avec une intensité infiniment plus grande que dans les entreprises de production. Le danger de mort n'est pas évité et constitue au contraire l'objet d'une forte attraction inconsciente [...] [C]es pertes atteignent même souvent une démence telle que les joueurs n'ont plus d'autre issue que la prison ou la mort.
> (Bataille 1967, 28)

The distinction between the fulfillment and loss of self offered by gambling and those afforded by the *peau* appears to be more one of form than one of essence: both partake of the demonic, and both occur through the unproductive consumption of the self operated by desire.

As for the repressive (and self-repressive) role which is proper to Raphaël's father, it can be aptly characterized by the following statement in *La notion de dépense*:

> [...] la contradiction entre les conceptions sociales courantes et les besoins réels de la société rappelle [...] l'étroitesse de jugement qui oppose le père à la

> satisfaction des besoins du fils qui est à sa charge. Cette étroitesse est telle qu'il est impossible au fils d'exprimer sa volonté. La sollicitude à demi malveillante de son père porte sur le logement, les vêtements, la nourriture, à la rigueur sur quelques distractions anodines. Mais il n'a même pas le droit de parler de ce qui lui donne la fièvre: il est obligé de laisser croire qu'aucune *horreur* n'entre pour lui en considération. A cet égard, il est triste de dire que *l'humanité consciente est restée mineure*: elle se reconnaît le droit d'acquérir, de conserver ou de consommer rationnellement, mais elle exclut en principe *la dépense improductive*.
>
> (Bataille 1967, 25; emphasis in the original)

The father, then, embodies the repression of desire, insofar as desire represents expenditure and loss. He symbolically represents the impossibility to give in to its demonic temptation. The father censors the pact established with gambling; he is the symbol of the castration of desire.

However, although Raphaël's father is a major symbolic figure in the novel, he does not have extensive narrative relief; he is not allotted enough space to fully and explicitly formulate his "repression-as-investment" utilitarian theory. We will find a more complete and sophisticated solution in the theories expounded by the *antiquaire*, whom Raphaël encounters shortly after having decided to postpone his suicide until the night.

In their meeting, *La peau de chagrin* reaches a first narrative climax. The pact scene, structured around the antique shop and the seemingly eternal old man's teachings, is presented in the first section of the text, *before* Raphaël's autobiography. By transposing the order of the events, Balzac here displaces the whole block of the demonic pact to the opening of the novel—the part to which, both in literary tradition and in the logic of dramatization, a pact scene normally belongs.

The antique dealer's theories can be said to innovate creatively upon the notion of the castration of desire. According to the merchant,

> L'homme s'épuise par deux actes instinctivement accomplis qui tarissent les sources de son existence. Deux verbes expriment toutes les formes que prennent ces deux causes de mort: VOULOIR et POUVOIR. Entre ces deux termes de l'action humaine, il est une autre formule dont s'emparent les sages, et je lui dois mon bonheur et ma longévité. *Vouloir* nous brûle et *Pouvoir* nous détruit; mais SAVOIR laisse notre faible organisation dans un perpétuel état de calme.

> Ainsi le désir ou le vouloir est mort en moi, tué par la pensée; le mouvement ou le pouvoir s'est résolu par le jeu naturel de mes organes. En deux mots, j'ai placé ma vie, non dans le cœur qui se brise, non dans les sens qui s'émoussent, mais dans le cerveau qui ne s'use pas et qui survit à tout.
>
> (*Peau*, 85)

We can recognize in these words an example of what Bataille called the self's "horror" toward unproductive expenditure. However, we soon learn in the further development of the *antiquaire*'s argument that this "horror" belongs to a category slightly different from the one embodied by the father:

> Rien d'excessif n'a froissé ni mon âme ni mon corps. Cependant j'ai vu le monde entier [...] enfin, j'ai tout obtenu parce que j'ai tout su dédaigner. Ma seule ambition a été de voir. Voir n'est-ce pas savoir? Oh! savoir, jeune homme, n'est-ce pas *jouir intuitivement*? [...]
> La pensée est la clef de tous les trésors, elle procure *les joies de l'avare* sans en donner les soucis. Aussi ai-je plané sur le monde, où mes plaisirs ont toujours été des *jouissances intellectuelles*. Mes débauches étaient la contemplation des mers, des peuples, des forêts, des montagnes! J'ai tout vu, mais tranquillement, sans fatigue; je n'ai jamais rien désiré, j'ai tout attendu.
>
> (*Peau*, 86; emphasis added)

While Raphaël's father evicts pleasure from the psychic horizon, the antique dealer intends to re-establish it on more secure foundations. Whereas the father eliminates it, the self-styled philosopher thesaurizes it. The first process is one of repression, the latter is one of sublimation; and there is something almost "artistic" in the old man's *(sa)voir*. Obviously, a price must be paid for this accumulative strategy: enjoyment has to be delayed, just as in the case of the amasser of money, who defers the fruition of his treasure. But there is no denying that, deferrral notwithstanding, in the antique dealer's shop desire still speaks. In spite of some superficial similarities, we are here far from the cold cynicism of Mephisto, who embodies the immobilization of pleasure and the pleasure of immobilization: Balzac's *antiquaire* talks of omniscience with the enthusiastic words of a man who has discovered the secret of how to successfully compete with God.

The old man's passion bursts forth with his every word:

> Là, dit-il en se frappant le front, là sont les vrais millions. Je passe des journées délicieuses en jetant un regard intelligent dans le passé, j'évoque des pays entiers, des sites, des vues de l'Océan, des figures historiquement belles! J'ai un sérail imaginaire où je possède toutes les femmes que je n'ai pas eues. Je revois souvent vos guerres, vos révolutions, et je les juge [...]
>
> Ceci, dit-il d'une voix éclatante en montrant la Peau de chagrin, est le *pouvoir* et le *vouloir* réunis. Là sont vos idées sociales, vos désirs excessifs, vos intempérances, vos joies qui tuent, vos douleurs qui font trop vivre; car *le mal n'est peut-être qu'un violent plaisir.*
>
> <div align="right">(<i>Peau</i>, 86-87; emphasis added)</div>

For the old man, *Savoir* is the mastery over the explosive mixture of the two components: desire and power to fulfill. It takes a superior being to command their dichotomy: Raphaël, for one, is certainly not up to the task.

Ironically, however, while in the first part of the novel the antique dealer controls with skill the economy of desire and fulfillment, later on things rapidly change: because of a wish of Raphaël's (who will by then own the *peau*), he will soon fall in love with a dancer. His enterprise will thus fail precisely because he has undertaken it with excessive empathy, and has over-enthusiastically espoused the cause of ataraxic superiority. As Nietzsche pointed out, it is impossible to kill passion with passion: one is left with a *second* passion instead (Nietzsche, *Morgenröte*, Bk. IV, # 411). Raphaël's doom will later be brought about by the contradictoriness of his desiring not to desire; here, the antique dealer precedes him on the path of inconsistent thought by a visceral, passionate defense of indifference.

At this point at least, the "liquidity" of Raphaël's desire (cf. his intention to drown himself, to become one with the river) is so overwhelming that all forms of pleasure are equivalent and equally hypnotizing to him. His only priority at this stage is delaying the loss: "J'ai besoin d'embrasser les plaisirs du ciel et de la terre dans une dernière étreinte pour en mourir" (*Peau*, 88). In these circumstances, it is quite immaterial in whichever way death may intervene: Raphaël takes the ultimate loss of the self for granted.

Bataille opposes on a theoretical level the two principles embodied respectively by the antique dealer and Raphaël:

> [...] la consommation doit être divisée en deux parts distinctes. La première, réductible, est représentée par l'usage du minimum nécessaire, pour les individus d'une société donnée, à la conservation de la vie [...]
>
> La seconde part est représentée par les dépenses dites improductives: le luxe, les deuils, les guerres, les cultes, les constructions de monuments somptuaires, les jeux, les spectacles, les arts, l'activité sexuelle perverse (c'est-à-dire détournée de la finalité génitale) représentent autant d'activités qui, tout au moins dans les conditions primitives, ont leur fin en elles-mêmes. Or, il est nécessaire de réserver le nom de *dépense* à ces formes improductives [...]
>
> Bien qu'il soit toujours possible d'opposer les unes aux autres les diverses formes énumérées, elles constituent un ensemble caractérisé par le fait que dans chaque cas l'accent est placé sur la *perte* qui doit être la plus grande possible pour que l'activité prenne son véritable sens.
>
> (Bataille 1967, 26-27; emphasis in the original)

The most important acquisition in Bataille's way of stating the problem is that it leads us to see with more clarity how the *antiquaire*'s delay of the direct pursuit of pleasure (a delay which he callls "la pensée": a subjective act seizing the world in its totality) is the equivalent of an attempt at moving toward the conservation of energy; and that it therefore implies a strong "structuring" of the self. In the same perspective, Raphaël's opposite choice of gratification, which equals dispersion of energy, clearly shows to entail the self's dis-orderliness and de-structuring.

*

There can be little doubt that the general notion of energy, with its social applications and implications, was recast in a new, revolutionary way by the European nineteenth century. The classic sciences of nature, previously grouped under the general notion of "physics", were re-thought and differentiated methodologically; altogeher new branches—the study of thermodynamics and electromagnetism, for example—were founded.[6] Similarly, the economists', including Marx's, analyses of wealth can be regarded on a global scale as inquiries into the ways in which a specific form of socioeconomic energy is accumulated, transformed, and magnified over historical epochs. In this view, then, the bourgeois revolution of the late eighteenth and early nineteenth century can be described as a revolution in man's ways of transforming, exchanging—and necessarily *consuming*—ever-growing quantities of energy. The forms of the general category of "energy" cover an extended spectrum ranging from the chemical to the artistic to the social.[7]

In the epistemology of the times, however, loss was far from being perceived as the necessary and inevitable other side of energy production. What followed from this situation was an often pervasive fear of the growth of entropy in the universe. In *Entropy and Art*, Arnheim has sketched both the thermodynamic notion in question and some of the catastrophic interpretations to which it occasionally gave rise:

> [E]ntropy is defined as the quantitative measure of the degree of disorder in a system [...]
> [T]he second law of thermodynamics is often formulated to mean that the material world moves from orderly states to an ever-increasing disorder and that the final situation of the universe will be one of maximal disorder [...]
> The second law stated that the entropy of the world strives toward a maximum [...]
> The sober formulations of Clausius, Kelvin, and Boltzmann were suited to become a cosmic *memento mori*, pointing to the underlying cause of the gradual decay of all things physical and mental.
> (Arnheim 1971, 7-9 *passim*)[8]

Hence, as Arnheim readily points out, follows the theorization that in the organic world there exists a general "striving [...] toward tension reduction" (Arnheim 1971, 45). Such a striving is the principle which Raphaël obeys in *La peau de chagrin*, and which the antique dealer, at least for the time being, manages to keep in check. In Balzac's terminology, the increase in entropy is the fulfillment of the *Vouloir-Pouvoir*; the old man's *Savoir*, by contrast, is its reversal into accumulation.

The psychic phenomenon at the basis of Arnheim's theory is the well-known one which so much concerned Freud in *Beyond the Pleasure Principle*. In Freud's words:

> The facts which have caused us to believe in the dominance of the pleasure principle in mental life also find an expression in the hypothesis that the mental apparatus endeavors to keep the quantity of excitation present in it as low as possible or at least to keep it constant [...]
> If the work of the mental apparatus is directed towards keeping the quantity of excitation low, then anything that is calculated to increase that quantity is bound to be felt as adverse to the functioning of the apparatus, that is

as unpleasurable. The pleasure principle follows from the principle of constancy [...] The tendency which we thus attribute to the mental apparatus is subsumed as a special case [...] of the "tendency toward stability" [...]
(Freud *GW* XIII, 5; *SE* XVIII, 9)

In terms of entropy, this corresponds to a more probable configuration of equally, homogeneously distributed potential energy. The fulfillment of the "endeavor" ("Bestreben") of the mental apparatus mentioned by Freud has as a consequence the breaking up of the pre-existing, less probable energetic distribution (or, if one will, energetic "structure").

In *La peau de chagrin*, Raphaël is the very incarnation of such a tendency toward fulfillment and "stability". Raphaël begins the novel by losing his last coin, by planning to commit suicide; and concludes it by exhausting his vital force. In all cases he *strives* toward the zero level of energy—be it financial (bankruptcy), geographic (the sea level), or physical (death). In terms of physics, Raphaël is the perfect heat exchanger. He embodies in the most extreme form the increase of entropy in the universe.

The antique dealer's choice of accumulation and deferral of desire has an opposite role to play; his psychological standpoint can be defined as the tendency that counters Raphaël's catabolic dissolution. Arnheim describes this by the two notions of *homeostasis* and *anabolism*.

Arnheim defines homeostasis as "an orderly state in the organism through the balancing of opposite forces [...] a steady stream of absorbed and expended energy" (Arnheim 1971, 47). As for anabolism, he develops the principle as follows:

> I describe [...] this counterprinciple as *the anabolic creation of a structural theme* [...] be it a crystal or a solar system, a society or a machine, a statement of thoughts or a work of art. Subjected to the tendency toward simplest structure, the object or event or institution assumes orderly, functioning shape.
> (Arnheim 1971, 48-49; emphasis added)

What Arnheim writes about any "object or event or institution" can be expanded to equally apply to psychic reality. The *antiquaire* in *La peau de chagrin* can be described as an "artist" in a metaphorical way; he does pursue a significant form of anabolic construction—the construction of his own self.

The anabolic process, or "creation of a structural theme", can be used to define not only the nature of art in general (*a fortiori*, of course, of Balzac's novel), but also the nature of the human self. Arnheim's argument implies that the human self can be described as *a (statistically) "improbable" anabolic configuration*, founded on the reversal of the tendency toward the increase of entropy. Translated into psychological terms, this proposition can be reformulated to state that the self *is an orderly structure cemented by the repression of the tendency toward tension reduction*; that is to say, by the repression of the pleasure principle.

The essential corollary of this formulation is that the immobilization of pleasure is a necessary condition for the construction of an articulated self—and thus the prerequisite for any form of psychic life. As Arnheim puts it,

> Mere orderliness [= the growth of entropy, C.T.] leads to increasing impoverishment and finally to the lowest possible level of structure [...]
> When it comes to the whole of human existence, whose only goal is its own fullness, [a] structural theme must not only be present but also as rich as possible.
> (Arnheim 1971, 48-49)

Free-flowing desire, then, de-structures the orderliness of the self; thesaurization (repression, as in Raphaël's father, or deferral, as in the antique dealer) is the foundation of its structured hierarchy.

*

Freud's starting point in *Beyond the Pleasure Principle* is the explanation of the apparently paradoxical predominance of the *Wiederholungszwang* over the striving toward pleasure.[9] He subsumes the apparent contradiction between the two into the general principle of the "conservative nature of life", which, according to him, can explain both. The basic instinct inherent in life would thus be the "urge [...] to restore an earlier state of things" ("*ein dem belebten Organischen innewohnender Drang zur Wiederherstellung eines früheren Zustandes*") (Freud *GW* XIII, 38; *SE* XVIII, 36; emphasis in the original).

But the ultimate "earlier" state of organic life is the inorganic one—i.e., for the living structure as a whole, non-existence. Hesitatingly Freud suggests that the pleasure principle "seems actually to serve the death instincts" ("das Lustprinzip scheint geradezu im Dienste der Todestriebe zu stehen"—*GW* XIII, 69; *SE* XVIII, 63). Elsewhere, he suggests that "the pleasure principle is [...] a tendency operating in the service of a function whose business it is to free the mental apparatus entirely from excitation" ("Das Lustprinzip ist [...] eine Tendenz, welche im Dienste einer Funktion steht, der es zufällt, den seelischen Apparat überhaupt erregungslos zu machen") (*GW* XIII, 67-68; *SE* XVIII, 62).

It is not difficult to recognize in Freud's statements the theoretical equivalent of the concept of loss of energy through desire, or desire as essentially unproductive, which Bataille describes in *La notion de dépense*. The two texts converge toward the common notion that the ultimate goal of fulfilled desire is the disintegration of the self at the lowest level of potential energy. This, if one prefers, would also be Arnheim's quoted "lowest possible level of structure" (Arnheim 1971, 49).

Raphaël's words during the "pact" scene with the old man are thus particularly significant:

> Donc je commande à ce pouvoir sinistre de me fondre toutes les joies dans une joie. Oui, j'ai besoin d'embrasser les plaisirs du ciel et de la terre dans une dernière étreinte pour en mourir.
> (*Peau*, 88)

By accepting to conjugate (in the antique dealer's terminology) his own "Vouloir" with the "Pouvoir" contained in the hide's magic essence, Raphaël finally expresses the death wish which, all along, has governed the economy of his desacralized demonism. The old man is justified in exclaiming sarcastically: "Vous avez signé le pacte, tout est dit [...] Après tout, vous vouliez mourir? Hé bien, votre suicide n'est que retardé" (*Peau*, 88). It is hardly surprising to see the category of the demonic reappear here in connection with the desire for death; Freud points out that the compulsion to repeat is commonly perceived and described as "demonic" (*GW* XIII, 36-37; *SE* XVIII, 36). In the act of accepting his demonic contract, in his "signing up for death" Raphaël strives for the final loss of self in a uniquely direct, compulsive-conscious way: the theme of the "quest for death", here so much more explicit than in *Faust*, is the trait that makes Raphaël's pact so peculiar. As Isaac aptly stresses, in this frame the talisman is only "an après-coup realization of a life already committed to *dépense*" (Isaac 1983, 742).

Faust has inverted (or, more exactly, sublimated) his own quest for death. Out of a drive toward regression into the inorganic he has fashioned an impulse projected forward. He, too, entertains thoughts of suicide; unlike Raphaël, however, he finally discards them, depriving death of consciously positive connotations. Faust's "demonic" desire obtains final satisfaction and leads to de-structuring the self *only after a long detour*—only after he has completed his long exploration around the world and concluded his crusade against the principle of fixed pleasure: "Do you not hear, I have no thought of joy!" (*Faust*, v. 1765; Kaufmann, 189). By contrast, Raphaël's choice is a conscious and explicit one: desire burns him in a direct way. When, in the third part of the novel, he realizes his desperate situation, it is too late for him to reverse his first option (partly because his very act of *desiring to kill desire* can easily be inscribed into the same logics of volition which it allegedly intends to disavow).

Freud perceptively writes about *Faust*:

> What appears in a minority of human individuals as an untiring impulsion towards further perfection can easily be understood as a result of the instinctual repression upon which is based all that is most precious in human civilization. The repressed instinct never ceases to strive for complete satisfaction [...] and it is the difference in amount between the pleasure of satisfaction which is *demanded* and that which is actually *achieved* that provides the driving factor which will permit of no halting at any position attained, but, in the poet's words, "Presses ever forward unsubdued" ("ungebändigt immer vorwärts dringt") (Mephisto in *Faust I*, Study room) [...]
> Only a word to suggest that the efforts of Eros to combine organic substances into ever larger unities probably provide a substitute for this "instinct towards perfection" whose existence we cannot admit. The phenomena

that are attributed to it seem capable of explanation by these efforts of Eros taken in conjunction with the results of repression.
(Freud *GW* XIII, 44-45, 45; *SE* XVIII, 42, 42-43)

The passage highlights the parallelism-opposition of Faust's and Raphaël's paths. Faust's mobilization of the self leads him to the "lowest possible level of structure" after long peripeties in the perennial quest of the Other Pleasure, the pleasure of ever-changing Otherness; Raphaël's inertia comes about by instant combustion, in direct presence of gratification. Faust's pleasure is ever-projected, hypothetical, i.e. located in Other Time; Raphaël's is always in the present moment. This explains why the dispersal of Faust's energy takes a whole lifetime to be accomplished, while Raphaël's loss of self is consummated in the violent blaze of the few months spanned by the events of *La peau de chagrin*.

In the last analysis, Bataille's historical approach to the concept of unproductive expenditure allows us to position diachronically the theoretical notions which operate in Balzac's novel. Bataille's assumption is that the specific way of conceiving and fashioning energetic loss is determined by the class structure of each given society. In Bataille's terms, for example, the type of consumption activated in *La peau de chagrin* can be described as belonging to a general category of expenditure, the trans-historical "Notion de dépense"; but it can also be understood as a specifically nineteenth-century bourgeois form of it.

The unmasking of the perversity of the bourgeois economic mechanisms is the point which Balzac and Bataille's œuvres have in common from the vantage point of a second-level reading of the texts. It is not quite a matter of forcibly calling Balzac once more (to paraphrase Victor Hugo) "un écrivain révolutionnaire [...] qu'il le veuille ou non" (cf. Butler 1983, 262); the point is, rather, to evaluate soberly the essence of the social mechanisms described by Balzac, now that the glamor and the attractiveness which so hypnotized the would-be aristocrat and emotionally colored his discourse have long vanished and we no longer live in the historical context that motivated his foregrounding of personal empathy. The main advantage of Bataille's perspective is that it can define one and the same phenomenon both as, in principle, inevitable and justified anthropologically—and as deleterious in its concrete historico-political manifestations.

*

After the scene in the antique shop, the reader is now ready to see Raphaël move from the river back and up toward society. Now Raphaël has fresh potential energy, *and* the obligation to use it: desire has been replenished. The demonic contract has, in Arnheim's sense, re-structured his self.

Raphaël's first energy quantum is spent on the spot. When he learns about the destiny of death to which he has condemned himself, he takes immediate revenge—and tells the antique dealer:

> [...] je *désire*, pour me venger d'un si fatal service, que vous tombiez amoureux d'une danseuse! Vous comprendrez alors le bonheur d'une débauche, et peut-être deviendrez-vous prodigue de tous les biens que vous avez si philosophiquement ménagés.
> (Peau, 88; emphasis added)

By virtue of the hide's supernatural powers, the theorist of the thesaurization of desire is thus, significantly, condemned to submit himself to the principle which a dancer perfectly symbolizes—that of absolute mobility. Balzac's text will later show in detail this dramatic energetic reversal, "demonic" again in its literal application of the Dantesque principle of *contrappasso* organizing the Hell of the *Divine Comedy*.[10]

After having cursed the *antiquaire*, Raphaël proceeds from the shop to an orgy (to which he has desired to be invited). There, at the banker Taillefer's, he meets a crowd of self-styled philosophers, as well as a group of courtesans led by the "reines du plaisir" Aquilina and Euphrasie. After the libations and the pleasures afforded by the situation, while the other guests of Taillefer's lie around the *hôtel* in exhaustion, Raphaël is prompted by his friend Emile to "confess" to him (and to the reader) his life's story—which he sets out to do. Here ends the first part of the novel, justly entitled "Le Talisman" after its unquestionably most powerful protagonist.

The section of the novel which Balzac entitled "La femme sans cœur" scans events that comprise Raphaël's family life (with, for example, the reference to the father in the first gambling episode), as well as his friendship with Rastignac and his encounter with the one woman who, in *La peau de chagrin,* does "have a heart": Pauline. It may thus seem somewhat odd that Balzac decided nonetheless to label this division after Fœdora only; and critics have often remained perplexed when trying to explain this difficulty. Such an incongruity, however, can be overcome if one keeps in mind that the "empty" woman, Fœdora, is a *type général*, a symbol of society as a whole. As Balzac himself noted in his handwritten post-scriptum to the epilogue of the novel: "Fœdora [...] elle est partout, c'est, si vous voulez, la Société" (*Peau*, 294).

If one permutated the two terms according to Balzac's suggestion and entitled this section "Society", all elements would fall into place. It would then be perfectly natural to see Raphaël, in the midst of the eminently social ambience of the orgy, evoke the contradictory class factors which shaped his life and rendered it such as it is in the moment of his painful confession to Emile. If this part of the novel is viewed as an analysis of the social circumstances determining individual lives, then apparently disparate elements can be opposed to each other in a significant fashion: the squandering that ravaged Raphaël when he was dominated by Fœdora would be the element opposed to the homeostasis which reigned in his life when, as a poor student, he was living under the protection of Pauline's (and Pauline's mother's) self-sufficient world. At the same time, the father's past fanatic principle of utilitarianism can be identified as the necessary, chronological as well as existential, counterpart to the ostentation and waste which characterize Taillefer's orgy (and which on the face of it show no apparent teleology). Assuming the socio-historical dimension to be the organizing principle of this second section of the novel is the most fruitful way to tie together many diverse characters and to make sense of Raphaël's anguished flashback. The word "confession" aptly describes the latter: many of his formulations strikingly echo the historical *ouverture* to de Musset's quasi-autobiographical *La Confession d'un enfant du siècle*.

In a complex work, P. Barbéris has given a convincing general interpretation of the *mal du siècle* characterizing the fictional Raphaël de Valentin as well as many of his real peers in the generation of 1830. According to Barbéris,

> Le thème central du mal du siècle est [...] celui du vide, de l'absence à soi-même. Mais, d'apparence ou d'expression psychologique ou morale, il a, en fait, des causes historiques précises [...]
> Le mal du siècle résulte du conflit entre le vouloir-vivre, justifié par certaines promesses de la "civilisation", et les possibilités objectives, avec tous les retours sur soi que cela suppose [...]
> Le mal du siècle est la conscience d'une dissonance entre l'Homme et l'Histoire [...]
>
> (Barbéris 1970, I, 111-12)

It is true that for example the Jeunes-France, the young Gautier, etc., express the progressive and potentially liberating aspects of the constitutional monarchy put in place by the 1830 revolution. The political atmosphere in France was then indeed more encouraging than in the rest of Europe stifled by the Holy Alliance, where even the economic rise of the bourgeoisie was hampered by feudal strictures. Outside France and few other areas, such a desacralization of political power did not take place until much later in the century—by which time the specter of 1848 had already warned the aristocratic ruling class of the dangers implicit in any type of political concession. Nonetheless, the fact remains that French society suffered deeply from an equally grave imbalance of an opposite sign. If most European societies were still oppressed by a deficient development of the market economy, France was under strain because of the excessively rapid, chaotic expansion of capitalism (at least in certain sectors). The *Enrichissez-vous!* suggested by Guizot, when turned into the existential rationale justifying an industrialization *à la hussarde*, yielded the peculiar results which we find depicted, to name but the most famous example, in Balzac's *Illusions perdues*—whose theme is precisely the commodification of all types of intellectual resources, from the artistic to the scientific.

Possibly inspired also by the impressive testimony of Stendhal's *œuvre*, Lukàcs wrote in his fundamental essay on *Illusions perdues*:

> [The] heroic period came to an end with the fall of Napoleon, the return of the Bourbons and the July revolution. The ideals became superfluous ornaments and frills on the sober reality of everyday life [...]
> The drive of ideals, a necessary product of the previous necessarily heroic period, was now no longer wanted; its representatives, the young generation schooled in the tradition of the heroic period, was inevitably doomed to deteriorate [...]
> They demanded a place for themselves and politics refused it to them [...]
> It was the tragedy of a whole generation.
> (Lukàcs 1950, 48-49)

Lukàcs points out that *Illusions perdues* is a tragicomic epic showing how "the spirit of man is drawn into the orbit of capitalism. The theme of the novel is the transformation of literature [...] into a commodity, and [the] complete 'capitalization' of every sphere of intellectual, literary and artistic activity [...] Its real subject is the advance and victory of capitalism" (ibid., 49, 53).

Barbéris thus aptly characterizes in political terms the apparently apolitical phenomenon of the melancholy we encounter in *La peau de chagrin*:

> Le mal du siècle est l'un des symptômes les plus voyants des "maladies infantiles" du capitalisme aussi bien que de la poussée anticapitaliste [...] Tout concourt à établir un décalage entre les ambitions et les possibilités, pour le "plus grand nombre", d'accéder à des emplois [...]
> Le mal du siècle, Balzac nous le montrera avec force, caractérise la période ascendante du siècle [...] Le mal du siècle correspond à une certaine jeunesse de la bourgeoisie [...] Le mal du siècle est celui d'une jeunesse qui n'avait pas encore définitivement désappris à croire.
> (Barbéris 1970, I, 126, 127)

In sum, it would be impossible to overlook the obvious "political" dimension (in the broadest sense) of French Romanticism. There were specific historical circumstances which caused Raphaël's *Weltschmerz* and rendered it much more than a fictional episode within the *Comédie humaine*.

In this sense it is useful to establish once more a connection with Bataille's *La notion de dépense*. Bataille draws the historico-economic curve of a psychological category; in so doing, he sets in movement the border between the two fields and mobilizes categories traditionally considered impermeable to each other. There seems to be a liberating overdetermination in the possibility of applying to *La peau de chagrin* both the historico-economic and the psychological implications of Bataille's notion of energetic loss.

According to Bataille, expense without return being the indispensable prerequisite for the very existence of civilization, the affluent classes' main social responsibility is that of serving as catalysts and functional consumers of wealth—as if the socially privileged were the equivalent of sacrificial priests for the energetic surplus of society.[11] After having established what he calls "la dépense fonctionnelle des classes riches" and "la perte ostentatoire [...] universellement liée à la richesse comme sa fonction dernière" (Bataille 1967, 35, 35-36), Bataille goes on to illustrate their historical peripeties:

> Dans les sociétés dites civilisées, l'*obligation* fonctionnelle de la richesse n'a disparu qu'à une époque relativement récente. Le déclin du paganisme a entraîné celui des jeux et des cultes dont les riches Romains devaient obligatoirement faire les frais: c'est pourquoi on a pu dire que le christianisme avait individualisé la propriété, donnant à son possesseur une disposition entière de ses produits et abrogeant sa fonction sociale [...] à la dépense païenne prescrite par la coutume, le christianisme a substitué l'aumône libre [...]
>
> Tout ce qui était généreux, orgiaque, démesuré a disparu: les thèmes de rivalité qui continuent à conditionner l'activité individuelle se développent dans l'obscurité et ressemblent à des éructation honteuses [...]
>
> Autour des banques modernes comme autour des mâts totémiques des Kwakiutl, le même désir d'offusquer anime les individus et les entraîne dans un système de petites parades qui les aveugle les uns contre les autres comme s'ils étaient devant une lumière trop forte [...] seules la générosité, la noblesse ont disparu et, avec elles, la contrepartie spectaculaire que les riches rendaient aux misérables.
>
> En tant que classe possédant la richesse, ayant reçu avec la richesse l'obligation de la dépense fonctionnelle, la bourgeoisie moderne se caractérise par le refus de principe qu'elle oppose à cette obligation. Elle s'est distinguée de l'aristocratie en ce qu'elle n'a consenti à *dépenser* que *pour soi*, à l'intérieur d'elle-même [...]
>
> A ces conceptions humiliantes de *dépense restreinte* [emphasis added] ont répondu les conceptions rationalistes qu'elle a développées à partir du XVIIe siècle et qui n'ont pas d'autre sens qu'une représentation du monde strictement *économique*, au sens vulgaire, au sens bourgeois du mot. La haine de la dépense est la raison d'être et la justification de la bourgeoisie [...]
>
> > (Bataille 1967, 36-38; emphasis in the original, except where otherwise stated)

Bataille's notion of *restricted expenditure* explains well the apparent paradox of the retentive, anabolic character of Taillefer's "bourgeois orgy". The ultimate purpose of Taillefer's liberality is an interested one—namely, the founding of a new paper voicing a tamed, piloted opposition against the liberal-bourgeois government (*Peau*, 91). Accordingly, the attitude of Raphaël's friends toward expenditure consists in a cynical hedonism in which the notion of pleasure is governed by an obsessively utilitarian intention. The celebrations offered by Taillefer in *La peau de chagrin* thus deserve being described as a specifically *bourgeois* orgy in the sense sketched by Bataille: there the ultimate goal is not the consumption of energy in pleasure, but rather accumulation, profit (both financial and political). It is clear how wide a gap separates the expenditure principle that permeates Raphaël's life from the one commanding the greedy convives of Taillefer's. For all the power he has accumulated in the *peau*, Raphaël is a stranger at the orgy; he is an outcast, since his energetic strategy is the inverse of the mainstream one.

To be sure, Balzac's novel contains at least one other character who shares with Raphaël the uncertainties and vicissitudes of the young man striving for success in society: Rastignac. Rastignac, in fact, at one point even goes so far as to set out in despair and gamble for survival, just as Raphaël would; having won, he then generously shares his small fortune with his friend, thus allowing him to go through a fresh cycle of dissipation. However, the spirit of Rastignac's actions runs precisely counter to the principle of direct consumption of the self in pleasure which they apparently advocate: his squandering is yet another example of anabolic investment. As he pointedly tells his friend at the very moment when he is about to introduce Fœdora to him,

> [...] ne nous arrêtons pas aux hommes, interrogeons les résultats. Toi, tu travailles? eh! bien, tu ne feras jamais rien. Moi, je suis propre à tout et bon à rien, paresseux comme un homard? ... eh! bien, j'arriverai à tout. Je me répands, je me pousse, l'on me fait place; je me vante, l'on me croit; je fais des dettes, on les paie! La dissipation, mon cher, est un système politique. *La vie d'un homme occupé à manger sa fortune devient souvent une spéculation*; il place ses capitaux en amis, en plaisirs, en protecteurs, en connaissances. Un négociant risque-t-il un million? Pendant vingt ans il ne dort, ni ne boit, ni ne s'amuse; il couve son million, il le fait trotter par toute l'Europe; il s'ennuie, se

donne à tous les démons que l'homme a inventés; puis une liquidation, comme j'en ai vu faire, le laisse souvent sans un sou, sans un nom, sans un ami. Le dissipateur, lui, s'amuse à vivre, à faire courir ses chevaux. Si par hasard il perd ses capitaux, il a la chance d'être nommé receveur-général, de se bien marier, d'être attaché à un ministre, à un ambassadeur. Il a encore des amis, une réputation et toujours de l'argent. Connaissant les ressorts du monde, il les manœuvre à son profit.

(*Peau*, 145; emphasis added)

It is typical that economic and existential notions here incessantly metaphorize each other. In the world of reification, the animate becomes inanimate, the inanimate animate; friends become sacks of gold, sacks of gold "trot" amiably around Europe. Far from giving the uncanny effect which is often the result of the confusion of the two realms, discourse here pushes normalization to the extreme: in the fairytale world of the "best" of all possible economic systems, the spiritual can absurdly be commensurable with the material, because money has become the common measure of all things.

One could not state more clearly than Rastignac the fact that in the bourgeois society the dissipator is actually an investor; and that even loss acquires a value insofar as it can become profitable in the long run. In different but analogous ways, both Rastignac and Taillefer partake of the homeostasis-anabolism which is active in Fœdora, Raphaël's father, and the *antiquaire*; the novel's "bourgeois orgy" illustrates the praxis—and Rastignac's teachings to Raphaël furnish the theory—of an economy which moves entirely within the logic of ultimate fixation of desire, and fully deserves to be described by Bataille's term of "restricted expenditure". In the bourgeois society of *La peau de chagrin*, all roads to the expenditure of desire are blocked; its flow is tolerated only as an investment yielding higher returns, in an immobilization which (with the partial exception of the antique dealer's almost mystical quest for divine *Savoir*) essentially means emotional castration.

It is not surprising that Fœdora, "la femme sans cœur", should be the symbol of such an emotionally castrated society (cf. Danger 1982, 229). All personal traits of Fœdora's individuality have withered; her only interests reaching beyond the public appreciation of her physical and social image are, simply and literally, financial ones.

The maximum tragedy to which her balance could be exposed is measured in percentage points. Indeed, such is Fœdora's energetic success in the society with which she is identical that in her case a demonic contract would be inconceivable. Her universe is a machine ticking in the ideal steady state of homeostasis—and this one condition suffices to decree her "thermodynamic" success within the *Comédie humaine*.[12] She is a usurer in the psychological realm; the closest parallel to her in Balzac's universe is Gobseck, the usurer of the financial world.

The mention of Gobseck here is not an accidental one; his role is exemplary in connection with the physico-economical principles expounded in *La peau de chagrin*. His life is a fundamental point of reference for all reflection about Balzac's views on energy—and his death all the more so. At the end of the novel bearing his name the reader witnesses tangibly, and with the full force of Balzac's metonymic energy, the intensity of the conflict leading a major character to the castration of desire.

In a long and detailed page, the narrator-witness describes what could be termed the materialization of the psychic damage entailed by the choice of blocking the emotional flow of the self:

> Dans la chambre voisine de celle où Gobseck était expiré, se trouvaient des pâtés pourris, une foule de comestibles de tout genre et même des coquillages, des poissons qui avaient de la barbe et dont les diverses puanteurs faillirent m'asphyxier. Partout fourmillaient des vers et des insectes. Ces présents récemment faits étaient mêlés à des boîtes de toutes formes, à des caisses de thé, à des balles de café. Sur la cheminée, dans une soupière d'argent étaient des avis d'arrivage de marchandises consignées en son nom au Havre, balles de coton, boucauts de sucre, tonneaux de rhum, cafés, indigos, tabacs, tout un bazar de denrées coloniales! Cette pièce était encombrée de meubles, d'argenterie, de lampes, de tableaux, de vases, de livres, de belles gravures roulées, sans cadres, et de curiosités. Peut-être cette immense quantité de valeurs ne provenait pas entièrement de cadeaux et constituait des gages qui lui étaient restés faute de paiement. Je vis des écrins armoriés ou chiffrés, des services en beau linge, des armes précieuses, mais sans étiquettes. En ouvrant un livre qui me semblait avoir été déplacé, j'y trouvai des billets de mille francs.
> (Balzac 1951, II, 670-71)

This passage is a true mirror-image of the description of the antique dealer's shop—with one essential difference. There, accumulation is a sign of the *antiquaire*'s frenzied desire for knowledge; here, it is deteriorated, reversed into its psychological shadow—the frenzy of folly. At the representational level, the novel manages to justify Gobseck's madness by ways of his increasing senility; but the reader immediately recognizes that the conceptual chain runs quite in the opposite direction. The theme of repression run amok demands here, as a narrative consequence, Gobseck's *retombée en enfance* (his obsessional neurosis). Gobseck's death impressively materializes the waste of humanity implicit in the strategy of accumulation of withheld energy which he has pursued for his whole life. This strongly graphic episode represents in concentrated form a sort of Balzacian narrativized essay on "instincts and their vicissitudes".

Whereas in *La peau de chagrin* Fœdora's castration is passed under silence in the text and is itself textually "castrated", the usurer's loss as a living being is eventually exposed and illustrated in *Gobseck*. Gobseck's case shows, once and for all in the *Comédie humaine*, that bringing (to use the same wording of *La peau de chagrin*) "la mort dans la vie" is perhaps, in the short term, an energetically efficient way to run and manage the psychic balance—but ultimately nonetheless also a castrating choice. The existential price paid for the attainment of homeostasis and the immobilization of desire proves to be intolerably high.

*

Raphaël's infatuation for Fœdora has by now transformed him into a perfect machine for the dissipation of energy:

> Riche à millions, j'aurais toujours joué, mangé, couru. Je ne voulais plus rester seul avec moi-même [...] Galérien du plaisir, je devais accomplir ma destinée de suicide.
> *(Peau,* 202)

Nowhere else is the equivalence pleasure = suicide pursued with such obstinacy.

When Raphaël is reduced to his last coin, we have finally reached the moment when the text opens. It is at this point in narrated time that the beginning of narrative time (with the gambling episode, the casino, Raphaël's thought of drowning himself) finds its place in the chronological sequence.

The second section of the novel is now moving quickly toward its conclusion. Raphaël completes his narration to Emile and becomes again aware of the reality that surrounds him; this immediately reminds him of his destitute state. But then he suddenly recalls that he has just acquired the magic hide: he thus wishes to forget Fœdora and to become a millionaire. The next morning, Raphaël is told that he has inherited six million francs. The hide has shrunk, and he can measure exactly what amount of his vital energy has been transformed into money. Suddenly understanding to their full extent the implications of the "exchange rate" of desire, he declares that he no longer wishes anything and begins a life haunted by the fear of his own fatal power (*Peau*, 210-11).

All of the time he has left to live stands under the sign of the destructivity of desire. And, after Fœdora's magic disappearance, Raphaël's desire is essentially incarnated in Pauline.

Pauline is the ideal locus for a study of Raphaël's discontinuous, stop-and-go strategy in the handling of energy. With and around her, the protagonist of the novel repeatedly switches between the anabolic tendency which is exemplified by the antique dealer and the dispersive, consumptive one which is typically his own. Pauline is then, on one hand, a figure of the sublimation of the sexual drive, when she inspires Raphaël to energetic constraint, artistic expression, and more in general pursuit of self-control; on the other hand, she is also fatal temptress, when she unintentionally causes her lover's death by consumption.

The first of the two roles predominates in the central section of the novel, Raphaël's autobiographic flashback. There we learn that, while the women of the *grand monde* care little for the destitute poet, the poet himself, who is at that stage renting a room from Pauline and her mother, lives happily in the company of the two angelic, protective women. Raphaël finds with them a sublime / sublimated fulfillment. In a room which he calls "un sépulcre aérien", " [une] cage digne des Plombs de Venise" (*Peau*, 137), he attains a uterine, pre-natal peace high above the hustle-bustle of the city.[13] Thanks to this tranquillity, Raphaël can spare his modest economic resources; he can concentrate his energy on his studies. He writes a comedy and—in a clear *mise en abyme* of the very theme of the novel—the treatise *Théorie de la volonté*.

The quiet, steady state attained in the garrett could in a sense be described as Raphaël's materialized equivalent to the antique dealer's screen of indifference toward worldly desires; Raphaël's barren room could be put in parallel with and in opposition to the obstructed shop. One difference, however, is essential: while the old man (at least until the next peripety) has managed to effectively neutralize desire, Raphaël has not renounced it. While the *antiquaire*'s desire is sublimated, Raphaël's is only momentarily repressed and circulates beneath the surface as a disruptive element:

> Parfois mes goûts naturels se réveillaient [...] J'étais rongé de vices, plongé dans la débauche, voulant tout, ayant tout; enfin ivre à jeun, *comme saint Antoine dans sa tentation*.
>
> (*Peau*, 139; emphasis added)

Pauline is clearly the object of a conscious strategy that aims at avoiding the expenditure intrinsic to the fulfillment of desire. Balzac significantly visualizes the notion of immobilization when he has Raphaël tell the listener / reader:

> Je m'étais ordonné à moi-même de ne voir qu'une sœur en Pauline [...] j'admirais cette charmante fille *comme un tableau*, comme le portrait d'une maîtresse morte. Enfin, c'était mon enfant, *ma statue*. Pygmalion nouveau, je voulais faire d'une vierge vivante et colorée, sensible et parlante, *un marbre* [...]
>
> (*Peau*, 141; emphasis added)

Reversing Pygmalion's feat, turning live desire into motionless stone: such are the telling images used to illustrate Raphaël's enterprise of *immobilizing desire in representation*.

Raphaël's subsequent encounter with Rastignac easily unanchors the young poet's hesitating, fragile homeostasis. A single speech by the *viveur*—his lecture, referred to above, on the notion of investment through dissipation, dissipation *as* investment—

suffices to reverse Raphaël's freezing of desire. Raphaël thus gradually consumes his energy (physical, intellectual, economic) in the Fœdora episode. We saw how the pact with the devil concluded this parable, when human energy became exhausted and supernatural help had to relay it.

The anabolic role which Pauline has in the retrospective part of the novel then changes dramatically in the third and last section, significantly titled "The Agony". Here, Raphaël gives up all hope to maintain his original project of containing desire, and not only can but must yield to the logic of fulfillment.

Little wonder, therefore, that, after the climactic episode of the inheritance announced to Raphaël at the banquet, "The Agony" tells us of Raphaël meeting Pauline by chance at the theatre and—for once—freely wish that she love him (*Peau*, 227).[14] After this turning point, as the *antiquaire* had foretold (*Peau*, 88), the episodes that follow are a mere retardation of Raphaël's death. The beginning of plenty is here more than ever the beginning of the end; and Raphaël's agony proves to be at the same time the slow agony of narration. Retarding episodes—Raphaël's consultation with the doctors; the treatment at Aix; life with the peasants in Auvergne—do not modify the general trend. Ironically, the progressive, irrecuperable dispersion of the hide's energy gives this part of the novel its peculiar atmosphere of an accelerating rush toward the end.

In a last flare of desire, Raphaël finally dies in Pauline's arms:

> Le moribond chercha des paroles pour exprimer le désir qui dévorait toutes ses forces; mais il ne trouva que les sons étranglés du râle dans sa poitrine, dont chaque respiration creusée plus avant semblait partir de ses entrailles. Enfin, ne pouvant bientôt plus former des sons, il mordit Pauline au sein.
>
> (*Peau*, 292)

It is, of course, possible that Raphaël's agony represents here a reminescence of the gruesome end traditionally attributed to the literary characters who consign themselves to the devil. Doctor Faust's death, as it appears in the sixteenth-century chapbook, may have been an indirect source for Balzac. More important, however, is what the text implies at the theoretical level. In the moment of the apotheosis of desire, Balzac is showing, one last time, the fundamental equivalence between desire and loss of self, between pleasure and death. The final episode of *La peau de chagrin* symbolizes once more the ultimate convergence of pleasure and castration.15

We should, however, make a distinction between two forms of the castration of desire in *La peau de chagrin*: namely, an *a priori* one, operated through the preventive freezing of the soul; and a final one, setting in at the distant *point de fuite* of the self dissolved by pleasure. The first is the one practiced by Fœdora and Raphaël's father (and, in his own peculiarly mystical variant, by the antique dealer); Raphaël envisages it in vain when he is a guest in the golden prison under the roof. The second one applies in the case of Raphaël's agony.

The first type of castration is an *anabolic* one, which immobilizes the self by blocking it in a structure that (in Arnheim's terms) tends toward complexity (the complexity of the the antique shop being but an extreme illustration of the concept). It is based on the repression or sublimation of desire, that is to say, on the reduction of entropy. Rigidity and frigidity are the notions that best describe this form of castration—both terms having the advantage of referring at the same time to the physical as well as to the psychic universe. As is well exemplified by the immense power of the characters of the *Comédie humaine* who undergo it, this type of freezing of the self takes place at the highest possible point of potential energy. On the other hand, the highest point of potential energy is also the most "improbable", i.e., the most unstable one.

By contrast, the second type of castration, which describes Raphaël's final state in the novel, is due to the greatest possible stability—namely, death. Again in Arnheim's terminology, this form of castration can be characterized as *catabolic*: it is based on the principle of fragmentation and unanchoring of the self, which brings it to a state of absolute simplicity. Raphaël's catabolic castration is based on the fulfillment of desire, or, to say the same in thermodynamic terms, on the growth of entropy. Mobility, exchange and energy dispersal—also both physical and psychic concepts— are the traits that best define this form of "fulfillment". As Raphaël repeatedly shows in *La peau de chagrin*, this mobile-dispersive castration of the self sets in at the lowest point: namely, after all potential energy has been transformed into kinetic. The teleology of consumption is clear if we consider that such lowest point of potential energy is the most "probable" one.

On one hand, then, it is essential to stress that in *La peau de chagrin*, as Bersani puts it, "the strategy of emotional castration seems like an effort to control a fate of castration: the smaller, voluntary mutilation of desire is designed to protect Raphaël from a more massive destruction *by* desire" (Bersani 1970, 46). On the other hand, there is an intrinsic symmetry between two different and complementary principles in the novel. Raphaël alternates between an anabolic form of castration (the resistive one) and a catabolic one (the final one). The same opposition between the two variants is active in the other characters of the novel and structures their ways of directing their own dialectic of energy.[16]

*

La peau de chagrin essentially asks a single major question: is there no possibility of a mediation between these poles, apparently opposed to each other? Is there no world-immanent *third way* above the two mutually exclusive ones, apt to resolve the energetic *demonism of desire*? That is to say, is desire an ultimate curse for the psyche, necessarily destined either to succumb to repression—thus immobilizing the self in emotional death—, or to take the upper hand—thereby leading it to disarticulation? Balzac's answer is a negative one: for him, there is no way out of the dilemma. In the course of his autobiographic narration, Raphaël reveals the degree to which one can delude oneself:

> Réalisant ces fabuleux personnages qui, selon les légendes, ont vendu leur âme au diable pour en obtenir la puissance de mal faire, le dissipateur a troqué sa mort contre toutes les jouissances de la vie, mais abondantes, mais fécondes!
> (*Peau*, 197)

The rest of the novel is there to prove that Balzac does not believe in the "abondance", in the "fécondité" of desire: for him, dissipation remains dissipation as pure loss.[17] In portraying Raphaël's ill-fated pact, *La peau de chagrin*, which is in all other respects a completely modern, demythologized novel, quite unexpectedly and paradoxically complies with one of the most conservative historical traits of the genre—namely, the condition that the pact with the devil be, in the long run, but a fool's bargain for the human being who contracts it.

As for an ultimate answer to Balzac's energetic aporias, one could perhaps be found in a reflection organized along the lines which Bataille sketches in concluding *La notion de dépense*.

In opposing the notions of "useful" accumulation and "wasteful" dispersion of energy, analogous to Arnheim's terms of anabolism and catabolism, Bataille establishes between the two a dialectical correlation which could justify distinct functions for both:

> [...] il devient possible, toute réserve abandonnée, d'assigner à l'utilité une valeur *relative*. Les hommes assurent leur subsistance ou évitent la souffrance, non parce que ces fonctions engagent par elles-mêmes un résultat suffisant, mais pour accéder à *la fonction insubordonnée de la dépense libre*.
>
> L'immense travail d'abandon, d'écoulement et d'orage qui constitue [la vie humaine] pourrait être exprimé en disant qu'elle ne commence qu'avec le déficit de[s] systèmes [fermés, qui lui sont assignés dans des conceptions raisonnables]: du moins ce qu'elle admet d'ordre et de réserve n'a-t-il de sens qu'à partir du moment où les forces ordonnées et réservées se libèrent et se perdent pour des fins qui ne peuvent être assujetties à rien dont il soit possible de rendre des comptes. C'est seulement par une telle insubordination, même misérable, que l'espèce humaine cesse d'être isolée dans *la splendeur sans condition des choses matérielles*.
>
> (Bataille 1967, 46, 44; emphasis added)

Raphaël is absorbed by the notion of concrete, specific desires; what causes his castration and loss of self is materially fixed, immobilized in representation. Goethe's Faust, by contrast, turns his struggle against this type of desires into his conscious principle—to the point of betting his soul against them. Raphaël's death symbolizes despair; Faust's, hope.

In both cases, then, fixation is what transforms the Other of desire into a threat; conversely, the overcoming of the threat can only be mediated (as Faust does) by a definite *unanchoring of desire from representation.* The result of such an unanchoring would then be the transformation of desire back into that ever-shifting Other which Bataille calls "the non-subordinate function of free expenditure" of the self.

III
Vautrin and Utopia

Balzac does not suggest a generally valid psychic solution to the aporias of desire. For him, all humans are subject to the *usure*—usury *and* wear—caused by demonic desire, irrespective of what kind of pact may ally them with the demonic source of energy. There is, however, one exception: Vautrin. And the exception is a remarkable one. When all merely human characters are caught in the deadlock, by his very movement Vautrin proves that there is a way out.

Balzac did not conceive the notion of an unanchoring of desire from representation (or, in other terms, its dissociation from what Faust would have called the *Augenblick*—the freezing of the moment); he wants instead to envisage a solution that is adequate to his own view of desire as an "object-ive", specific appetite. An imitation of Faust's never-ending, metaphysical quest would probably have seemed "empty" to him (the closest parallel being perhaps Louis Lambert, who not by chance sinks into folly). Given these circumstances, Vautrin represents Balzac's ideal solution. Vautrin's peculiarity is that of projecting total fulfillment within finitude. His essential features are, firstly, that he has demonic energy, yet is not a demon, or any incarnation of one; secondly, that he commands superhuman, but not super*natural* forces; finally, that he proposes dilemmas of success and failure, and only considers good and evil as abstractions impossible to verify in reality.

In and with Vautrin, Balzac chooses to suspend the question of the pact with the devil, and to foreground the question of the mastery of pure energy instead. In a different formulation: Vautrin shows how in Balzac's world, short of meeting the devil, one can actually *be* a devil—provided that one is as exceptional as Vautrin, that is.

Vautrin therefore plays a double role. On one hand, he is energetically "demonic" when he proposes to share his immense resources with Rastignac and Lucien de Rubempré. On the other hand, however, he is also psychologically human when he is affected by his protégés' vicissitudes, helps them (as he does with Calvi in *Splendeurs et misères*), or suffers for and through them (most visibly, when Lucien commits suicide). Humanity is indeed Vautrin's most striking peculiarity, when we match him against the other demonic figures that can be encountered in stories of demonic pacts. Whereas elsewhere the devil usually appears as sarcastic and mocking toward its partners, Vautrin loves his own creatures—so much so that Milner refuses to see in him a demonic figure: "On ne s'imagine guère un Satan passionné" (Milner 1960, II, 45). Whereas in the historical development of the theme of the pact with the devil the being which gives power and the one who desires to use it are normally distinct, and the pact showing the convergence of their interests as a rule foregrounds the contrast of their personalities, in Vautrin the two roles completely collapse into one.

Half man and half demon, Vautrin could be called an "anti-Christ" in the literal sense of the word: a sort of suffering, human devil in the world of criminality. His milieu is an anti-world which competes with, but is by no means inferior to, the hypocritical one of the "respectable" circles. In fact, the recuperation of Vautrin to society at the end of *Splendeurs et misères des courtisanes* intends to show, among other things, the reward deserved by Vautrin's humane qualities in an official world in which—Balzac's rhetoric spares no ammunition to stress this—the "human" being is essentially a beast.

Obviously, a transcendental apotheosis in the style of Faust's could never be applied to Vautrin in Balzac's novelistic world—such devices belonging of necessity to the conventions of the allegorical poem.[18] Yet the essential intentions are remarkably similar, and, if *La Comédie humaine* finally bestows upon its most powerful hero the totally world-immanent apotheosis of the command of the Parisian police, this simply happens because there can be no divine providence succoring a character who boasts being "Providence itself". The success crowning Vautrin's *Streben* is essentially the final reward allotted by Balzac to someone who can invest his feelings nobly in a corrupt world, at the cost of being beyond the notions of good and evil as these are generally understood in and by society.[19]

However, just as Christ, the mediator figure in the world of Grace, is by definition unique, so is Vautrin, the inimitable humane devil of *La Comédie humaine*. His solution is not attainable to the merely human character. When normal beings must choose between either repressing desire ferociously (Bette, Gobseck, Grandet, among many others) or being consumed by it (Claës, Lambert, old Goriot, Hulot, Raphaël de Valentin), they obey the logic that applies to humans. The same does not hold for Vautrin. Vautrin collects all mutually exclusive qualities; in *La Comédie humaine*, he is the only one who can suspend the physical, thermodynamic laws of expenditure of energy and loss of self through desire. Vautrin is the only character in Balzac who can dispose of all the energy deriving from demonic powers, without being consumed by the catabolic action of localized hedonism. Vautrin illustrates the fact that the ultimate answer to the aporias of desire and vital force is in Balzac not allying oneself with the devil—but *becoming* the devil himself. Such is the extent of Balzac's investment in his human-demonic Overman figure.

Stating that in Balzac's fictional universe Vautrin combines the two normally incompatible opposite poles of desire and energy amounts to suggesting that there is a clearly delineated utopian dimension to Balzac's view of his favorite character. Indeed, Balzac construes Vautrin as a generalized oxymoron—as a coincidence of the opposites supported by an ideal, visionary intention. Vautrin is an image of Balzac's utopian desire for absolute fulfillment of the self, projected onto the psychological plane. The shift of Utopia toward an interiorized dimension must be explained with the circumstance that in Balzac's view of society, permeated with total pessimism, there is no point of cleavage allowing to depict it in an exteriorized, topological form. Vautrin represents Balzac's psychologization of Utopia, or (which is to say the same) his acknowledgement of the impossibility of projecting *any* Utopia "proper" onto the realistic side of the universe of narration.[20]

The interiorization of the utopian dimension in Vautrin becomes even more evident when contrasted with another one that has an established status in criticism: the well-known ideal role that prisons have in Stendhal. In Stendhal, the fulfillment of the self's desire is strongly tied to spatial representation; the locus of happiness is defined in a quintessentially three-dimensional space. As Brombert puts it:

> C'est l'écriture stendhalienne qui se conçoit finalement dans un espace idéal. "Quel bel endroit pour composer une tragédie, que la Grande Chartreuse" (*Journal*, 534). Une page presque onirique—il s'agit d'un de ses premiers textes—annonce la vocation de la prison aérienne. Le jeune Henri Beyle imagine une "vallée délicieuse" [...] [les artistes et les philosophes] "habitent tous une tour d'immense structure située exactement au milieu de la vallée [...] "
> On songe en effet à tous les "lieux élevés" où les personnages de Stendhal découvrent la sérénité: le rocher de Julien, la tour gothique à Besançon, les figures de la verticalité dans *La Chartreuse*. L'isolement et l'élévation topographique correspondent aux moments de plus intense ferveur poétique [...]
> (Brombert 1975, 91, 78)

Stendhal's "happy prison" is then a particular manifestation of an absolute triumph of spatiality in Utopia. This is entirely consistent with the canonic notion: from Thomas Moore and Rabelais's Abbey of Thélème to Bulgakov's *The Master and Margarita* (which is particularly relevant in this context because it, too, ties Utopia to the theme of the pact with the devil), the fulfillment of desire is organized along spatial coordinates and connected with a tangible *locus amœnus*. In a word, the three-dimensional pattern represents the normative standard.[21]

By contrast, Balzac's emotional investment in the utopian ideal takes a non-spatial path; and his locus of "desirable impossibility" becomes an interior reality. The satisfaction of the *fantasmes* of desire is not distributed over a series of discrete points in space, but rather, contained in the *coincidentia oppositorum* of Vautrin's character. The spatiality of Utopia can then be left to float in an extreme degree of remoteness: the Indre valley of *Le lys dans la vallée* could hardly be called a shelter from the struggles of the world; and the southern United States mentioned in *Le père Goriot* have a function and a meaning only insofar as they can—once more—serve as backdrop for Vautrin's omnipotence.

Vautrin combines all opposites: on one hand, he can reconcile Balzac's "thermodynamic laws" of desire; on the other, he is able to collapse the demonic and the human role into one. Such a coincidence of opposed principles can be found in at least two further characteristics of Vautrin's: namely, in his political attitudes, and in his sexual preferences. Viewing him as the utopian convergence of all determinations explains his much-debated political *arrivisme révolutionnaire* (which would otherwise remain a mere a contradiction in terms), as well as his pronounced but not activated homosexual affection toward the friends-sons with whom he allies himself in *La Comédie humaine*. In short, the choice of leaving all determinations equally co-present in Vautrin is Balzac's way of raising him above all possible fixations and limitations in one identity only. Vautrin must be Raphaël *and* the antique dealer: he must cumulate all identities, if he is to soar above the common-mortal world of the loss of energy in desire—if he is to attain a utopian dimension capable of endowing him with the absolute non-determination of a God.

Thus, in spite of what Affron justly calls the recurrent "patterns of failure" dominating the characters of *La Comédie humaine* (Affron 1966, 133-41)—in spite, in other words, of the evident cynical pragmatism that is required for success in Balzac's fictional world—it is clear that, at least when depicting Vautrin, Balzac's *écriture* still partakes of an aesthetic of fullness. In such an aesthetic of plenitude of the text, language still adheres to its ultimate referent, and can still attempt to formulate images of a fulfilled Utopia.[22] Balzac's language constantly strives to effectively fill silence and fantasmatically present the exhaustion of desire by satisfaction. Vautrin incarnates such a striving: he is the living image of fulfillment. Perhaps a major reason for the contradictory fascination exerted by Balzac on his readers lies in the fact that the stage of his novels, the (as he repeatedly calls it) sordid "Hell" of Parisian society, in the long run serves as a triumphal background for his utopian-paradisiac apotheosis of energy. Balzac's amazing paradox is that his Utopia of power, his images of plenitude, are derived from a universe of lack, and that his desire for perfection is steeped in, and expressed by, a fictional world inhabited by the crassest imperfection.

At the opposite end of the spectrum, Flaubert will repudiate "Vautrin-ism": he will ridicule the very attempt to construe the image of the fulfillment of desire. He too will assume narratively the emptiness of society; above all, however, he will *reduplicate* it with a language which also refuses the ambition to express plenitude. In Flaubert's novels, negation doubles itself when the evacuation of society is mirrored by the silence of the language which would describe it. For Flaubert, the utopian fulfillment of desire exists only in representation; it takes the form of self-illusion and self-deceit (as in *L'Éducation sentimentale* or *Madame Bovary*), or else it becomes strictly an hallucination, in which the very notion of the self is no longer definable— as in *La Tentation de Saint Antoine*.

The ontological status of the demonic in Flaubert reflects this state of affairs: it traces an anti-climactic curve in the existential dignity of the textual device called the devil. Balzac's belief in a form of secular demonism is a highly original transitional form between the *absolute density* of "orthodox" evil and the *absolute emptiness* about to be displayed by the notion of the demonic in the Flaubertian world.

Notes to Chapter One

[1] By contrast, an excellent proof of the dangers lurking behind the mere mechanical reproduction of the contract scene, which takes over the surface plot without radically re-thinking the motivations for it, is offered by the artistic failure of (for example) Soulié's *Mémoires du diable*.

[2] True, by the end of *Illusions perdues* Lucien's *esprit* is already consumed: all he can sell to Vautrin is a mask, an empty token without intrinsic contents—his puppet-like body. This, however, may well be a mere evolutionary mutation necessary in capitalism: Lucien must adapt and become an expropriated "proletarian of desire" in a society governed by the survival of the richest. Even Vautrin is, in a sense, only an artisan devil, threatened by the anonymous demonism of modernity.

Illusions perdues expounds Balzac's views on the obsolescence of the traditional demonic pact in a world in which desire has become an industrial-capitalistic process.

[3] Again, both realistic and fantastic postulates are here represented with equal weight.

[4] This is not the only gambling episode in Raphaël's life. In the second part of the novel—which, in a long flashback, narrates the hero's adolescence and early experiences—the reader learns that at some point during the previous year Rastignac had already shared with Raphaël the profits of a lucky visit to the casino (*Peau*, 194).

[5] The passage in question strongly confirms Bersani's claim that "Balzac takes very little trouble to obscure the masturbatory fantasy recognizable in this fable" (Bersani 1970, 46)—even *before* the talisman appears in the novel.

For the link between masturbation and gambling, cf. the last part of Freud's *Dostoevsky and Parricide* (Freud *GW* XIV, 416-18; *SE* XXI, 177-96, esp. pp. 193-94).

[6] Accordingly, various branches of science are portrayed and contrasted in the third part of *La peau de chagrin*: the thrust of reality breaks through from under Balzac's parodic intentions.

[7] On the notion of production-dispersal, cf. also "Lois de l'économie générale", in Bataille's *La part maudite* (1967, 66-78).

[8] However disconcerting the theories of some anguished philosophers of science may have been, the fact remains that the second law of thermodynamics is a reality—a reality which Feynman verbalizes as "the one-way behavior of the entire universe" (Feynman 1961, 46/9). In particular, Carnot's cycle of perfectly reversible energetic transformations is a merely theoretical one; as Feynman puts it, "[T]he hypothesis of Carnot, the second law of thermodynamics, is sometimes stated as follows: heat cannot, of itself, flow from a cold to a hot object [...] Carnot assumed that it is impossible to extract the energy of heat at a single temperature [...] While the process of making work go into heat can take place at a given temperature, one cannot reverse it to get the work back again" (Feynman 1963, 44/4, 44/3).

[9] An extraordinary anticipation of Freud's remark can be found in Dostoevsky's *Poor Folk*, when, in his peculiarly grotesque *skaz*, Makar Devushkin writes to

Varvara Alekseevna: "And then, well, the memories of all my past bring me down [...] [I]t's a strange thing: I'm oppressed, but the memories of it, somehow, are pleasant" ("A vot vospominaniya-to obo vsem moem prezhnem na menya tosku nagonyayut [...] [S]trannoe delo—tyazhelo, a vospominaniya kak budto priyatnye") (Dostoevsky n.d., 9).

[10] The antique dealer's fragility proves that he is not an incarnation of the devil. He is in charge of administering demonic power; yet, unlike Goethe's Mephistopheles or the devils of more traditional narrations, he is far from owning that power himself. The best definition of the old man would perhaps be that of a devil's notary or secretary: he has demonic, supernatural energy at his disposal, yet he is human and harbors human feelings. The combination of demonic powers and human nature is not too dissimilar from the one which Balzac (obviously with a completely different emotional investment) attributes to Vautrin.

[11] It would be tempting to inscribe René Girard's theory of the eternal return of the sacrificial lamb into the Bataillean principle of the functional annihilation of the surplus.

[12] This may well be the factor which, catalyzed through subconscious envy, fascinates Raphaël's inefficiency.

[13] The analogy with Stendhal's paradisiac prisons is here striking.

[14] Here, ironically, the *peau* does not shrink: she loves him already.

[15] As P. Danger aptly suggests, Raphaël's death is "un inceste suicidaire" committed with the mother-sister figure Pauline (Danger 1982, 244).

[16] In spite of the differences that oppose the *antiquaire* and Raphaël on the narrative level, an evident trait which they share is the final victory of the catabolic principle. The old man's infatuation with the dancer Euphrasie, which Raphaël witnesses at the theater, is a form of revenge: not only a personal revenge of Raphaël's, but also, on the symbolic plane, a revenge of desire. This episode illustrates the tendency of entropy to grow in spite of all attempts to keep it in check: the old man's extreme sentimental investment represents the sudden transformation of "improbable" potential energy into a kinetic avalanche which will bring him to the final, most "probable" state—death.

[17] Goethe's *Faust* upholds the notion of desire and eventually justifies it metaphysically; however, it can only do so by proposing a peculiar, unique form of shifting desire, devoid of static pleasure (the "I have no thought of joy!" of v. 1765; Kaufmann, 189). Furthermore, Faust's non-hedonistic, anguished desire can circulate effectively only because its value is guaranteed and countersigned on High. According to strictly terrestrial standards, Faust *is* guilty; and it is only a literal *deus-ex-machina* intervention that saves him in the end.

[18] In *La peau de chagrin*, appropriately for an *étude philosophique*, we come close to such a solution in Pauline's elevation to mythical status, which is one of the features of the epilogue.

[19] My usage of the concept of "striving" is aimed much less at claiming analogous philosophical meanings for Vautrin and Faust (which they simply do not have) than it is at pointing out Vautrin's peculiar conflation of roles with respect to the structure

on which Goethe's poem is based. On one hand, Vautrin "strives", as Faust does; on the other hand, he dispenses power to his partners, as does Mephisto.

[20] The interiorization of the features of Utopian desire clearly parallels the interiorization of the category of the demonic operated in *La peau de chagrin*.

[21] Examples of "spatial Utopia" could be multiplied at will in drawing, for example, from European Romanticism (the Mediterranean countries, the Caucasus, the Orient, etc.). The very etymology of the word, of course, foregrounds spatial dimensionality.

[22] Balzac's aesthetics are made to correspond to the "gold standard" of the realist novel, characterized by the "signifiant convertible", in Goux's *Les monnayeurs du langage* (Goux 1984, esp. pp. 191-202).

2

Disrupting the Canon, Pulverizing the Self: Flaubert

I
Desire In Textual Wilderness

> Now for the wilderness!
>
> Byron, *Cain*

During the nineteenth century, the French public long ignored (or worse still, underestimated) Goethe's *Faust* because, as Baldensperger perceptively put it, "some people saw in it above all an extremely badly written tragedy, others a very hazy philosophy" (Baldensperger 1904, 124). This example aptly illustrates the decisive importance which the correct choice of a canon has in the process of literary evaluation. What is truth on one side of the aesthetic watershed is error on the other; and the task of the critic is, ideally at least, that of proposing the "correct" criteria for interpretation. In the real world, however, as F. Vodichka points out in his "The History of the Echo of Literary Works", the relationship between artist and critic is at best a dialectical one (Vodichka 1964, 72), and a philological assessment of the literary norm can, in practice, only be attempted retrospectively, once the norm itself has been relativized by further evolution.[1]

In his ground-breaking "Standard Language and Poetic Language", Mukarovsky stressed that the history of literature may be described as a series of successive shifts in the foregrounding of different compositional elements, so that each of these sequentially becomes the "dominant" of a given period—or, *a fortiori*, of a single work. The initially new foregrounding gradually wears out and becomes automatized, an ossified frame in turn calling for its own replacement. A literary norm is then, by definition, always a transitional formation. Bakhtin developed this point further by stressing the notion that in literature the diachronic succession of codes takes the form of a series of reaccentuations, each reflecting different authorial intentions, in which aesthetic "revolutions" are but the turning points of an essentially continuous line. (For Bakhtin, then, literary revolution and literary evolution arguably are but the two dialectically related sides of one and the same metamorphic process). Such turning points are the moments when obviously not *the* canon, but *a* canon disintegrates. The old sets are inadequate, but there is no clearly defined new standard (cf. the "gold standard" in economics) against which to measure it. No wonder, then, that those are precisely the moments of disarray in which "the echo of the literary work" can suffer most deeply in the transition from a literary norm to another one incompatible with it.

Although recent criticism, with its emphasis on the deconstruction of codes, has been somewhat more in tune with Saint Antony's obstinate, perdurable alterity, the fact remains that Flaubert's anchoritic work has elicited an amount of criticism incomparably less impressive in size than the more canonical parts of his *œuvre*. Antoine's disruption of the literary canon, and the pulverization of the self which accompanies it, to a certain extent still seem to be disquieting to a part of the critics. This imbalance calls for correction: it is simply unsatisfactory to assume that Flaubert's so painstakingly researched and documented grotesqueness-monstrosity could have no *specific* functional, semantic role within a carefully orchestrated plan.

It may well prove impossible to state ultimately what *La Tentation de Saint Antoine* "really" is. *La Tentation* is such a defyingly, mockingly subversive text, that seizing it is likely to be a hopeless enterprise. Similar in this (as well as in many, Other thematic features) to Montaigne's *Essais*, it acts out the disruption, indeed the disintegration, of old canons, but it consciously refuses to establish a new one: "vouloir conclure" is, for Flaubert, itself stupid. It would be easier to say what *La Tentation* is not; or perhaps, more fruitfully, to analyze how it works. If one wants to decode Flaubert's "comble de l'insanité" in order to render it readable, intelligible (and hopefully, at long last, also *intelligent*), the best approach is to examine its components, its mechanism, its voices—all distributed far more intentionally than a first deceiving impression would suggest.[2] To do so, it will be necessary to disentangle the apparent cacophony of registers and to analyze each of them carefully in its own terms, and not merely as a contrastive negativity. If we address specific questions: "What is the text about? How do the hallucinations work together, and against the centralized character?", we may be able to make sense of Flaubert's anthropoclastic ire. We may then find out that the answer to the problem of why the *Tentation* pulverizes the self—and the canon along with it—is really one and the same as the answer to another more representational one: what does it mean to *adore the devil*?

*

In presenting a part of Goethe's *Faust* to the French public, Mme de Staël praised it by writing that (in spite of its evident defects) "il fait réfléchir sur tout et [...] sur quelque chose de plus que tout" (de Staël 1968, I, 367). What *La Tentation de Saint Antoine*, first and foremost, has in common with *Faust* is, indeed, the conscious striving to be a "book about everything". On the other hand, we do know from the *Correspondance* that Flaubert was also constantly fascinated with the possibility of writing "un livre sur rien [...] qui se maintienne par la force de son style, comme la terre [...] se maintient dans l'air" (1852) (Flaubert 1980, II, 31).[3]

One of the most revealing paradoxes of *La Tentation* can be detected here. The more the story of Saint Antony breaks with conventional narrativity and soars into the perfectly non-justified level of what Flaubert called "la gueulade métaphysique"—in other words, the more it becomes a book about "nothing"—the more it encompasses the World-All, the Universe as a theme. It is highly significant that the two works by Flaubert which with most determination veer away from the canon of the realist novel, *La légende de Saint Julien l'Hospitalier* and *La Tentation de Saint Antoine*, thematize respectively sadism with parricide, and sadomasochism with deicide (more exactly, a repressed desire for deicide). In these two texts there is almost "nothing" in the ways of representational literature; yet there is undoubtedly "everything" from the psychological point of view. It seems as though plot and character, with all related conventions, were inversely correlated to thematic breadth; and as if the liberation of fantasy could only take place through rebellion against the (paternal) authority of narrative norms. What is certain is that *Saint Antoine*'s first deicide is committed against the authority of the laws of the novel: the crime is put in place symbolically in the structure, long before it is thematized by the text. The absolute liberty which *La Tentation* and *Saint Julien* allow to the free association of ideas is a striking return to the *orgies of the imagination* contained in Flaubert's early works, in which—from fratricide to parricide to incest—nothing was prohibited.

Granted, just exactly *how* "everything" is portrayed in *La Tentation de Saint Antoine* is far from being self-evident. In Flaubert's time as well as in ours, most critics have seen in the work an arbitrary collection of visions, arranged (if the notion of "arrangement" is granted at all) in a more or less haphazard way. This opinion is, at least *prima facie*, justified by Flaubert himself, who, in writing to Louise Colet about the first version of the *Tentation*, defined it as "un collier de perles" lacking the thread which should unite them. The critic's task is then to attempt to put the "thread" back into the "necklace". My hypothesis is that the sub-text underlying Saint Antoine's history, and repressed and censored by it, is Byron's *Cain*;[4] and that Antony's temptation is the Œdipal parricide which Cain symbolically commits in revolting against God, and in metonymically killing the brother instead of the father. As is well known, Byron's *Cain: A Mystery* ends with the expulsion from the "Land without Paradise" into the territory farther East: in that same "wilderness" (v. 544) Saint Antoine waits and meditates in solitude, haunted, in the depth of his subconscious, by an uncanny perception which he cannot possibly bring to exact anamnesis—by the vague *recollection of having once been Cain*.

The specificity of the *Tentation* vis-à-vis its Byronian model can be expressed thus: just as in *Cain*, in Flaubert's work, too, the devil demands to be adored; however, because the saint indefinitely refuses to accede to such a request, his hallucinations also continue indefinitely. They will only cease after the saint's vision of the mystical union with matter has satisfied his desire, some type of suspension of the paternal God-principle is attained, and atonement with feminine Matter is granted. The nature of the difference between Antony and Cain is clear: Flaubert's "saint" does not ally himself with the devil and does not enter parricidal rebellion, because the pulverization of the self which he experiences in the course of the temptation process gradually leads him to the disarticulation and disintegration of his conscious being—to a *devenir la matière* which takes place at the molecular level, altogether cutting off the organized, rational-paternal notion of self. Revolt at the level of psychological macrostructures proves to be superfluous, since infiltration "from underneath" bypasses the interdiction.

The "string" which I would like to propose for the reading of the only apparently sparse "pearls" of *La Tentation* is thus the following one. First, in section I, the scene of the temptation is presented. Then Antony undergoes a series of attacks by repressed desires, physical (section II) and later intellectual (section III). In these three sections, the devil-figure(s) represent "good" Mentors—"good" relatively, i.e. in the sense that they propose enjoying fruits all forbidden with varying degrees of intensity. The devil-figure(s) here entirely fall into the category which Jones described as "the son who defies the Father".[5]

After the course of traditional temptations has been fully run in sections II and III, sections IV and V represent Flaubert's own innovation in the possibilities of literary hallucination. Heretics and Gods of the past appear here as an abstraction and intellectualization of visions which had been made tangible in the preceding part of the work. However, unlike for example Gérard de Nerval, who is "crossroads of all mythologies" (Richer 1970 [1963], 22) and indiscriminately accepts all faiths, Antoine here turns them all down. In these sections, Hilarion is the main metamorphosis of the devil; he, too, is a "good Mentor", in the sense that he does not threaten Antony but, on the contrary, guides him through his visions of what could be called "non-Œdipal" religions. (With this term I mean that they are not based on the axioms which structure the father-religions grounded in the Œdipus complex). Here the devil-figure(s) leave their rebellious aspects in the background and take on the traits of what Jones calls "the Father toward whom is felt admiration".

Thereupon follows section VI, in which the devil appears in person and takes Antony on the traditional ride through the cosmos. The devil peculiarly begins as a good Mentor—i.e., as an admirable father-figure—but, in a sudden reversal, finally threatens Antony with the hypothesis of absolute cosmic Nothingness. He is to be identified here with Jones's "Father toward whom is felt hostility".[6]

The next section, VII, can be divided into two parts, which obey opposite tendencies. The first one lies "beyond Good and Evil": since the devil has proven to be as threatening as the Father-God, only pure nightmare remains. The monsters attack Antony; the borderline between life and death is effaced. This is the most anti-canonical part of *La Tentation*. In its literal, primeval Chaos, even the notion of the demonic is corroded and abolished. Finally, the second subunit—which closes the work—portrays the disappearance of the monsters. The devil is absent from the conclusion also. At dawn, Antony's vision of the mystical union with Life-Matter is followed by the apparition of Jesus Christ in the sun.

In a sequence such as this, the demonic temptation is clearly *paralyzed* by Antoine's abolition of the conscious self and of all fixed desires. Cain is here neither refused nor refuted; he is overcome, de-structured. The dispersion and pulverization of the self which is begun in the first sections grows asymptotically toward the end, until the moment of the comforting (or perhaps torturing) *da capo* experienced at sunrise: "Antoine fait le signe de la croix et se remet en prières" (Flaubert 1964 I,

571B; henceforward *Tentation*). The novelistic convention of "the end" of a plot could not be derided with more lucidity: another night will come after the liberation, and after that another day, *ad infinitum*.

Reading Cainite revolt beneath the surface of Flaubert's *Saint Antoine* can contribute to explain the apparently incongruous fact that, while the saint has countless *visions*, Flaubert's title always referred to a singular temptation. There is *one* parricidal temptation; there are *many* derivative hallucinations. The multiplication of the latter is merely the inevitable and predictable consequence of the protracted repression of the former. A significant parallel can be found in Freud's *The Uncanny*:

> In Nestroy's farce, *Der Zerrissene* [*The Torn Man*] [...] the fleeing man, convinced that he is a murderer, lifts up one trap-door after another and each time he sees what he takes to be the ghost of his victim rising up out of it [...] [h]e calls out in despair, "But I've only killed *one* man. Why this ghastly multiplication?"
> (Freud *GW* XII, 267; *SE* XVII, 252)

Here as in Nerval, the anguish experienced in facing the uncanny proliferation of figures is connected with the paternal threat—due in this case to the Saint's subconscious guilt feelings. One wonders how Flaubert would have reacted to Nietzsche's provocative aphorism in *Human, All-Too-Human*: "In every ascetic moral the human being adores a part of himself as a God, and must for this purpose demonize the rest" (Bk. I, Ch. III, # 137).

With varying degrees of perplexity, many critics have observed that Antoine's visions do not truly "tempt" him. The point is that they do not intend to: the visions have the purpose to baffle and confuse Saint Antoine and cause him to despair. That they may, accessorily, baffle and confuse the reader as well, is indeed true; but this, in a sense, only proves that Flaubert knew what effect he was pursuing, and pursued it effectively—even for the twentieth century. After all, one of the main objections raised to the *Faust* chapbook of 1587 as a work of literature is that the riddles there proposed to Faustus and solved by the devil were too easy: the protagonist, so the argument convincingly runs, could have obtained that knowledge from any learned theologian of his time, without having to forfeit his soul's salvation for it.[7]

The whirlpool of beings which hurl themselves at Antoine is merely a façade, behind which the repressed meaning remains one and one only: the desire for revolt, abjuration of God, adoration of the devil, deicide. The hallucinations are but traces of a guilt feeling that does not arrive at self-awareness. Antoine, the "saint" (and here a substantial amount of textual contamination with the "saint" of Croisset ought to be suggested by the critic) never arrives at a liberating realization about the nature of his desire. The drive is so strongly feared that it is repressed altogether; and the self is literally drowned by the emblems of Impossibility—the Monsters.[8] The alternative route prefigured in the *Tentation de Saint Antoine* for the flow of desire is the abolition of the unified personality: fulfillment in the mystical union with Matter.

II

La Tentation de Saint Antoine: The Book About Everything

The *Tentation* challenges the reader with a series of discrete interpretive knots, generally not coinciding with the work's partition in sections, each of which calls for logical consolidation and a separate treatment.

The first such knot is to be identified with the role of the Seven Sins and logic (to be found in sections I, II and III of the *Tentation* of 1872). Here, the narrator's voice wavers between the desire to imitate God and the reality of the tortured saint.

Then follows a second problematized point, which is the ultimate nature of the heretics and of the *défilé* of the Gods (corresponding to sections IV and V). This is the part where Antony experiences the fascination of what I have proposed to call "non-Œdipal selves".

The third problem presented by the text is the ambiguous role of the flight through space on the devil's back (corresponding to section VI), in which Antony imitates

Cain and Gustave's own Smarh. He appears at first as an enthusiastic, then as a terrified "Star-Seer".

Later on, a fourth phase materializes with the appearance of the monsters (first part of section VII). Here the saint endures the assaults of Death, Lust and infinitely numerous grotesque beings—as he puts it, "Animals beyond Conception".

Finally, the fifth and perhaps most impregnable concept which the text attempts to formulate is the ever-increasing shattering of the self. Mineralization and final convergence toward the *Unio Mystica* lead to the sequence of scenes: blue sky—beach—Unicorn (which corresponds to the end of section VII and of the whole work).

Sins, de-œdipalization of desire, flight through space, monsters, and mineralization of the self in a panic mystical union: the five steps represent the *crescendo* which materializes Antoine's forbidden Cainite desire—at the price, however, of de-materializing character and plot alike. In the text as a whole, Antoine's desire, unable to be formulated in the conscious wish to rebel against the Father-God, is a catabolic force which aggresses the self and disintegrates it into a series of unstructured impulses that strive to seep in to the source of life from under the dam of the Œdipus complex.

The Quest For the Ultimate Sin

> Hypocrite qui s'enfonce dans la solitude pour se livrer mieux au débordement de ses convoitises!
>
> *Tentation*, 534A

Saint Antony is the symbol of Flaubert's "bad faith": he represents the awareness of the failure awaiting Flaubert's attempt to *become God*. Imitating the inimitable—the Father: this is the task of which Antoine proves incapable. The saint's figure symbolizes the inanity of the effort to seek out God in the desert and successfully challenge him. In showing that the hermit fails to be superior to humanity, *Saint*

Antoine amounts to a confession; the story of his temptation is a de-narrativized autobiography. But at the same time, perhaps paradoxically, the *Tentation* is also the protracted attempt to recuperate the very loss to which it confesses. Declaring decay from divine status and admitting to finitude become textual devices enabling Flaubert to stage his own omnipotence as the narrator of the text. Every hallucinatory image in the text is double-faced; each is a catalysis of anguish *and* a revenge against it. The task of relativizing Antony is accomplished through the absolutization of his narrator Flaubert—and, in turn, renders it possible.

It is not surprising to see that the saint does not dwell on (much less give in to) any of the figures in the gallery of desire. Totality is aimed at; no "sin" can, in and of itself, sufficiently mobilize the two halves of authorial projection—the saint's weakness, and the narrator's omnipotence. If the colossal enterprise of the *Tentation*, the prefiguration of a *Unio Mystica* achieved by agitation of the self, is to succeed, Antony must go through every possible hypnotization, as the narrator must go through every single display of power. Only through such a peculiar "training" can the self (both the protagonist's and the narrator's) be successfully directed to the disintegration indispensable to annul the unhappy consciousness of the structured identity. *La Tentation* is a type of Flaubertian *reverse askêsis* (i.e., a "reverse training") in which all figures of desire successively co-participate in the disarticulation of Antoine's ability to say "I". The observation has been made by some critics that the sins' obsessive interplay abolishes them all in a sort of reciprocal *jeu de massacre*.[9] The purpose of the sins, however, is not that of vanquishing the self: their purpose is to prepare the first stage of its disarticulation—a disarticulation which the following sections on the heresies and the Other Gods will raise to progressively higher levels.

Accordingly, it is only appropriate that the "spectaculaire retour du refoulé" (Bem 1979, 42) should begin with the constitution of the self which is later to be disrupted. Section I of the *Tentation* essentially consists of Antoine's evocation of memories from his pre-monastic life. This procedure could also be justified within a representational narrative strategy, but in fact it has a deeper sense: it intends to put in place the entity which the following sections will be in charge of tearing apart.

A significant example for the definition of Antoine's identity can be found in the anamnesis of the feminine Trinity reigning in the saint's home at the time of his youth. To the self threatened by desire, the Eternal Feminine symbolizes a world where no lack is experienced. Leaving such a world in order to follow the Father-God's call is retrospectively perceived as a fall from paradise.

> Tous me blâmaient lorsque j'ai quitté la maison. Ma mère s'affaissa mourante, ma sœur de loin me faisait des signes pour revenir; et l'autre pleurait, Ammonaria, cette enfant que je rencontrais chaque soir au bord de la citerne, quand elle amenait ses buffles. Elle a couru après moi. Les anneaux de ses pieds brillaient dans la poussière, et sa tunique ouverte sur les hanches flottait au vent. Le vieil ascète qui m'emmenait lui a crié des injures. Nos deux chameaux galopaient toujours; et je n'ai plus revu personne.
> (*Tentation*, 523B)

If the source of this particular episode (one to be added to the innumerable ones already pointed out by the critics) is the story of Perceval, it is at the same time clear that Antoine's quest for reintegration will never know the deliverance awaiting Perceval. While Saint Antoine is a modern seeker, he is also a desperate one, whose Grail is, by definition, absent—indeed, the figure of Absence itself.

In section II, the devil silently leads the attack of the traditional seven sins. As Nadeau indicates, the devil himself had said in the first version of the *Tentation*: "les péchés sont dans ta poitrine" (Nadeau 1969, 81)—the visions arise from within. Self-flagellation brings about sensual memories, the sadomasochistic vision which Antoine has of sharing Ammonaria's martyrdom. Suffering and pleasure are undistinguishable: "Quel supplice! Quelles délices! Ce sont comme des baisers. Ma moelle se fond! Je meurs!" (*Tentation*, 530B). When the Queen of Sheba appears, she appropriately concludes the Seven Sins episode: she recapitulates them all in one symbolic presence. Not by chance, she says: "Je ne suis pas une femme, je suis un monde" (*Tentation*, 532B).[10] The sexual aspect is by no means absent from the discourse; it is, in fact, its culmination. But the other temptations—bodily pleasures, power, glory, pride—all accompany it.

A revealing episode, unexpected in a context of adult sexual enticement, is the following:

> Ah! quand tu seras mon mari, je t'habillerai, je te parfumerai, je t'épilerai [...]
> Ce tissu mince [...] est la fameuse toile jaune apportée par les marchands de la Bactriane [...] Je t'en ferai faire des robes, que tu mettras à la maison.
> *(Tentation*, 531B)

One could conclude that the devil-Queen is here "féminité perverse et virilité", that "la reine de Saba est un hermaphrodite, ou plutôt [...] un travesti"; and that "la première tentation d'Antoine [...] est donc de devenir femme entre les mains d'un personnage dominateur, au sexe ambigu" (Danger 1979, 188). Yet it may be possible to suggest the alternative solution that in the Queen of Sheba episode the saint's desire is oriented toward infant sexuality. This would explain Antoine's desire not so much as one of inversion of sex, but as an abolition of it: hair removal and maternal care as return to the perfect bliss of the nursling. The insistence on being perfumed and clothed by the Queen is indicative in this sense. The Queen's immense power, paralleling the pan-sensual nature of her sexuality, is an additional reinforcement of the mother-figure as it appears to the infant. (Royal couples are the standard projections of the parents' figures in the child's family romance). In synthesis, all appearances seem to comfort the view of a sublimated fantasy of mother-seduction: seduction *of* as well as *by* the mother permeates Antoine's imagination.

Two more details are particularly significant. The Queen oscillates between extreme power and extreme vulnerability; she needs the hermit. When the latter, "terrified", refuses her incestuous offers, she walks away limping. Upon her arrival, however, there had been no question of such limping; on the contrary, the stress had been laid on her phallic potency: " [...] ses mains chargées de bagues se terminent par des ongles si pointus que le bout de ses doigts ressemble presque à des aiguilles" (*Tentation*, 531A). The impression is that the Other World from which she is coming is not only the world of her omnipotence, but also the world of her castration; and that she needs the son as a savior against the castrating father.[11] Furthermore, the Queen makes an avowal which could come from any of Flaubert's early works (*La Grande Dame, Un parfum à sentir*, the dreams of *Mémoires d'un fou* ...): "La nuit, je pleurais, le visage tourné vers la muraille [...] je t'aime! Oh! oui! beaucoup!" (*Tentation*, 531A). Between the son's conflicting feelings toward the mother—compassion for her who is persecuted, and resentment against her who has betrayed—compassion takes here the upper hand.

The Mother-Queen identity is further reinforced by a reference to the "primal scene" of parental coitus. The Queen evokes it when she proposes marriage to Antony and offers him, among her marriage presents, "quelque chose de rond [...] un petit coffret chargé de ciselures" (*Tentation*, 532A). The box or *étui* is a well-known sexual symbol;[12] she is thus here proposing incest. Thereupon, the father-figure is allusively evoked, and the child is tempted by the suggestion of at last satisfying the haunting curiosity about the true nature of the beginning of life:

> Mais si tu savais ce que j'ai dans ma petite boîte! Retourne-la, tâche de l'ouvrir! Personne n'y parviendrait; embrasse-moi; je te le dirai.
> (Elle prend Saint Antoine par les deux joues; il la repousse à bras tendus).
> C'était une nuit que le roi Salomon perdait la tête. Enfin nous conclûmes un marché. Il se leva, et sortant à pas de loup ...
> (Elle fait une pirouette).
> Ah! ah! bel ermite! tu ne le sauras pas! tu ne le sauras pas!
> (*Tentation*, 532A)

The stream of desire is here reversed in order to be tolerable to the self and consciously formulable: the Queen does what *Antoine* wishes she did. The "saint" can thus reassuringly decline the incestuous proposal. If Antony were to accept, the fulfillment of such totality of desire would be non-representable in language, beyond the articulated mind's conception. Antony is here still too bound to his structured self to be able to float freely in the Flaubertian Ineffable. The physical training, the *askêsis* of the *Tentation* toward mystical union must continue.

The Queen of Sheba comes from the same world of self-sufficiency and plenitude in which Antony's boyhood memories live on: she is a reincarnation of the feminine

Trinity, Mother-Sister-Friend, which Antoine had abandoned in order to follow his destiny of confrontation with the Father. In a sense, here she arrives too soon: Antony is not yet ready to leave structured consciousness behind. The communion with the source of life, which was lost after infancy and offered by the Queen, will only return at the end of the *Tentation*, after both the "son" and the "mother" have lost their anthropomorphic selves and have become pure movement, pure energy. This may well be the inevitable precondition for the secret of the Sphinx to be seized.

The de-structuring of the saint's rationality is then prepared in section III, when the devil-figure Hilarion appears. Through the presentation of the traditional themes of doubt, *superbia* and *curiositas* (cf. Hempel 1970, 20-22), Hilarion manages to elicit from Antoine the same assent which Lucifer had obtained from Cain:

> *Hilarion*: Désires-tu connaître la hiérarchie des Anges, la vertu des Nombres, la raison des germes et des métamorphoses?
> *Antoine*: Oui! oui! ma pensée se débat pour sortir de sa prison.
> (*Tentation*, 535A)

The "secret of life" which the Mother-Queen had promised thus lurks at the end of the longer road taken by Antony: by the end of section III, he is prepared—and willing—to embark upon the quest for the lost mystery. The following two sections will then provide the necessary mobility of the self; their massive process of dis-assimilation and de-structuring of forms will be the equivalent of a *Bildungsroman* in the negative. What Antony now needs to experience in order to have access to the mystical union is a *novel of disintegration*—of which Hilarion promptly proceeds to be the reverse Mentor.

Section III of the *Tentation*, then, represents the *entre-deux* between the earlier, physical road to desire, in which the self is still unified, and the de-materialized, de-narrativized ways to it portrayed in parts IV and V, which explore rejected Christian theories and multifarious God-figures of world religions. The physicality of the pleasures earlier proposed by the Seven Sins will there be sublimated into the pleasure of the "knowledge" announced.

However, while the voyage to be led by the anti-Mentor Hilarion is a more abstract one, it is also, by its very nature, a more essential one in its exploration of the forms of desire: it is not a movement away from them, but rather a more in-depth repetition. At the end of section III, Hilarion's intellectual destabilization of Antony's has assured the transition from the erotic to the heretic.

The Other Fathers: The Fascination With Non-Œdipal Selves

> Le monde est l'œuvre d'un Dieu en délire.
>
> *Tentation*, 536B
>
> Mon cœur se soulève de dégoût devant ces Dieux bestiaux, occupés toujours de carnages et d'incestes!
>
> *Tentation*, 558A

The "basilique immense" (535B) of the heresies and the Gods is by far the longest unit of the *Tentation*. Defined in various negative ways by readers in quest of representational narrative conventions, this part is nonetheless the essential nucleus of the *Tentation*, and, provided one approaches it by applying the proper norm, perhaps its most fascinating one.[13] As Reik lucidly writes,

> [In] this great, grandiose Twilight of the Idols [...] the founding idea of the great work comes to the fore in the most perfect fashion. The hallucinations of the saint are but objectifications of his repressed instincts and thoughts.
> (Reik 1912, 56)

The usage which Reik makes of the notion of "Twilight of the Idols" is an intentional one: by a transparent allusion, it establishes a parallel between Flaubert's work and Nietzsche's, and points out the radical doubt—the radical deicide—which subtends the thought of the two authors.

The readers will unfailingly become lost in the *selva selvaggia* of the dozens, hundreds of religious fathers and families, unless they keep in mind that, as Bem puts it,

> [...] la tentation du néant universel, tout intellectuelle d'apparence, est la transposition des conflits engendrés par la mort (le meurtre) du Père symbolique. Derrière la tentation du néant se lit la tentation de TUER LE PERE.
>
> (Bem 1979, 67; emphasis in the original)

Whereas (to paraphrase Lukàcs) the "destruction of reason" is operated in Byron's *Cain* through Lucifer's verbal arguments, in *La Tentation* it is exposed *in the act*: the absurdity of the Law of the Father is not predicated, but performed.

A detailed discussion of the figures exposed by Flaubert is outside my scope; all I can do here is show the general tendency which the two sections IV and V have in common. My main hypothesis is that Antoine's glancing at sects and religions other than the standard form of orthodox Christianity allows him (and, obviously, Flaubert) to examine and desire "non-standard" forms of family configurations. In these families, the confrontation with the father is not filtered through the Œdipus complex—or, even when such is the case, it is resolved in a "non-Œdipal" manner (that is to say, in ways that differ from the Christian two-pronged alternative: submission *vs.* revolt and punishment). This is the meaning conveyed by the concepts of "Other Fathers" and "non-Œdipal selves". Specifically, by a "non-Œdipal self" I intend a self for whom the Œdipal postulates are not valid—thereby consciously pursuing a methodological parallelism with the notions of Euclidean *vs.* non-Euclidean geometries, in which the elimination or modification of one of the axioms entails a complete uprooting and rearrangement in the chain of theorems. Needless to say, I am here bracketing the philosophical question about the existence *in praxis* of what could be called (to continue the analogy further) non-Œdipal *spaces*. Such spaces are described in the *Tentation*; but their relation with Being lies only at the extreme horizon of the world of literary criticism. Asking whether non-Œdipal selves can exist in everyday experience may well amount to the same as asking which one of the many is the ultimately "true" geometry of the empirical universe. Art, of course, is by definition the laboratory—the *space*—where such identities can be devised.

One may then be justifiably tempted to ask why Flaubert felt that the religious metaphor was a particularly apt way to experiment with non-Œdipal constellations. This appears to have happened because the kaleidoscope of world beliefs offered him *historical proof* of the fact that *all* configurations could be conceived with equal dignity and seriousness, as they actually had been *before, after,* or at any rate *outside* Christianity. In a text that is at the conscious level "le comble de l'insanité", it will not be surprising if all subconscious desires become "le comble de la normalité": this *normalization of the monstrous* strategically ensures absolute permutability (and therefore perfect legitimacy) of all desires—the forbidden ones first and foremost.

I will limit myself here to a brief rationalization of the contrast between Saint Antony's (and Flaubert's) religion and other religions of the ancient Mediterranean world. In "A Psychoanalytic Study of the Holy Ghost Concept", Jones writes:

> The most striking characteristic of the Christian solution as compared with others, such as the Mithraic, is the way in which [...] atonement is achieved through surrender to the Father instead of through openly defying and overcoming him. This surrender, the prototype of which is the Crucifixion, is periodically repeated in the ceremony of the Holy Mass [...]
> In this way the Father's wrath is averted and the Son takes his place as co-equal with Him. In the banquet is lived over and over again both the celebration of the original deed of killing and eating the Father and the remorseful piety which desires re-union and identification with him.
> (Jones 1964, II, 359)

We are all familiar with these facts; and, of course, so is Saint Antoine. But when the "saint" is told—to mention but a few examples—that "Au sommet du ciel le plus haut se tient la Divinité impassible; en dessous, face à face, sont le Fils de Dieu et le Prince des ténèbres" (Manès, *Tentation*, 536A); or that "Le Père, pour punir les anges révoltés, leur ordonna de créer le monde" (Saturnin, 536B); or that "Le monde est l'œuvre d'un Dieu en délire" (Valentin, 536B); or perhaps that "Le Saint-Esprit est féminin!" (Les Elkhesaïtes, 537B),[14] he is inevitably petrified by these hypotheses, because they all shed a new, revolutionary light (certainly revolutionary for him) on the meaning of his own sacrifice to the superior Law of the Father.

When there are too many fathers, there no longer is any father at all; and repressing desire has been a pointless sacrifice. The clash with the heresies is but the beginning of the disruption of the self which will reach its nadir at the end of the flight through space on the devil's wings. The "saint" will then say:

> Comment? mes oraisons, mes sanglots, les souffrances de ma chair, les transports de mon ardeur, tout cela se serait en allé vers un mensonge ... dans l'espace ... inutilement [...]
> (*Tentation*, 565A)

Here, the Christian heresies begin preparing him precisely for such a despair.

Before reaching that phase, however, the saint still has to be confronted with the shattering reality of the Other Gods of section V. These Gods are even further removed from Christian-Œdipal solutions, thus making it clear that Flaubert's choice to present Heresies and Other Gods in precisely this sequence is due to the lucid intention of gradually intensifying the estrangement effect. The three following instances are particularly apt for comparison and contrast with Christianity: the Great Goddess Cybele; Isis; and Ormuz, the Persian God, father of Mithra. To Flaubert's dialogized-dramatized presentation I shall here prefer the analytical one given by Jones in "Psychoanalysis and the Christian Religion":

> In the Near East [...] a number of religions developed in which the Great Mother played a central part, and later on in Rome they competed for a time very seriously with early Christianity. The typical version of the story they incorporated was that of the Dying God, the God who fell victim to malign influences, but whose body was always found and resuscitated by the Great Mother. Thus the priests of Cybele, often self-castrated, would hold a recurrent festival in which on the third day Attis, her son, would again be brought to life through the ministrations and intercession of his mother.
> (Jones 1964, II, 205)

The corresponding scene in the *Tentation* appears with an even stronger emphasis on the mother's sexual desire for Atys (555B-556B). In Flaubert's text, Atys's wish to identify with the mother is so violent that "his virility horrifies him"; he castrates himself in order to resemble her more.

As for the Gods of Egypt,

> Isis [...] displayed a similar beneficence to Serapis-Osiris, periodically restoring him to life. Many features of her religion are reminiscent of the Christian ritualism. There was holy water, there were tonsured priests (now only symbolically castrated), and the Goddess herself was known as the "Mother of Tenderness" and the "Mother of Sorrows" (*Mater Dolorosa!*) The believers achieved the assurance of a happy immortality, through identifying themselves with the risen Osiris.
>
> (Jones 1964, II, 206)

Accordingly, Flaubert portrays Isis looking for Osiris and longing for him (*Tentation* 557A-558A). Antony's disarray is intense, if short-lived: in viewing images of non-Christian desire, he must ask himself: *why not I*? The "disgust" which he refers to after having seen Isis disappear (558A) is more likely to be an antiphrasis—a reaction-formation covering what is in actual fact envy.

The most telling of all religions centered around a son-figure, however, is clearly Mithraism. As Jones puts it,

> Mithraism [was] characteristically the religion of soldiers [...] [T]he young Son-God resolutely opposes the father and becomes the Master of his own fate. Early in his career he struggled with the Sun and forced [him] to do him homage. In the central ceremony of the Mithraic religion he faces a bull, a typical father-symbol—here representing the Persian deity Ahura-Mazda—and slays him. It is significant that he is represented as doing this unwillingly, averting his gaze as he deals the fatal blow with his knife, as if to indicate some regret for the parricidal deed. After accomplishing it he ascended to heaven, and doubtless ruled there, whence he succors those who believe in his heroic powers.
>
> (Jones 1964, II, 206-07)

The corresponding episode in the *Tentation* shows the Father-God (here Ormuz) summoning his son for help:

> [...] je devais un jour, grâce au temps sans bornes, vaincre définitivement Ahriman.
> Mais l'intervalle entre nous deux disparaît; la nuit monte! A moi, les Amschaspands, les Izeds, les Ferouers! Au secours, Mithra! prends ton épée! Caosyac, qui dois revenir pour la délivrance universelle, défends-moi! Comment? ... Personne!
> Ah! je meurs! Ahriman, tu es le maître!
>
> *(Tentation, 555A)*

The narrator so much identifies with the son Mithra that his looks, too, are turned away at the moment when the fatal blow is dealt. It is as though the narrating voice were Mithra's and shared Mithra's concern—to render parricide more acceptable.

In sum, parricide operates in the heresies and Gods sections of *La Tentation* not only in the evident attempt (which Hilarion eagerly apppropriates) to dismiss *dos à dos* all the incompatible religious beliefs, but also, and even more importantly, in the actual content of the beliefs themselves. A direct authorial investment on Flaubert's part must therefore have been quite active in many of the non-Œdipal situations portrayed—as if obsessively suggesting the idea that the themes of *liberation from Œdipus* echoing from the most remote history of humanity indeed are the founding structure of *La Tentation de Saint Antoine*. This hypothesis is confirmed by many minute details. To mention but one, when Adonis's lover cries over the dead body of her beloved, longing for the moments when he would take her in his arms "toute frémissante de rosée, ô Soleil!" (*Tentation*, 556B)—obviously a sensual image—Antoine immediately thinks of the Mother of Jesus. Here again, it is not, or in any case not only, the mere whirlpool of heresies and religions that dazzles Antony; it is their *specific contents* that astonishes him. The great numbers make the impact only more powerful, but the essence of the matter lies in their meanings.[15] Behind an apparent impression of chaos, the overarching principle that structures the episodes is Flaubert's fascination with the heresies' non-standard solutions of the Œdipus complex.

The saint does not particularly adhere to one or the other: he lets his self float among all of them, without choosing to direct his desire in a specific direction. His conscious self is suspended, dis-organized; it is "everywhere". After having been corroded by doubt in section III, he now has a diffused identity: his *curiositas* (in the theological sense) tears him apart. With their uninterrupted parade of pan-demonic drives, Sections IV and V of *La Tentation* represent an attempt to de-œdipianize the unified desire of the character by fragmenting the character's conscious self. Such is the necessary next logical step one has to take after having conceded, with J. Bem, that "la mobilité incessante propre au rêve caractérise bien le texte de la *Tentation*" (Bem 1979, 226), and that the artist's gesture of defying the Father-God is but a "way around" his Law. If the Œdipal interdiction blocks desire at the level of macrostructures, Antoine prefigures a countermeasure: fragmented, pulverized desire seeps through in a molecular state. "Real" selves may not literally endure the narrative process of fragmentation through desire (cf. Achilles in Kleist's *Penthesilea!*)—but such may be precisely the advantage of non-representational speculation and experimentation.

A surprising blunder contained in the subsequent *Credo* (an error which seems to have so far gone unnoticed in the *Tentation*-criticism) then once more draws our attention to the excruciatingly complex intertextuality of Antony's discourse. To Hilarion's disquieting lecture in comparative religion, the saint responds as follows:

> Je crois en un seul Dieu, le Père,—et en un seul Seigneur, Jésus-Christ,—*fils premier-né* de Dieu,—qui s'est incarné et fait homme,—qui a été crucifié—et enseveli,—qui est monté au ciel,—qui viendra pour juger les vivants et les morts,—dont le royaume n'aura pas de fin [...]
> (*Tentation*, 559A; emphasis added)

Is the specification: "eldest" Son of God necessary here? Given the general methodology of *La Tentation de Saint Antoine*, we shouldn't be surprised if Flaubert had a source for his "premier né" too. But the philological question is here, as elsewhere, merely the first layer of the "ideological" one. The fact remains undisputable: Christ is not the *first* son of the Christian God; he is the only one. Even if Flaubert had a source, why did he choose to use it in this particular way? I hold that Antoine's viewing the Crucified as his eldest / elder brother is indeed significant: he may well elevate the elder one to divinity as a reaction-formation for having wished to crucify him.

La Tentation echoes the Cainite themes of Flaubert's adolescence works and affords an occasional glimpse into the subconscious implications still active for the author. Here the pacifying role of consciousness is obvious; and Christianity appears as the main barrier against parricide-fratricide and the ensuing threat of castration.[16] As Jones put it, in Christianity "th[e] identification [with the Son-God] re-establishes the loving harmony of the primal family situation and abolishes all the jealousy, rivalry and hostility latent in it" (Jones 1964, II, 207).

However, the mythical figures of Greek cosmogony immediately come to dissipate Antoine's illusion and to remind him of the inescapable Law of Time: "Les dieux doivent finir. Uranus fut mutilé par Saturne, Saturne par Jupiter. Il sera lui-même anéanti. Chacun son tour; c'est le destin!" (*Tentation*, 559A-B). Castration proves once more to be the principle haunting the *Tentation*'s centered selves—the inevitable conclusion of a desire not sufficiently mobilized to circumvent repression by the super-ego.

Antoine's only hope for deliverance lies in mobility. He pursues freedom by precisely that means when, terrified by the devil, he accepts to fly over the universe on the wings which promise to give him liberating knowledge. Not until the end of the flight will he realize that, in terms of a fulfilling unanchoring of the self, the devil has, literally, Nothingness to offer. The mobilization of desire will then have to be taken up again, after the deceptive *cul-de-sac* of demonico-paternal science.

Saint Antony the Star-Seer

> So on the seventh day, toward night, I returned home and slept three days on end.
>
> Doktor Faustus the Star-Seer
> (*Wolfenbüttel manuscript*, Pt. II, Ch. 25)

> And here I am, for all my lore,
> The wretched fool I was before.
>
> Goethe, *Faust*, vv. 358-59

Gustave precociously undertook the sublimating quest for knowledge about the world: from his early adolescence on, his works show him intent on fathoming the ultimate metaphysical questions. He was still a boy when he set out—as the narrator of the Faust chapbook puts it—"die Elementa zu spekulieren" (*Historia* ... 1963, 41). The devil of the *Tentation* had been flying over the cosmos ever since the time of *Voyage en enfer*, which Gustave wrote at age thirteen. Later on, in 1839, came the even more significant demonic flight of *Smarh*—the text from which section VI of the final version of 1872 was developed.

Since the flight above the universe represents such a resilient moment in Flaubert's imagination, to the point of being the generating episode of the whole Antony text, it is only appropriate to contrast it briefly with Flaubert's main sources of inspiration. In *Cain*, Lucifer functions as a good Mentor giving real knowledge as to the nature of the universe. If his science was deadly for Cain, Lucifer himself was in no way responsible; responsible was to be held only He who had "planted the tree". The knowledge promised by Lucifer is not a lie: "The tree was true, though deadly" (Byron 1901, V, 246; Act II, Sc. II, v. 167). Lucifer's words do not even remotely imply that man should regret having abandoned the Garden of Eden; in fact, the hypothesis underlying his thought (and thereby subtending his whole ideology of revolt) is that Eden was quite literally a fool's paradise, to be paid for at the cost of the brutishness of submission and naïvety. One may agree or disagree with Lucifer's ideas, but not accuse him of proposing an ambiguous role for science.

As for Flaubert's other, less direct source of reflection, Goethe's *Faust*, it is clear from its first few scenes that science and knowledge are there equally unlikely to threaten the self's quest for the absolute. They are ever-insufficient, and the mere passive repetition of the fathers' heritage constrains and suffocates Faust; but heritage *there is*, and Faust's breaking away from the Word and into Action is a gesture destined to build upon the Word and vivify its spirit. Faust aspires to be united with the Macrocosm, because he has *already* absorbed science and can thus afford to be above the pettiness of earthly affairs. The mobility of his desire would be inconceivable without its scientific basis and its disinterested foundation. Faust minus science would not be Faust—he would be another Luizzi from some other *Mémoires du diable*.

In principle, the two opposite logical possibilities in the *Tentation* would thus seem to be the following: through the contact with Science offered by the devil, the saint could be won over to a new "faith" or to a new existential conviction (as is the case in *Cain*); alternatively, he could refuse to do so and persevere in his own project. (Persevering is, in a nutshell, precisely what Faust does: the more the devil's teachings try to limit him within the contingency of finitude, the more Faust remains Faustian and expands desire *ad astra*). In the first case the devil would prove to be a "reliable Mentor-figure"; in the latter, it would be an inadequate one, a weak one to be rejected.[17] In both cases, the human could be a winner and attain a higher self-awareness: whether through education received from a stronger being, or through trials successfully endured against a principle eventually proven to be inferior. However, the characteristic trait of the devil of *La Tentation* is that he takes neither of the two paths just sketched. In a very close re-elaboration of the Satan appearing in *Smarh*, Saint Antoine's devil in fact chooses a destructive, perverse strategy: by sharing with him reassuring knowledge about the nature of the universe, he at first solicits the Saint's trust; then, once he has acquired some hearing on the Saint's part, he plunges him into despair, roundly declaring that all is illusion.

The decisive turning point is to be found in the moment when the devil glides from expounding the omnipresence of God to denouncing his indifference:

Le diable: [...] il n'y a pas de fond, pas de sommet, ni haut, ni bas, aucun terme; et l'Étendue se trouve comprise dans Dieu qui n'est point une portion de l'espace, telle ou telle grandeur, mais l'immensité!
Antoine (lentement): La matière ... alors ... ferait partie de Dieu?
Le diable: Pourquoi non? Peux-tu savoir où il finit?
Antoine: Je me prosterne au contraire, je m'écrase, devant sa puissance!

Hence the logical conclusion:

> [*Le diable*]: Et tu prétends le fléchir! Tu lui parles, tu le décores même de vertus, bonté, justice, clémence, au lieu de reconnaître qu'il possède toutes le perfections! [...]
> Ce n'est donc pas une personne!
> *Antoine*: Comment? Mes oraisons, mes sanglots, les souffrances de ma chair, les transports de mon ardeur, tout cela se serait en allé vers un mensonge ... dans l'espace ... inutilement,—comme un cri d'oiseau, comme un tourbillon de feuilles mortes!
> (Il pleure).
> (*Tentation*, 565A)

The devil could still recuperate the Saint's despair if he tried to propose an alternative, antagonist interpretation of the world. But he has painted himself into an ontological corner: if God "is not a person", how can he be accused? How could one revolt against him? Or *is* there a devil, if the Universe is but a mass of atomized divinity? The devil is here resolutely striding toward his own suicide.

It thus comes hardly as a surprise that the logical chain winds back on itself in a gesture of self-elimination:

> [*Le diable*]: [...] A moins que le monde étant un flux perpétuel des choses, l'apparence au contraire ne soit tout ce qu'il y a de plus vrai, l'illusion la seule réalité.
> Mais es-tu sûr de voir? Es-tu même sûr de vivre? Peut-être qu'il n'y a rien!
> (*Tentation*, 565B)

This may indeed distress Antoine; but no despair can be strong enough to elicit adoration for a non-existent being. In the flight-through-space section of the *Tentation*, science clearly backfires on the devil; and the net result of his efforts is strictly nil. This had also been true in the drama of Gustave's first anchorite, Smarh: there, Satan had said that "la science, c'est le doute, c'est le néant, c'est le mensonge, c'est la vanité" (Flaubert 1964, I, 195B). On one hand, we have the severity of the Law of the Father-God; on the other, one finds the devil's corrosive, self-phagocytizing doubt. Paradoxical as this may seem, Saint Antoine's nightmare consists in the fact that at the crucial moment when he despairs of God, even the devil fails him. Apparently, this is a *non sequitur* of the *Tentation*. But the contradiction can be overcome if we realize that the converging threats of God and the devil point to an essential symbolic identity of the two figures. More than perhaps anywhere else, the devil is here but a decayed double of the divine figure.

In Gustave's case, the reason for such a double identity has been explained convincingly. While, on one hand, the Father-God figure "naturally" incarnated for him the essence of the taboo repressing desire, the strong analytico-scientific aura which Flaubert senior—the famous archdoctor—was inclined (and proud) to emanate also "naturally" caused the devil's traditional attributes of insight and sharp dialectics to be attracted into the paternal gravitational field. The result is, as J. Bem puts it succintly, that "le diable de *La Tentation* est un docteur Flaubert à peine camouflé, avec ce que cela comporte d'admiration enfantine et de refus violent" (Bem 1979, 195). Sartre, too, stresses Gustave's subconscious identification between the Father and a nihilistic devil (Sartre 1971, I, 562). Evidently, this is the powerful psychological reason which motivates what the critics have described as Flaubert's parallel rejection of Faith and Science.

The consequences are not difficult to see: throughout the text, the "saint" represents a self in quest of a *cogito*—in quest, that is, of a way to define its own existence. Because, to the very end, the God he calls out for in the desert eludes him and refuses him such a guarantee, Antony floats among hallucinations which are all the more threatening the more they are vague, all-pervasive, deprived of "definition" (in the photographic sense). He could opt to seek no *cogito* at all, and let his self float with the visions in a sort of Nervalian coincidence of all opposites—yet this is precisely what he stubbornly refuses to do: strenuously saying "I" is his constant effort. This is why the silence-absence of God's guarantee anguishes him so deeply. When the devil appears, it is only consistent that Antony pursue with him the quest for a foundation of his being; alas, the devil too refuses to provide the saint with the founding axioms he needs. The universal nothingness which the devil suggests brings Antoine back to his starting point of despair.

The final recognition that fulfillment can come only by abandoning all striving for organized consciousness will appear only later to Saint Antoine, after the preparation afforded by a long anabasis through monster-land and toward the sources of life. For the moment, however, the devil's refusal blocks Antony's self in the dead end of hyperbolic doubt. Hence the Saint's feelings of fear and resentment toward the devil-father who, by denying the existence of all things, essentially denies himself to the son's desire. In the *Tentation de Saint Antoine* the devil gradually reveals itself as the monstrous portrait of a father deformed by the son's hostility.

This explains the general feeling of sadness lingering over Antoine's episode of flight through the universe. In Saint Antoine there is no trace of what Brombert perceptively calls "voluptuousness of the infinite" (Brombert 1966, 197): more exactly, Saint Antoine's space flight is the only locus in *La Tentation* where such voluptuousness does *not* burst forth with intense sensuality. Antony's fear before, during and after the voyage contrasts strikingly with the Rabelaisian-bulimic travel lust of Spieß's Faust; *a fortiori*, it contrasts with the enthusiasm of Cain looking down upon the Universe and universal history and becoming "intoxicated with eternity". Antony's melancholy comes about because the hoped-for alternative Mentor is finally unmasked as an empty one. Here, a pseudo-father leads him—and leads him nowhere. Goethe's Faust did have a destination in his final flight: he had someone awaiting him in his ascent toward "En-haut".

*

The devil no longer appears in the seventh and last section of the *Tentation*, essentially because the doubt aimed at Antony cannot but corrode the very entity which had emitted it. *Sic transit*: an unglorious end thus meets the saint's "universal" curiosity. Alluding to the topos of flight as sexual symbolism, Reik wrote:

> Antonius is abducted by the devil into the air so that he may learn the secrets of the world. The curiosity for truth, the instinct for research arises only by a sublimation of infant-sexual curiosity. The top layer of the wishes that brought about this vision was, then, the Faustian motive of the thirst to learn about the creation of the world. It is the infant curiosity about the creation of the individual, projected into the Universe [...]
>
> (Reik 1912, 61)

However, modern science has here appeared as stating that the mistery of life is not very mysterious at all—or, worse perhaps, that it is not one worth being pursued in the first place. For Antony, even eating the fruit from the treee of knowledge can reveal nothing of substance about the genesis of Being, if it very possibly just reveals the depressing truth that "maybe nothing exists".

"Animals Beyond Conception"

> Si j'allais avoir envie ...
> [Rest of the sentence censored by the author].
>
> *Tentation*, 570A
>
> ... and no one can now find the way to it.
>
> Gogol, *The Viy*

The monster episode of the first part of section VII is what best justifies Flaubert's own admission that "the subtitle of *La Tentation de Saint Antoine* could be: *le comble de l'insanité*" (quot. in Thibaudet 1935, 188, and Brombert 1966, 213).

After Antoine has been abandoned by the devil, he is overcome by despair. The moment of his return to earth brings about the sobering recognition of the mindless *hybris* implicit in trying to comprehend the sense of the Universe as a whole, i.e., in trying to grasp its totality as an object by means of the intellect available to a unified subject. This is the despair expressed by the saint's "Et j'avais cru pouvoir m'unir à Dieu!" (566A)—perfectly echoing Faust's annihilation after the *Erdgeist* has contemptuously turned him down. As we approach the end of *La Tentation*, we at last fully realize to what extent Flaubert has reaccentuated the concept of the devil-contract: here, hyperbolic emphasis on the process of desire dwarfs the narrative conventions of the traditional pact, and drains of all signification the notion of the exchange of "services" for a soul.

Akin to Faust at the beginning of Goethe's work, Antoine is now mesmerized by thoughts of suicide. In the *Tentation* of 1872, we here find the scission of what, in the first version, had been the hallucination of the "lascivious Virgin". The seduction of and by the Mother of Christ—of obviously incestuous character—has become too intolerably explicit for Flaubert, and has accordingly undergone subconscious censorship. Thus, the originally unified mother-prostitute type is split into the two complementary figures Mother + Ammonaria, who, for greater emotional distantiation, are then further transformed respectively into *Mort* and *Luxure*.[18] Reik writes:

> Psychologically, the most important modification is the elimination of the temptation by the Mother of God. The same voice which incites the Saint to embrace the statue whispers to him: "It would not be the first time. She has sinned with Pantheras, a Roman soldier ... " This is an explicit accusation of prostitution, brought about by the voice (in Antony). The suspicion is directed against God's Mother, against the ideal feminine figure. But Mary is only a substitute for his own mother.
> The mother, then, has something of the prostitute ["etwas Dirnenhaftes"]— we now realize why Flaubert had to drop this scene, how great were the interior obstacles opposing its becoming-conscious and its objectification.
> (Reik 1912, 85, 183)

Lasciviousness and Death thus appear as the *ultimate* realities, the only ones left behind after the hallucinated parade of the Gods; in their dualism-unity, they appear as the nihilistic final statement about the world produced by the kaleidoscope of the *saeculum*'s non-Œdipal selves.

In the final version, the caesura between sections as well as a relatively higher degree of psychologization of the visions tend to obscure the directness of such a relationship; but in the first *Tentation*, "Mort" and "Luxure" are all that remains after the "great silence" which immediately follows the death of "the God of the armies" (*T1*, 470A). In other words, in *T1* the de-œdipianization of the self brought about by the grandiose Twilight of the Idols points explicitly to the essence of the drives at work: the (incestual) desire of Lasciviousness, and the (repressive-punitive) function of Death. In *T3*, the cards are somewhat shuffled; significantly, the devil appears between the two scenes and cordons them off from each other: a subconscious censorship of the text parallels the dissociation operated on the Virgin-figure. Clearly, the stakes of *La Tentation* are becoming intolerably high for the centralized subject.

This is the moment when "saint Antoine" moves beyond the categories of Christianity. In his own words, "la mort n'est qu'une illusion, un voile, masquant par endroits la continuité de la vie" (*Tentation*, 568A). Antoine feels "eternal"—not in an anabolic sense, but in a catabolic one. Antony pulverizes the self; in so doing, he goes beyond the boundaries of morality. Beyond God and the devil, he seeps through to Being *tout court*—he moves from the ethical to the ontological. The liberation of desire long planned and prepared in *La Tentation* can now be activated as the narrative self begins to float into an open space, and the waves of cosmic energy, "previously named Antoine" (to paraphrase the felicitous expression designating Gretchen in the apotheosis of *Faust II*), though existing as waves, lose the convergence that had tied them together in one point and made of them a psychic quantum. Having lost all individualization and merely streaming from a source of which we have now lost sight, the visionary self dreams of perceiving "the Forms":

> Mais la Substance étant unique, pourquoi les Formes sont-elles variées?
> Il doit y avoir, quelque part, des figures primordiales, dont les corps ne sont que les images. Si on pouvait les voir on connaîtrait le lien de la matière et de la pensée, en quoi l'Etre consiste!
> Ce sont ces figures-là qui étaient peintes à Babylone sur la muraille du temple de Bélus [...] Moi-même, j'ai quelquefois aperçu dans le ciel comme des formes d'esprit. Ceux qui traversent le désert rencontrent *des animaux dépassant toute conception* ...
> (*Tentation*, 568A; emphasis added)[19]

For Flaubert's Saint Antoine the monsters are knots in which the Being behind the Forms comes to materialization. The animals are "beyond", i.e. before conception: they are the not-yet-individualized self. The monsters are the chaos that is *before birth*. In a clear illustration of the principle which Reboussin calls "régression jusqu'à l'incréé" (Reboussin 1973, 80), the ab-normal animals attract the self that is undergoing disintegration, whose project is (as J. Bem puts it) "[de] contourner la Loi [du Dieu-père] par une œuvre de pure métamorphose" (Bem 1979, 138). The particles of the self, liberated from constraints, are attracted into the magma of animal forms, as they would be into a whirlpool of matter forcing them to break away from their original gravitational field.

In order to unsettle Antoine's centralized self and maintain it in a vibrating, liminal state of suspension, Flaubert has recourse to the monsters' marked *grotesque*—which, in his monograph bearing the same title, W. Kayser defines as follows:

> The grotesque is the estranged world ["die entfremdete Welt"] [...]
> The grotesque is the formulation ["Gestaltung"] of the "It", the ghostly "It" [...]
> [The formulation of the grotesque is] an attempt to conjure and subdue ["bannen und beschwören"] the demonic aspects of the world.
> (Kayser 1963, 184, 185, 188)

The monsters of *La Tentation* are, strictly speaking, an exorcism.[20]

The concept that is central to the grotesque—and thus to Flaubert's monsters, *qua* psychopomps on the path to Antony's disintegration and rebirth—is the one analyzed by Freud in *The Uncanny*. Freud's well-known essay addresses the paradoxical inversion of labels by which we describe as "estranged" ("Un-heimlich") the feeling we entertain toward a repressed content which is in reality most "familiar" ("heimlich") to our self. The feeling of the uncanny being the uneasy reverberation of the ego's refusal to admit to an unacceptable *déjà-vu*, the "monstrous" is arguably but a disguise intending to camouflage that which the self is not prepared to recognize consciously.[21]

As Jones writes in his theoretical analysis of the absolute culmination of the uncanny—the nightmare:

> In most of the dreams of adults, where the dream appears on the surface to contain no evidence of any desire, the operative desire is one that is inacceptable to the subject's consciousness and has therefore been repressed. This repressed desire can now be allowed to attain imaginary gratification only when it is not recognizable by the subject, so that it appears in another form by becoming *distorted, perverted and disguised.*
> (Jones 1951, 42; emphasis added)

La Tentation, then, works essentially as the proliferation of erudition destined to *distort, pervert and disguise* the linear movement of Œdipal desire. Within a basically oneiric frame, it "conjures", in order to "subdue" (in Kayser's terms), a long series of uncanny images—i.e., of familiar images, deformed in such a way as to make them resemble nightmares. Thus, the threat implicit in the forgotten meaning lingers on in an uneasiness which does not become aware of itself in the text. Because the fears and desires which Antoine's monsters exorcize are repressed, it is hardly surprising that, from the very beginning of the *Tentation*, Antoine should be steeped in a twilight of semi-consciousness, in a haze half covering and half revealing what is otherwise Unnameable.

*

Reik interprets a single one of the beastly apparitions of *La Tentation*—the hyena roaming around the burial site of Antony's mother.

> Such a vision ["Vorstellung"], which now appears so terrifying, once used to be a source of pleasure for the child. We know that instincts are symbolized by wild animals for [Saint Antony]. The hyena that sniffles through a wall-hole is therefore easy to interpret. It is easily comprehensible that fear should affect him as a consequence for the intensity of the moral rejection and of the later repression of the child's wish [...]
>
> The stronger the rejection of the image, the graver becomes the melancholy which derives from it [...]
>
> The source of Antony's interior struggle [is the] incestual love which [...] prompted him to leave the world behind.
>
> (Reik 1912, 63-64)

However, he offers no interpretation of specific monsters; and little has been done in the exegesis of these theratological hallucinations, except for the technical, philological identification of some sources (Seznec 1943, 212-17) or the classification of some of the most obvious allegories (Bem 1979b, 39, 42).

The monsters can be interpreted both on a general and on an individual plane. Firstly, in their diverse but undifferentiated totality, they certainly are a sign in language of the breakdown of all attempts to describe interpretively the universe: their chaos represents figuratively the threat of an army of signs in mad quest for their lost meanings. In this perspective, then, not only is the monstrous "meaningless" (i.e., without a referent)—but, far more importantly, conversely all that does not have a referent is "monstrous". Language itself has here become uncanny; and the concept of words as "mushrooms growing in one's mouth" of Hofmannsthal's Lord Chandos is but one step away. At the same time, however, the monsters are also connected with Gustave's personal imagery and have the complementary function of attempting to exorcise the demonic by the disguised formulation of a specifically individual desire. In this sense, the monsters of the *Tentation* do have an ultimate *content*, which justifies some traits of their deformities. Among innumerable interchangeable possibilities, Flaubert dwells upon a few peculiar ones: here as elsewhere, the eeriness of the monsters is in the last analysis not a haphazard phenomenon, but rather a semantically motivated one, in that repressed factors render certain configurations evidently *more uncanny* than others for the authorial voice.

The first relevant vision is that of the copulation between the Sphinx and the Chimæra. The attempted union of the two animals shows here just about everything that elsewhere (for example, in "la scène du fiacre" in *Madame Bovary*) fell victim to Flaubertian censorship. It was probably its mythological garb that, paradoxically, made its obscenity go unnoticed (or at least uncommented-upon).

The Sphinx's and the Chimæra's attempted coitus has been interpreted in the most abstract ways imaginable: as a metaphor, that is, of the "impossible marriage" between Science and Faith (Unwin 1979, 39), between "fantaisie et pensée logique" (Seznec 1943, 212), between "matière et esprit, Science et imagination" (Bonwit 1946, 207), to name but the most commonly recurrent ones. These interpretations, however, do not take into account the uncanny atmosphere in which the vision is steeped. While rational symbolism cannot and should not be ruled out, it seems that the hallucination ought to be rooted deeper in Saint Antoine's (i.e. in Flaubert's) consciousness—or rather in his subconscious. Their ultimate ground must then be sought elsewhere.

The presence of the Sphinx gives us a hint that should not be overlooked: after all, *Œdipus* was the man who solved its riddles. Antoine—his self now, as we saw, floating freely beyond the false appearances of voluptuousness and death—is here soliciting the crowd of "ultimate monsters" to show him the source of life: *while, before* life is created. Had he not desired to see monsters "on the other side of conception"? In other words, what Antony asks of the Sphinx and the Chimæra (the former in the male role, the latter in the female one), is to show him *in fieri* the cosmic fecundation whose effects have deluged him in the course of his innumerable hallucinations. The union of the two animals in the text represents the fantasy of witnessing what Freud calls "primal scene"—i.e., parental coitus (cf. Freud *GW* XII, 54-75, 155-56; *SE* XVII, 29-47, 119-20).

It should not be surprising that the parents appear here disguised as monsters. The child's desire is a subconscious one; it undergoes a certain degree of metamorphosis in order to be acceptable to the conscious self. Since the satisfaction of his curiosity is accompanied by the humiliation of his pride, it must be to a greater or lesser extent painful for him to view (or to imagine) the mother's unfaithfulness to him. Thus, the "monstrosity" of the humans involved easily appears as a projection onto the Other of the intense degree of emotional rejection which accompanies the vision. In this perspective, the monsters' final failure at copulating witnessed by Saint Antoine is arguably but a wishful-thinking invention of the child's; it obeys a logic of refusal of reality in which the emotionally inconceivable is translated into language as a physical impossibility. Significantly, such voyeuristic fantasies find a precise parallel in Gustave's earliest works, losing all collective-unconscious character and becoming firmly rooted in his individual experience.[22]

A section of *Mémoires d'un fou*, which Flaubert wrote when he was an adolescent, foreshadows the "monstrous copulation" in the desert so strikingly as to leave no doubt regarding the true nature of the allegedly highly metaphysical animals meeting, as the narrating voice puts it, "right next" to Saint Antoine, "almost touching his shoulder":

> Deux êtres jetés sur la terre par un hasard, quelque chose, et qui se rencontrent, s'aiment, parce que l'un est femme et l'autre homme! Les voilà haletants l'un pour l'autre, se promenant ensemble la nuit [...] et puis ils rentrent, poussés tous les deux par une ardeur sans pareille, car ces deux âmes ont leurs organes violemment échauffés, et les voilà bientôt grotesquement accouplés, avec des rugissements et des soupirs, soucieux l'un et l'autre pour reproduire un imbécile de plus sur la terre, un malheureux qui les imitera! Contemplez-les, plus bêtes en ce moment que les chiens et les mouches, s'évanouissant, et cachant soigneusement aux yeux des hommes leur jouissance solitaire—pensant peut-être que le bonheur est un crime et la volupté une honte.
>
> <div align="right">(<i>Mémoires d'un fou</i> X; Flaubert 1964, I, 237B)[23]</div>

The parallel between the "bêtes" is impressive: dogs and flies, Sphinx and Chimæra—all are interchangeable forms of the same paradigm.

A second, imposing illustration of the intrinsic meaningfulness of some Flaubertian monsters is then proffered by the threatening figure of the Catoblépas:

> (Buffle noir, avec une tête de porc tombant jusqu'à terre, et rattachée à ses épaules par un cou mince, long et flasque comme un boyau vidé.
>   Il est vautré tout à plat; et ses pieds disparaissent sous l'énorme crinière à poils durs qui lui couvre le visage).
>   *Le Catoblépas.* Gras, mélancolique, farouche, je reste continuellement à sentir sous mon ventre la chaleur de la boue. Mon crâne est tellement lourd qu'il m'est impossible de le porter. Je le roule autour de moi, lentement [...]
>   Personne, Antoine, n'a jamais vu mes yeux, ou ceux qui les ont vus sont morts. Si je relevais mes paupières—mes paupières roses et gonflées,—tout de suite, tu mourrais.
>   *Antoine.* Oh! Celui-là! ... a ... a ... Si j'allais avoir envie? ... Sa stupidité m'attire. Non! non! Je ne veux pas!
>
> <div align="right">(<i>Tentation</i>, 570A)</div>

The reader may justifiably ask: *envie*—of what? The ambiguity of the last version of the *Tentation* is here particularly embarrassing. However, the missing item can be restored thanks to the version of 1849:

> Si j'allais avoir envie de les regarder, ces yeux!
>
> <div align="right">(<i>T1</i>, 440B)</div>

The censorship operating in the 1872 version is remarkable. What the original text showed, and the final one removed, was the notion of a menacing confrontation, a sort of duel of glances, threatening Antoine with the punishment of death. Uncanny, revealing detail: the Catoblépas is the *only* monster of *T3* that addresses Antoine neither in the universal mode "Je / nous" (as most do) nor in the direct-impersonal mode "tu" (as a few others do), but rather in the direct-personal mode, by calling him "Antoine" and evoking death as directed precisely at him. It is hardly surprising that Antoine thereupon suffers symbolic death: after the Catoblépas's threats, he is literally flooded by reptiles and spun into a cocoon by spiders—the father's tentacular army. Antoine becomes a mere stump: death / castration is rendered visible in his immobilization.

The conclusion is clear: the Catoblépas is a deformed father-figure menacing to kill (or, by synecdoche, to castrate) Antoine for having dared to defy paternal power. Significantly, such an image of punishment surfaces as a subconscious afterthought at the end of a work that so overtly centers on suspension, reversal and abolition of the Father-God's precepts, as well as of the father-devil's nihilist logic. The Catoblépas represents here the punishment incurred for all the voluptuous, forbidden psychic errances through desire engaged in by the saint since the beginning of his hallucinations.[24]

This is the moment that spells the final abolition of the self called "Antoine"—i.e., literally called, named such by the monster. After the death incurred through identification, the only way out is now a symbolic return to life followed by a complete catabolism of the structures that can say "I". The fulfillment of desire through the mystical vision of Life thus requires resurrection, on one hand, and bracketing of the father, on the other: in such a world there will be no name-giving, no character, no "I" and no "Other"—no conflict in which a self could be defined against any Other one.

And now comes the *Licorne*, sweeping the sky from the clouds and clearing the horizon from the monsters. Antoine is freed. The fundamental question about the Unicorn is whether it may be read as a *third* vision provided with an intrinsic meaning—that is to say, whether it fits into a semantic chain connecting Antoine's imprisonment with the liberation in ecstasy which follows it and concludes the text.

An intrinsic symbolic meaning of the *Licorne* could be assumed if it were possible to tie its appearance to two features. One of the two would be the restoring of Antony to life; the second, complementary one, would be the marginalization of the father figure. Seznec confirms these hypotheses: "La Licorne, que seule une vierge peut capturer, est Jésus incarné dans le sein de la Vierge Marie" (Seznec 1943, 212, and 1949, 76). Christ is the one obvious traditional symbol of resurrection; *and* the saint's fantasy of being born from the Virgin Mary, i.e. by parthenogenesis, is perhaps the strongest possible way to downplay the paternal role—in a sense, a stronger one than revolt itself, since it implies refusing to acknowledge a principle with which even rebellion has to come to terms (if only to attack it).

In other words, the reasons that prompt Antoine / Flaubert to evoke Christ's (re)birth at this point in the *Tentation* coincide with those expounded by Jones:

> [Mary's] virginity when bearing Jesus [...] is not so much a tribute to her purity as a derivation from the son's Œdipus complex. The common infantile phantasy of one's mother being virginal signifies a repudiation of any part played by the father in one's birth—the wish to be independent of him—and the jealous distaste felt at the idea of sexual intercourse between the parents.
> (Jones 1964 II, 210)

Freud, too, points to the strong contextuality that exists between fantasies of rebirth and incestuous fantasies—the former being an "anagogical shortcut" for the latter (Freud *GW* XII, 136; *SE* XVII, 101-02). In short, the Unicorn brings about the breakthrough: its privileged relationship with the Virgin symbolizes the self's final separation from paternal Law and its direct accession to the cosmic principle of life.

When the last monsters vanish, there begins the movement toward matter operated by the observing glance, "previously named Antoine". Although the glance does not explicitly follow Faust on his way to the Realm of the Mothers, it nonetheless glides toward the same spheres of unanchored existence.

Etre la matière!

> Et il n'a plus peur!
>
> *Tentation*, 571B

The conclusion of the *Tentation* is articulated in four moments: at first Antony is transported to a sea shore; then he sees "life being born"; he desires to become, to *be* matter; finally, at dawn, he has a vision of Jesus Christ in the sun.

With the exception of the last one, these phases represent a continuous intensification of the disintegration of Antoine as a rational self. The sea animals attract him into the waves; they represent "sa nostalgie de la vie utérine" (Bem 1979b, 42). Then the borderlines between natural realms, between mind and matter, are blurred:

> Les végétaux maintenant ne se distinguent plus des animaux. Des polypiers, qui ont l'air de sycomores, portent des bras sur leurs branches. Antoine croit voir une chenille entre deux feuilles; c'est un papillon qui s'envole. Il va pour marcher sur un galet; une sauterelle grise bondit. Des insectes pareils à des pétales de rose garnissent un arbuste; des débris d'éphémères font sur le sol une couche neigeuse.
> Et puis les plantes se confondent avec les pierres.
> Des cailloux ressemblent à des cerveaux, des stalactites à des mamelles, des fleurs de fer à des tapisseries ornées de figures.
> Dans des fragments de glace, il distingue des efflorescences, des empreintes de buissons et de coquilles—à ne savoir si ce sont les empreintes de ces choses-là, ou ces choses elles-mêmes. Des diamants brillent comme des yeux, des minéraux palpitent.
>
> (*Tentation*, 571A-B)

The quest for the ultimate vision has led the observing eye from the realm of the proto-animals, through the realm of the proto-plants, to the mineral realm, and has animated the inanimate. As the extreme stage of a metamorphism which had begun gradually and then increasingly accelerated, all is now mobilized. The final fragmentation of Antoine's identity—which is not a factor given *ab initio* and more or less constant throughout the work, but quite on the contrary, the mystic point toward which the saint's desire strives—is here approaching. When such a goal will be attained in the divine vision, the mobilization will finally be much more radical than that of a simple "plurality" of voices: *All* will be in *all*.25

As Kayser points out, in principle the admixture of different natural realms is one of the essential devices, if not the main one, used to portray the grotesque (Kayser 1963, 183). In the case of the traditional grotesque, however, the goal aimed for is that of exerting a disquieting impression of uncanniness on the readers—to threaten accepted reality with collapse. This, however, is no longer the case in the last section of *La Tentation*; Flaubert writes of Antoine: "Et il n'a plus peur!" (*Tentation*, 571B). Far from that, the pulverization of the self is a liberation for him. The flowing-together of mineral, vegetal and animal mobilizes the self at the same time as it mobilizes the stone; anguish disappears when the vessel meant to contain it is shattered and falls into non-existence, non-definability.

The concept of a liberation deriving from the confluence of the realms of Nature and the abolition of the centralized subject is not exclusive to Flaubert; in fact, it structures Broch's novel *The Death of Virgil*, which depicts the asymptotic approach of death as the gradual blurring of the ability of language to represent an organized hierarchy of Being. Of the dissolving Virgil, Broch writes:

> More and more the flying and swimming animals were amassing to an impenetrably dense heap, increasingly commingled by monsters, the mass becoming increasingly monstrous, more and more threatened by uncreated and precreated elements [...]
> [N]o sort of isolation was any longer possible, none was permissible because everything was being resolved [...] an animal-fog losing itself in ultimate invisibility, absolved into starriness, absorbed into plantliness; the animal totality was swallowed by the night, [...] and the icy serpent had burst asunder, the icy serpent of time [...]
> [A]nd he, who even while in its midst might watch it, could watch it, must watch it, moved on by the animally-invaded plant-life, became like a plant himself, inside and outside [...]
> He was a seeing plant although he was not struggling back into anything, neither into beastiness [...]
> [I]nertia and movement, interchanged and time-exempted, united to an indistinguishable flowing rest [...]
>   (Broch 1976, 441, 443, 444; transl. Untermeyer 1945, 468, 470, 471)

The difference in emphasis is, of course, clear: in Antoine we have visions of an emotional type that derive from the repression of the deep-level drives of his eros. Contrary to Broch's, Flaubert's way of formulating in language the movement toward the fragmentation of the self into indistinct matter has a precise biological overtone— it specifically foregrounds the liberating aspect of the mystical vision of *life bypassing sexuality*.

The saint's blissful vision is doubly fulfilling: on one hand because it achieves the loss of the structure which suffers from the necessity to say "I"; but also, more in particular, because the images it portrays are precisely such as to abolish the very reproductive structure which had caused the saint's suffering in the first place. What the observing eye "adores" here is the all-comforting certitude of the general principle of non-sexual reproduction. The saint goes *back beyond sexuality* and finds in such a vision the reassuring state of rest which he had in vain sought in or against the family structure and its haunting complexes. This is likely to be the explicit sense of Flaubert's otherwise sibylline statement, reported by the Goncourts, according to which the Saint is finally defeated by "the cell—the scientific cell" (quot. in Nadeau 1969, 271). Since sexual reproduction is by definition the biological foundation of desire (be it biologically elementary, or organized and sublimated by communal life and culture), Antoine's pleasure in viewing the sexually undifferentiated cell indicates the bliss experienced in contemplating the abolition of the desiring process. The "androgynous" cell indicates to the observer the destruction, in its very root, of the absence called desire. This is the meaning to be attributed to the vision which the saint experiences once he has arrived at the realm "beyond fear": "Enfin il aperçoit de petites masses globuleuses, grosses comme des têtes d'épingles et garnies de cils tout autour. Une vibration les agite" (*Tentation*, 571B).

The next and final phase follows: the moment of *ekstasis* and *enthusiasm* proper (both in the etymological sense).

> O bonheur! bonheur! J'ai vu naître la vie, j'ai vu le mouvement commencer. Le sang de mes veines bat si fort qu'il va les rompre. J'ai envie de voler, de nager, d'aboyer, de beugler, de hurler. Je voudrais avoir des ailes, une carapace, une écorce, souffler de la fumée, porter une trompe, tordre mon corps, me diviser

partout, être en tout, m'émaner avec les odeurs, me développer comme les plantes, couler comme l'eau, vibrer comme le son, briller comme la lumière, me blottir sur toutes les formes, pénétrer chaque atome, descendre jusqu'au fond de la matière,—être la matière!

(*Tentation*, 571B)

What is aimed at here is no lesser a feat than the expression of the Unspeakable—the fundamental challenge posed to all mystical literature. Fulfillment being essentially non-representable, Flaubert's text has recourse to a finite number of choice figures: totality is hinted at by samples.

Accordingly, the vision is then represented in language in an oblique way, as an absence: in the past tense ("j'*ai vu*"), or in the conditional, as wish ("je *voudrais* avoir ... souffler ... porter ... être"). As in Hölderlin's blank spaces, in Faust's "Then I *could* tell the fleeing moment" (i.e., but cannot now), or in "Fulfillment", the unwritten Part II of Novalis's *Heinrich von Ofterdingen*, language falters and misses the visionary mark. At the end of the *Tentation*, the glance previously named "saint" or "Antony" is experiencing the *Gottesschau* which fulfills his progressive loss of self and completes his catabasis toward the supreme, divine indifference of matter. However, the interpenetration of intellect and vision, the *Unio Mystica*, cannot be predicated directly by the speaking voice; and the translation into thought, into language, empties the vision, which is always non-legible, non-writable, strictly speaking non-"thinkable". As Broch wrote in concluding Virgil's voyage through the pulverization of the self into death:

> [...] he floated with the word, although, the more he was enveloped by it, the more he penetrated into the flooding sound and was penetrated by it, the more unattainable, the greater, the graver and more elusive became the word, a floating sea, a floating fire, sea-heavy, sea-light, notwithstanding, still word: he could not hold fast to it, he might not hold fast to it; it was incomprehensible and unutterable for him, because it was *on the other side of language.*
> (Broch 1976, 454; emphasis added)

Antoine does not die; but he envisages with panic enthusiasm the disintegration of his own self. Clearly, the strongest attraction exerted on him by both the desexualized cell and animated matter (the two opposites that have converged and fused into one) comes from their perfect self-less-ness—from their inability to suffer. What elicits his excitement for *un-differentiation* is actually the moment of (psychological) *in-difference* which the former entails. The cell is "divine" not only because it participates in the movement of the cosmos, but above all because it repeats God's sovereign lack of passion. Becoming matter is here, once more,—becoming God.

It is easy to recognize here how Gustave's God-complex, which was present but had to remain frustrated at the level of psychological macrostructures (the competition with the father, the enterprise of literature as counter-creation, etc.) successfully returns at the microscopic level. The desire which the conscious self cannot satisfy is fulfilled by destructuring the "I" into visionary atoms: the Œdipal conflict cannot even be posited in the realm of the indifferent-undifferentiated Being. This is the full strategy of a process that can be described as the attainment of satisfaction by seeping in under paternal interdiction. Thus, while one can certainly concur, at one level, with Flaubert's statement reported by the Goncourts that Antony was "defeated by the scientific cell" (i.e., that subliminal drives fragment the "saint"'s claim to Christian credibility), one must also add that, in a different sense, the *Tentation*'s true victim is the Law of the Father: after having in vain tried to destroy it by revolt, its single adept finally transgresses it by assuming the shape of a disintegrated, unpunishable non-identity.

The essential striving of the *Tentation* must then be seen in its text-shattering intention to imagine a desire that would break away from the aporias of structured sexuality—an "alternative desire", that is, capable of achieving a radical abolition of the imprisonment in the entity called self. True, the ultimate goal of sexuality is also a loss of the self: such is Freud's well-known thesis in *Beyond the Pleasure Principle*. The crux of the matter, however, is that structured sexuality indeed seems to be the most circuitous possible way to reach the desired goal: a sort of exasperating, perhaps even pointless voyage through the antipodes of individualization, before finally reaching the loss-of-self of fulfillment. Hence, the *temptation*—no word could here more fittingly describe Flaubert's project—to take the shortcut through the destructuring of the self. Saint Antony's "training" could be described as the attempt to become God-Matter in and while bypassing the stage of the sexualized identity that calls itself "I".[26]

The fourth and last phase of this section then concludes the text: the sun rises, and Antoine sees Christ in the disk of the sun. "Consciousness has won" (Reik 1912, 75)—temporarily.

There is a remarkable balance between light and nocturnal visions at the end of the *Tentation*: the latter are transitory, but on the other hand the former also undergo a daily cycle which renders them fragile and contingent. It is true that the Law of the Father triumphs in the morning, and there is no question that Christ's appearance in the sun symbolizes the desire for atonement with him.[27] At the same time, however, it is also certain that the temptation to fragment the self into an "illegal"—or, at the very least, non-legal—mobility will mount yet another assault at nightfall, and again suggest the blissful satisfaction of mystical union with undifferentiated Being. The *eternal return* of the irreconcilable opposition Subject / Loss of the subject, Centralization of the self / Pulverization of the self, is sketched in the eternal repetition of day and night over Antony's symbolic solitude.

*

Antony is a mystic at bottom, yet he believes in nothing. No belief, no hallucination univocally vanquishes him; only the "ultimate vision" of a desexuated divine Matter replenishes his glance. He plays obedience against transgression, transcendence against immanence, and never really upholds either. He never adores, he never adheres: the alternation of the opposites suggests that, even for Flaubert himself, mysticism was only to be experienced in the mode of desire—as absence, as loss. The concept illustrated by the *Tentation* is that both God (with his *alter ego*, the devil) and matter are inadequate: the former two, because of their different but equivalent ways of threatening the sexualized self; the latter, because a de-sexualized, pulverized self is only imaginable as a transitory state, in the orgasmic agitation of a brief *Unio Mystica*. Antoine's *cogito* remains empty to the very end: if the Logos of the Law proves to be an oppressive-hallucinatory one, on the other hand the "I feel, therefore I am" ("I feel, therefore something is") of the union with Life remains a mere desire, to be explored and satisfied only in a fantasmatic (and peculiarly Flaubertian) *intermittence*.

In the reciprocal elision of opposite desires, what is certain is that for Flaubert the ineffable remains ineffable: try as much as one will to speculate "beyond Œdipus", reality will always bring the self back to its concrete contingency and identity. Thus, Flaubert's project to transform the self into an unstructured energy, capable of filtering through to the source of life from under Œdipal constraints, is a liberation which can only take place in the text and not in praxis. How could such a sustained mobilization of the self be possible in reality?

The self's liberation, however, can be brought into reality *by* the text—by literature. Since the text too belongs to praxis, all that happens in the text is, albeit in a mediated way, a part of praxis as well. In *L'Éducation sentimentale*, Flaubert makes one of his rare authorial allusions to the nature of literary fiction; he reports about Frédéric's laughable attempts to free himself from his "passion calamiteuse" for M.me Arnoux and writes:

> Frédéric [...] résolut de composer une *Histoire de la Renaissance* [...]
>   Peu à peu, la sérénité du travail l'apaisa. *En plongeant dans la personnalité des autres, il oublia la sienne, ce qui est la seule manière peut-être de n'en pas souffrir.*
> (Flaubert 1965, 207; p. II, ch. III; emphasis added)

Writing *is* the act fulfilling Flaubert's project of mobilization of the self.

Flaubert reminds us that Art is the only possible way to "become matter"—to seep through to Being, in atomic state, from under our being-in-the-world limited by time and space. *La Tentation* contains the victorious liberation of desire, not in the sense that Antoine's actions in the plot wring durable satisfaction from the omnipotence of the Father-God-Devil, or from the exhilarating indifferentiation of Matter; rather, it contains liberation because it enacts liberation *through language,* in the act itself of *speaking* absolute desire, "ce qui est la seule manière peut-être de *l'assouvir*". The true liberation does not take place for the self that is spoken of, but in the very subject that speaks, and that is thereby no longer merely its own "self". The mobilization of Flaubert's desire does not depend on the mobilization of Antoine's (even though it evidently projects itself into it): they belong to different planes, and authorial victory is assured independently of the outcome in the character's plight.[28]

However, Flaubert's struggle with style, his anguish to "write Perfection" at all cost, proves only too well that even in language victory is only transitory. As soon as the written text ends, the self, previously agitated, vibrating freely like the "petites masses globuleuses" that trigger Antoine's ecstasy, falls back into darkness and remains wrapped in a spiderweb of silence, frozen in the endless, "monstrous" immobility of the unwritten space.

III

Flaubert and the Evacuation of Utopia

"Vouloir conclure" may indeed be an "ineptie", as Flaubert claimed (*Correspondance* II, 239—quot. in Brombert 1966, 290); yet, outside Antoine's logic of the *Unio Mystica*, it may be a necessary one.

In Balzac the demonic is the treacherous force luring the self deeper into the disruptive process of desire. It is an aggressive, threatening element which leads to the castration of the subject. In this sense, Balzac's devil figure—whatever the text chosen—works in unison with the hedonism haunting his protagonist. Balzac's demonic, however, is not the initiator of the threatening spiral; rather, as in *La peau de chagrin*, it contributes the energy and the means necessary to prolong the exhausting roulette-game of desire. The devil is for Balzac no more "evil" than existence itself; and the world inherited from the fathers, cruel though it may be, is not evil, but dangerous at worst. Provided due precautions are taken—Vautrinian willpower above all—in Balzac the world can be fully *assumed*.[29]

In Flaubert the devil shows a clear tendency, increasing toward the end of the writer's life, to become a dialectical destructive element. In the works of Gustave's adolescence, the devil appears as the materialization of logical-paternal thought; later on, it becomes more and more perceptibly the logical annihilator of its own existence. Flaubert's devil is a suicidal atheist and nihilist: it is a philosophical Occam's razor which, in *La Tentation*, finally declares its own futility. In such an absurd world, empty of friends or foes, all that is left to the Flaubertian self is the somewhat morose mystical contemplation of the eternal co-essence of Death and Lasciviousness.

Whereas in Balzac the demonic has a threatening, but at the same time also a stimulating role, in Flaubert the devil falls short of its task and fares no better than its *alter ego*, the creator God, "dieu en délire" which it purports to attack. The devil is in Flaubert, at bottom, "un diable en délire": a *nullité*. In a stupid cosmos, both God and the devil cannot be but stupid; and besides, by the 1870's they have been far outvoted by the stupid bourgeois, whose numbers are legion. For Flaubert there are only two existential realms: the "desert" (of Art), which grants flashes of mystical union with the Absolute; and the "city" (Alexandria / Paris / the *sæculum*), which proves that the traditional notion of divine-demonic omnipotence is in bourgeois times but a *bêtise*. Little wonder that, conversely, for Flaubert the *bêtise* of the modern world is also omnipotent.

The bearing which the demonic has on Flaubert's view of the Utopian project is evident. If we define Utopia as the Alterity (whether geographical, historical or psychological) in which a programmed counter-discourse corrects the laws of reality and forces them to correspond to an "ideal" order (whatever "ideal" may mean for each individual author)—we must then admit that there simply is not sufficient tension for a Utopian project in Flaubert's world view. Utopia presupposes a radicalized polarity: between luxury and poverty in *La peau de chagrin* or *Illusions perdues*, between the Court and the Tower in *La Chartreuse*, between noble inventors and corrupt politicians in Gérard de Nerval's Faustian *œuvre*, between the golden age of Russian Romanticism and Stalin's 1930's in Bulgakov's *The Master and Margarita*, and so forth. But in Flaubert the polarity is invariably evacuated. In *Madame Bovary* the land of alterity, the land of counter-discourse, appears by definition as the pernicious escapism of a "bovaristic" mental creation; and in *La Tentation* the very emptiness of the Wilderness—the desert—symbolizes the non-existence of a second pole capable of creating an Other-Worldly space in competition with This-Worldly Alexandria. Flaubert's Other World is, simply, *the text*; but he has completely renounced all claim to the ontological existence (were it only a hoped-for one) of that which the text represents. Art, directly and in itself, becomes Utopia and begins to speak *as* Utopia when it is no longer capable of speaking *about* it.

The tragedy peculiar to Flaubert and to postromantic art with him (here the contrast with, for example, Nerval's indiscriminate *availability for faith* becomes astonishing) is that in the transition from Romantic Utopia-in-the-Text to Symbolist Text-as-Utopia the author's aesthetics became one of an increasing formal adoration for a textual beauty whose ontological existence was no longer even conceivable.[30] In the times of Romanticism there was an unspoken but persistently circulating hope that "the land where the lemon-trees blossom" may actually exist, somewhere in a distant subtropical climate; as the nineteenth century advanced, however, this persuasion faded into ridiculousness. While writing *Salammbô*, Flaubert in his letters prosaically mocked those who would believe him "dumb enough" ("assez godiche") to try and express in the novel something verifiable / falsifiable about contemporaneous Mediterranean Africa. The devil thus appears as both the psychopomp *and* the victim of the postromantic drifting of Utopia from the ontological to the aesthetic.

Emptiness is the distinctive trait of the Utopian slot in Flaubert's work. The world of the fathers (be they divine or demonic—or divine-demonic at the same time) is Smarh's and Antoine's nightmare: yet, for their creator there is no alternative in sight. Even though for him *le bourgeois est haïssable*, there is nothing to replace it with; and, while life in society is monstrous, the solitude of Art—as the *Tentation* well shows—breeds equivalent monsters. When the bourgeois have appropriated science—when reality has appropriated rationality—when the fathers have, for their purposes, appropriated even Cain's tremendously logical rebellion and turned it into an element of their social machinery (as Homais does in *Madame Bovary*)—what kind of revolt can then be conceived? Polarities disappear, and the traditional *révolté*, the devil himself, withers away. For the Hugo of *La fin de Satan*, such a resorption of the demonic figure takes place because, in the long run of world history, all is for the better; for Flaubert it takes place because, today already, all is for the worst. Demonic *action* is absent from Flaubert's world, as is the Utopian tension that would be necessary to sustain it: there being no fundamental conflict of a "demonic" principle against a paternal-divine one, no space is left for praxis.

Indeed, it is not by chance that all of Flaubert's demonic texts, from *Voyage en enfer* to the three *Tentations*, take negligible pleasure in plot development. This essentially happens because Gustave has no demonic *story* to tell; what he does intend to do is to denounce and accuse. *Voyage en enfer* can be said to consist of the narrator's hallucinations; *Smarh* and *La danse des morts* are processions of diverse visions, similar to the ones later to parade in front of Saint Antoine. Faust has fathers against whom he can meaningfully rebel in order to find his own way into the world; his Mephistopheles and his God are Other Fathers with and between whom the knots of narration can be tied. But in Flaubert the human partners of the devil only have the alternative between different-indifferent, equivalent ways in which to acknowledge God's and Satan's coinciding insignificance. Flaubert's despair is the twilight in which all idols are equally, repulsively gray.

From Faust's frenzied hyperactivity, in a few decades we have now arrived at a diametrically opposed ways to mobilize the self: Antoine's vibrating hyperpassivity. From the cosmic union attained through an immense enlargement of desire, almost an explosion of the self into the Universe, we have reached the zero point of a cosmic union won by a gradual regression, by the reduction of desire to the identification with the unstructured—by the fusion of self and non-self. Whereas Faust's (conditional) supreme moment comes with his visionary cumulating-upon-himself of the fates of "the millions", thus encompassing as much humanity as is conceivable, Antoine's (hypothetical) supreme moment coincides with his vision of himself deposing the human garb, not only fantasmatically but physically as well, to gradually become One with monsters, minerals, and matter. Faust wants to expand humanity to the spaces of wild, unreclaimed land; wilderness is for him an obstacle to be bent. Antoine moves away from the hypocritical monsters-believing-themselves-human that haunt Alexandria and seeks out the last retrenchment of humanity among the monsters of the desert.

By evacuating Utopia, Flaubert historically reverses Faust's desiring process: mobilization can take place in him only in a movement toward the atomic, not toward the cosmic. Accordingly, a centralized, anthropomorphic notion of the demonic becomes with him an entirely absurd notion. The advent of modern aesthetics has caused the devil's second, decisive ontological Fall.

Notes to Chapter Two

[1] As Tynyanov wrote in his essay on "Dostoevsky and Gogol", "every literary inheritance [*priemstvennost'*] is primarily a struggle, the destruction of an old unity and the new edification of old elements" (Tynyanov 1969, 302).

[2] Flaubert labored constantly (1848-1872) to "tune" those voices and to find an ideal arrangement for the episodes, which would correspond to the most satisfactory climactic sequence. On the modifications undergone by the text in its three extant versions, cf. Pantke 1936, 145-46, and Bem 1979, 47-62. I will be referring here to the third version, whose structure is in my opinion the most revealing of the three, at least in the perspective which I have chosen. I will examine a small number of episodes which, in the progression from $T1$ to $T3$, confirm that the "impossible anamnesis" of Cainite wishes was at the root of the first version as well—only to be more strictly censored in the third one.

[3] The "book-on-nothing" principle simply illustrated Flaubert's desire to break away from the conventions of nineteenth-century fiction, to whose rigid canon he had to discipline himself while writing *Madame Bovary*.

[4] After all, Cain, too (just like Gustave) was thought to be the "enfant raté" of the family—as Sartre's well-known *L'idiot de la famille* stresses.

[5] This and all subsequent references to Jones are to be found in Jones 1951, 166-80.

[6] This section is the one that is most directly derived from Flaubert's early work *Smarh*; it is the one which most clearly bears the imprint of Smarh's flight through space.

[7] Cf. Smeed 1975, 82 ("The Unanswerable Questions").

[8] One wonders, in this sense, to what extent Gustave's own negative feelings against his bourgeois brother may have been a mere safety valve dispensing him from consciously directing his aggressivity toward his father. One Homais is necessary as demonic caricature, if a father-figure, a Larivière, is to be purified of all resentment and reassuringly loved without reserve.

[9] As Butor puts it, "Si chaque régiment en particulier est d'autant plus séduisant qu'il est avec les autres, ne vont-ils pas se neutraliser? Le jeune homme tenté ne saura plus lequel choisir [...] [E]n lisant mainte page, n'avons-nous pas l'impression que ce montreur d'images se presse par trop de changer sa projection, que s'il avait seulement attendu quelques instants encore, le saint n'aurait pu résister davantage, qu'il est sauvé par la tentation suivante?" (Butor 1974, 216-17).

[10] The critics agree that the Queen's sexuality has been strongly de-emphasized (it has been transferred, one could suggest, to the fantasy of Ammonaria). Robert writes that the saint is "émerveillé comme un enfant devant le spectacle que lui offre cet être fantastique, mais non point sexuellement troublé" (Robert 1982, 111); Bem states that "la reine de Saba n'apporte à Antoine que son discours" (i.e., the "énigmes du sphinx" which she proposes to him) (Bem 1979, 102).

[11] This is the son's compensatory fantasy; sublimation reverses the symbolic flow of desire, and here the "Saint" turns down the "Queen", rather than the reverse.

[12] Cf. Freud's *The Theme Of the Three Caskets* (*GW* X, 26; *SE* XII, 292).

[13] To mention but some of the recent ones: "lacking interest" (Buck 1966, 59), "cacophonic", "boring" (Bardèche 1974, 148, 154), "painfully boring to read" (Unwin 1979, 31), "la partie la plus morte de l'œuvre" (Thibaudet 1935, 183), or [peopled with Gods] "annulling each other in the parade" (Nadeau 1969, 80).

[14] On the subject, see Jones's quoted "A Psychoanalytic Study of the Holy Ghost Concept", in Jones 1964, II, 358-73.

[15] This is not to deny the obvious surface meaning of the parade (namely, that all gods are to face inescapable disappearance), but rather to confirm it. The death of the Judeo-Christian God is both inferred diachronically by the series of the episodes and prefigured synchronically within each of them.

[16] Danger discusses the passage in question in view of the castration complex (Danger 1979).

[17] Other alternatives are, of course, possible. The orthodox view holds that the devil is (in my terminology) both strong (i.e., "sufficient" in terms of power) and unreliable (i.e., treacherous in the way he makes use of science). This is clearly the case in Spieß's *Faust* as well as in Klinger's—in the former, for the purpose of humiliating man; in the latter, in order to extol him.

[18] For a detailed comparison and comment of the parallel passages in the two *Tentations*, cf. Bem 1979, 41 and 86-90. Cf. also Séginger 1984, 66.

[19] In his introduction to *Faust* (I and II—1840) (Goethe 1969, 10, 14) Nerval, too, writes about the return of the "Forms beyond". Antoine's position, however, is radically different. The eternal souls of Nerval's metempsychosis always retain absolute identifiability. Because they clearly retain their individual *self*, Nerval's pantheon should be described not only as one of pantheism but, first and foremost, as one of polytheism.

The figures of Nerval's Realm of the Mothers are displaced; Antoine's visions, by contrast, are disassembled. Heroes dwell in the former; theratological combinations roam about the latter.

[20] Lombard defined Flaubert's aesthetics in the *Tentation* as one of "grotesque triste", "illogisme [...] plein de pensées secrètes" (Lombard 1934, 47). Similarly, Brombert stresses that the chaotic "animals beyond conception" excite, if anything, Antoine's melancholic *ennui* (Brombert 1966, 207-08). However, the melancholy elicited by the monsters encompasses more than just Flaubert's denunciation of the "tragic ineptness of Christian humanism" (Brombert). For such a denunciation, even the surface-level nausea provoked by the "heresies" and Other-Gods sections would have furnished sufficient material. The *grotesque* goes deeper than the conscious refusal of faith; it is tied to the subconscious complexes centered around the theme of the demonic.

[21] Accordingly, Reik draws a parallel between the *Tentation* and the *Légende de St. Julien l'Hospitalier* and convincingly argues that in both St. Julian's and St. Antony's case "the animals which they pursue are their own instincts, which have fallen prey to repression and surface again in the dream" (Reik 1912, 71).

²²To show how active the conflict was for Gustave, suffice it to refer here to the discussion of the *scène primitive* of *Mémoires d'un fou* which can be found in M. Robert's *En haine du roman* (1982, 64-70).

²³By interpreting the monsters as "Other" than Saint Antoine, I do not mean to deny that, by a process of interiorization, they can also be identified by the Saint (i.e., by Flaubert) with his own "monstrous" self. In other words, I agree with Bem's thesis that the monsters represent also Flaubert's own ab-normality, his e-normous uniqueness, catalyzed in tangible form (Bem 1979, 136-37).

²⁴"The Identity of Gogol's *Viy*" (Rancour-Laferrière 1978) exhaustively treats the problem of incestuous guilt and punishment by glance, both in the specific Gogolian context and in psychoanalytical theory. Most of his indications could be applied to Flaubert's Catoblépas—many of them verbatim.

²⁵Séginger writes repeatedly (Séginger 1984, 22, 34, 37, and *passim*) of what she calls "identités périphériques de Saint Antoine", "sujet polyphonique", "[un] Je qui menace toujours de se dissoudre dans le vaste On des représentations plus ou moins anonymes": this finally applies here fully to Antoine in his last stage.

²⁶Reik himself may be intuitively admitting this fact when he writes that "Antony's famous cry *Etre la matière!* is explained by the desire to be freed from all torments of conventionally determined sexuality, to be an elementary creature" ("von allen Qualen der konventionell gebundenen Sexualität frei zu sein, ein Naturgeschöpf zu sein") (Reik 1912, 184).

²⁷In his discussion of the Schreber case, Freud repeatedly stresses the symbolic equivalence between father and sun; cf. *GW* VIII, 240-316; *SE* XII, 3-82, esp. the postscript.

²⁸As Foucault writes: "[C'est] *le Livre* [qui] est le lieu de la Tentation" (Foucault 1967, 15). And, as J. Bem points out, "le diable n'est que la figuration allégorique d'un principe [...] [C'] est tout le texte de la *Tentation* qui est diabolique" (Bem 1979, 278).

²⁹For Gérard de Nerval the opposite is true. In Nerval the devil symbolizes precisely everything that is morally intolerable and unjust in the world; it is the symbol of paternal reactionarism. The repulsiveness of Nerval's materialistic devils symbolizes the infant *beautiful soul*'s refusal of the world. In his work, Gérard radically dismisses even the most innocent of the mundane satisfactions promised by the demonic pact. It was perhaps the unusual strength of his world-rejection that motivated his particularly strong belief in the ontological substantiality of the devil's existence.

It is indeed striking to observe how consciously Gérard writes himself away from the "demonic" world of reality, and into the purification of poverty and death. Gérard's rejection of the Devil-Father-World takes place, deep in the poet's soul, with such a degree of *happy consciousness* (all the more impressive by contrast with the unhappy *rentier* Flaubert) that the modern reader staggers in noticing how little self-hatred is contained in Nerval's self-annihilation.

On this, more *infra* (*Appendix*).

³⁰Likely, in fact, the former happened *because* of the latter.

3

Bulgakov: The "Evil One" and the "evil ones"

> Den Bösen sind sie los, die Bösen sind geblieben.
> The Evil One is gone, the evil ones remain.
>
> Goethe, *Faust*, v. 2509

I
The Diffraction of Evil

The first half of the nineteenth century was characterized by a high degree of epistemological optimism. The systems of philosophical idealism (Fichte, Schelling, Hegel), which placed the self at the center of material reality, not only played an influential role as cultural vehicles of a certain centripetal view of the the world, but, even more importantly, were in and of themselves the expression of an atmosphere in which ontological primacy went to a self-founding—and thereby necessarily world-founding—"I". So, for example, Novalis could write that Nature "is an encyclopedic systematical index or plan of our spirit" (Novalis 1981, 399).

In spite of its often politically conservative, at times even outright reactionary political implications and interpretations, the philosophical anthropocentrism of the Romantic period in a sense relayed and brought up to date the basic postulate of Renaissance and Enlightenment: namely, the notion of man preceding all things. The

Romantic quest for infinity and cosmic union may have been variously experienced or interpreted, existentially as well as politically, by different authors—but in each of them it arguably represented a striking form of solipsism, and perhaps its very apotheosis: the subject's almost amorous partner became no lesser a being than the whole Universe itself. It may be suggested that Flaubert's Antony, with his painstakingly and maniacally narrativized "dérèglement de tous les sens" (Rimbaud 1960, 344), renders virtually to perfection the archetype of what could be called the Romantic self's orgasm with and in the cosmos; and there can hardly be a doubt that Antony's position as the Self-of-the-Desert is a metaphorical representation of the subject's founding role in idealistic epistemology. For the Romantic soul, the world may be as rich and full of signs as a fairytale-like speaking landscape, or, by contrast, as barren and silent as an existential desert of the Thebaid; but the self always stands firmly in its center—if only to yearn for the fulfilling experience of the moment when the limiting necessity of "saying I" can be deposed. The enthusiasm of the time for the theme of the pact with the devil reflects its intoxication with what can only be termed, in the broadest sense of the word, the humanistic world view of an epoch passionately desiring to be *chercheuse d'infini*.

It is not surprising that the vast majority of the pacts with the devil of the Romantic epoch should be tributary to this form of subject primacy. When dealing with early nineteenth-century pacts, one has the impression of working in an almost complete vacuum of social-moral responsibility: it is as though the very fact of celebrating individualism rendered the contract at worst morally neuter, and could always recuperate even the protagonist's most selfish deeds. In this sense Romanticism certainly proved to be the swan song of individualistic anthropocentrism in Western civilization.

The second part of the century changed things dramatically. Wherever we want to place the epistemological shift, and to whatever complex convergence of social and scientific causes we wish to attribute it, the fact remains that, as the nineteenth century wore on, the experimentation with innocent individual desire and its morally neuter demonic sponsoring gradually waned. The scientific, industrial, social evolution which took place after 1848 fragmented the devil: the part of it which was to remain problematic became interiorized (very much in the direction sketched by *La peau de chagrin* or *La Tentation de Saint Antoine*), while superficial features were abandoned—to return, emptied of all intellectual significance, only in commercial "literature". In *The Queen of Spades*, Pushkin could still experiment playfully with the demonic contract and offer a convincing portrait of man's subconscious drives by translating them into the apparently light-hearted language of a purely Schlegelian *Witz*;[1] by the time of Dostoevsky, however, Romantic irony had long disappeared from the world—in a supra-personal, supra-national process which went far beyond conscious individual choices in matters of aesthetics. The Romantic individualistic (and individualized) foregrounding used traditional narrative structures in order to experiment with certain aporias of desire; postromantic works discarded those structures altogether, neglected problematizing desire, and focused instead on finding new ways of addressing what Kant had called the "radical evil" in the human being. Postromanticism shifted the focus from a restricted solipsistic notion of demonism to the inquiry into humanity's moral responsibility toward its being-in-the-world.

This did not mean that the whole demonic side of reality then received any less attention than it previously had; it simply applied to the devil as the *personification* of the demonic and its anthropomorphic catalyst. Dostoevsky's *The Demons* and *The Brothers Karamazov*, with Ivan's visions and the parable of the Grand Inquisitor, Thomas Mann's *Doktor Faustus*, and virtually the entire opus of Bernanos, are perhaps the most eloquent literary landmarks exemplifying the generalized diffraction of the originally unified Evil One into the human souls. Modernity, in a sense, rises from combining Balzac's interiorization of the demonic with Nerval's moral-political engagement against evil—and subtending them both with Flaubert's evacuation of Utopia.

Precisely here, however, seemed to lie the beginning of the end for the theme of the demonic contract. The devil of modernity—the "devil in man" permitting some of the most profound insights into human nature ever achieved by Western culture—is by definition no longer the devil outside man with whom a bargain can be struck. The shadow appearing to Ivan Karamazov is explicitly presented by the narrator as "a nightmare", the product of the character's "illness" (Part IV, Bk. XI, Ch. 9). For Dostoevsky its existence is *real* ontologically rather than psychologically; but its concrete appearance to man is filtered by man's own pathological condition. Dostoevsky's devil exists "as such"; but it certainly does not exist with the specific anthropomorphic traits which Ivan's imagination lends to it. In *The Brothers Karamazov*, the Evil One's true presence is the matter of a game of reconstruction: the reader has to piece it together with all the fragments of materialism, selfishness and lack of universal love distributed, with varying degrees of moral sanction, among the brothers Ivan, Dmitri, and Smerdyakov (as well as old Karamazov himself). The devil of the Karamazov's—and of all humanity—is a figure created in a mirror-game: not in the least less real, but certainly very much less personified than its counterpart of the Romantic period. For Dostoevsky, the devil has become too dark and magmatic to be accommodated in the monodimensional pattern of a pact.

The works by Bernanos and Mann referred to above reinforce the same notion. *Doktor Faustus* is structured in such a way that it can be read and made sense of without resorting to the hypothesis of the transcendental existence of a principle of evil; more exactly perhaps, the novel seems to strive for an ultimate convergence and coincidence of the transcendental and the immanent explanations. In commenting Leverkühn's anguished attempts to find a new (post-Mannian?) artistic expressive form beyond the "pitiful [...] aristocratic nihilism" of parody (Mann 1971, 242), J. B. Russell writes:

> Mann's own position was ambiguous. "From the very beginning", he observed, "the devil makes his presence felt in the novel, but appears personally to arrange the pact in the middle. Zeitblom tries hard not to believe in his reality. So do I". The devil himself says, "You see me, so I am here for you. Is it worth asking whether I am real? Isn't what is real what really works; isn't reality experience and feeling?" [...]
> Is Zeitblom finally seeing the devil, or is this a hallucination of his own? Mann does not intend a definite answer, for he felt the power of the demonic intensely and was aware that we have no way of knowing whether it is an external or an internal reality.
>
> (Russell 1986, 285)

Was the devil at work in the backstage of Nazi Germany *the Evil One*, or the sum total of *the evil ones*? Mann—and, with him, all contemporary readers horrified by the prodigies of twentieth-century evil—subjectively may well be somewhat less persuaded of the ontological reality of the "impure force" than many Romantic writers who depicted the devil as a real character in their works. The fact remains that in an epoch increasingly averse to the personification of the devil this existential conviction *must* objectively be filtered through the diffraction of the devil as a no longer unified and centralized being.

In fact, in modernity there seems to circulate a persisting conviction that catalyzing univocally the notion of evil in a specific, extra-human character would rather subtract from than add to the poignancy of the human's moral choices. Even for the author who in our century has most adamantly upheld and thematized the existence of the devil, Bernanos, the anthropomorphization of the principle of evil has never seemed to be a viable literary procedure, solid enough to become the support of a demonic "plot" and pact: Bernanos's devil has nothing to offer—it is absolute negation.[2] In these circumstances, the devil-compact today not only seems to be an aesthetically outdated example of non-literature / non-art; on the philosophical level, it also appears as a form of moral escapism, a hypocritical game with the very principle of evil, prompted only by the public's bourgeois boredom—or, on the authorial side, by a purely commercial interest in the least problematic recesses of human desire.

The persistence in literature of the concept of the demonic, coupled with a strikingly marked retreat of the theme of the pact proper, is, on the whole, a development diachronically far less accidental than it may seem to be at first sight: the tragic moral responsibilities of man, which were barely imaginable for the writers of the Romantic period, have become fully evident in the last one hundred years. In the century that has led from the repression of the Parisian Commune to the worldwide refusal to fuel indefinitely the Viet-Nam war—through all the intermediate cataclysms, impossible for the word to express as they are for the mind to grasp—it is only too understandable that the notion of the demonic should have shifted from the religious-individualistic view of the early hedonistic pacts to the social one of the twentieth-century immanent notion of the demonic. Here, of course, lies one of the great paradoxes of European letters: namely, the fact that pre-Romantic demonic literature was socially much more engaged than the often frivolous, petit-bourgeois minor (and at times minimal) demonic works of the so strongly devil-oriented first part of the nineteenth century. Klinger's and Goethe's Fausts already presented a clear movement toward the historico-social dimension and the connected implications of man's choices: society, which was absent from the self-absorbed heroes' world before 1770, looms larger and larger in the *hybris* of the relentless rebel, as well as in the expiring alchemist-engineer's preoccupation with reclaiming land from the sea. Klinger's and Goethe's texts are thus the ancestors of the modern, "engaged" attitude. The demonic genre's growing response to moral liability is also the feature which, their differences aside, the demonic works of Dostoevsky, Bernanos and Mann have in common with one another—and with many of the most important ones in our century.

In short, while an increasingly complex state of affairs in the portrayal of the devil as an anthropomorphic figure has harmed the literary representation of the demonic contract, it could persuasively be argued that most of the change has been for the better; and that, far from impoverishing our introspection into the depths of the human psyche, this development has served the purpose of refining our analysis and rendering it more adequate to a new epistemological epoch. In shifting from the Romantic problematization of desire to the modern problematization of the moral choice, man eventually becomes a social being in the full sense of the word—i.e., a planetary, global being. Something, undoubtedly, has been lost: not only, for example, the possibility of developing humorous and light-hearted, often lavishly brilliant devil figures, but also the opportunity to conceptually probe some disquieting aspects of human desire—be this Faustian or hedonistic, intellectual or frivolous, selfless or selfish. However, what has been gained in the course of the modern and post-modern reaccentuation outweighs the loss: no longer a literary character, the devil can today be more explicitly and objectively the Other within the conscience of man. As Espronceda's devil says in *El diablo mundo*:

> You engendered me, you mortal, and even gave me a name; in me you put your own torments, you put your rancor into my soul, your anxiety into my mind, your fury into my breast, your blasphemy on my lips [...] and I am a part of you, I am the sleepless spirit that excites you and raises you from your nothingness to Other regions, with thoughts of an angel, but with a man's pettiness [...]
> And my Hell is the heart of man.
>
> (Espronceda 1982, 183-85)

Today, even the writers who personally believe in the existence of the Evil One do not allow it to appear as a character in the text; rather, they present it as a nameless force that can turn the single humans into as many evil ones.

After having diagnosed the loss of status suffered by the curiosity of "experimenting with desire" in contemporary demonic literature, one wonders whether the time has then come to decree the end of a once glorious literary tradition. In this view, devil compacts would be gone forever, relinquished or repelled into a more rudimentary epistemic epoch still tampering with discussions for / against / around fulfillment. In the best hypothesis, a reversal of this tendency would be postponed until a later, as yet not foreseeable period of humanity's quest for truth.

Indeed, most anthropologically oriented "Histories of the devil" stop at this stage. And histories of literary pacts certainly do. It would seem as though in recent times, without a single exception, the very proposal of a pact story had been considered to be aesthetically in bad taste, if not, in Sartrean terms, morally a sign of "bad faith" altogether. In that view, the latest aesthetically as well as morally viable pact with the devil in literature would have to be traced back to some remote pan-European Romantic past.

Only this is not so. The middle of the twentieth century offers us one of the most disruptive pact stories written since the inception of the genre—disruptive, in any case, for the established canons. The text I am alluding to happens to be saturated precisely with humorous and even light-hearted, often lavishly brilliant devils; at the same time, it is also fully tragic in its addressing the question of man's moral choices, as well as in its depicting the reduction of desire to survival instinct in a specific form of the modern dehumanized world. The text in question is Bulgakov's kaleidoscopic, mythico-realistic novel *The Master and Margarita*.

II
The Master and Margarita: Utopia In Times of Anguish

> Je voudrais être Dieu pour faire des farces.
>
> Flaubert at age seventeen (*Agonies* IX)
>
> Veliky kanuler. Satanà.
>
> The Great Hoax. Satan.
>
> Bulgakov[3]

Bulgakov's last and most important novel, the one at which he worked for longer than the last decade of his life (he left it partially unfinished at the moment of his death in 1940), is a work of excruciating complexity. In its intertwining of realism and myth, tragic and ironico-grotesque episodes, divine and profane, antiquity and present times, *The Master and Margarita* is comparable only to Goethe's *Faust*—by which it was inspired. Its emphasis, however, is radically different. As we shall see, the ultimate question asked by Bulgakov's demonic novel rather resembles the one proposed by Hölderlin's poetry: "To what purpose poets in times of anguish?"— "Wozu Dichter in dürftiger Zeit?" To what purpose poetry, humanism, Utopia, in historical times of distress? Bulgakov's answer is that precisely then Utopia must be upheld more than ever; that precisely in times of suffering man must shake off the temptation to let himself slide into a moral Limbo—into the perhaps comforting, but certainly stagnating reduction to mere survival.

The devil appears in *The Master and Margarita* as the unmasker of the vices of humanity. The *razoblachenie* ("disclosure", "denunciation", "laying bare") of the tricks performed by the uncanny magician Voland which is promised in Ch. 12 of the novel ironically turns out to apply instead to their mirror image—the dishonest tricks of the human world. The apparition of the foreigner-devil and his retinue in Moscow is the laying bare, operated by an outsider, of the "black magics" which man organizes in society. The images of reality and illusion are here reversed: what at first appears as magics is but sound justice; what used to be accepted as "reality" was but the swindle, the demonic lie, of an essentially distopic social structure. While the utilization of the Stranger as a relativizer of the ambience described is not unique to Bulgakov, what is typical of *The Master and Margarita* is the text-founding role which the device assumes in it—as is confirmed by the fact that the narrator upholds to the end the devil's moral claim to act in the name of another Order, incomparably more perfect than the human one.

Two historical levels are active in the novel: Judaea under Tiberius, and Russia (specifically Moscow) in the 1920's-30's. By internal references, the novel further develops a third level of historical events: the Russia of the Romantic epoch, dominated by Pushkin's figure. In the modern part (occupying most of the narrative space) the group holding power in society is an association of positivistically-minded, variably selfish and shallow Soviet intellectuals, called MASSOLIT.[4] While the "literary" group is in theory devoted to the spreading of mass literacy, it is in actual fact bent on the mere preservation of its own considerable economic privileges, in a context of generalized poverty and oppression. More akin to a caste or to a mafia organization than to a literary association, the MASSOLIT dwarfs *Lost Illusions'* dilemmas and moral scruples into a touchingly childish-amateurish, "pre-scientific" innocence, and illustrates to perfection the systematic sale of one's soul to an evil principle—here, a perverse social machinery whose political side is never shown, but which the reader immediately identifies as Stalin's regime of terror.

The Master, for his part, is the author of a novel about a naïve philosopher by the name of Ieshua, nicknamed Ga-Notsri (Bulgakov 1969, 30; henceforward *Master*), who, in the Roman province of Judaea governed by Ponty Pilat, had the suicidal lack of commonsense to assert his belief in the goodness of the human race, and was therefore crucified for the sake of the local *raison d'état*. Such a generous faith is obviously as dangerous in Soviet Moscow as it was in Ershalaim almost two millennia before: the members of the MASSOLIT declare the Master's book unorthodox, and in their articles tear apart the "novel about Ponty Pilat".[5]

This causes a dramatic crisis in the Master's life. In the basement where he has lived and written under the protection of his custodian angel Margarita, he is overcome by a deep depression: he burns his novel. He is then "caused to disappear" from Moscow for a while (an obvious allusion to the *GULag* forced labor camps). He loses sight of Margarita, and finally takes refuge in an insane asylum on the outskirts of Moscow, where he declares himself incurable (*Master*, 189). In the meantime Margarita, far from giving up her quest for him, tries all she can to find him again and persuade him to rewrite his novel.

This is the *Vorgeschichte* that animates the plot before the beginning of narration. The actual text begins in the middle of the events: a mysterious stranger by the name of Voland[6] wreaks havoc on the comfortable self-assurance of a number of members of the MASSOLIT and their peers in the administration—one of them, Berlioz, slips and falls under a streetcar and is beheaded, another goes mad and is hospitalized in the same asylum where the Master is, another is arrested for the inexplicable fact that the roubles he accepts as kickbacks suddenly turn into dollars, yet one is magically spirited off to Yalta, etc. The height in the disruption of the snug routine of terroristic totalitarianism is reached in the mass scene at the Moscow Variety Theater, in which it is implicitly argued that a society can never be better than the sum total of its members—and vice versa. With the help of a retinue of disguised, grotesque adjutants, Voland, who claims to be a prestidigitator but is in reality Messir Satanà himself, artfully exploits the greed and vanity of the "new man" allegedly created by a system calling itself Socialism: he manages to send people out in the street without clothes and to have others stampede for the possession of demonic ten-rouble bills. All this "modern" section is steeped in a tragicomic light reminiscent of Gogol's world of grotesque puppets, in which the borderlines between the animate and the inanimate, the human and the bestial, are crossed in both directions. By contrast, the "novel about Ponty Pilat" (of which four chapters at different points alternate with the Moscow plot) is monoglossically epic, expressed in an elevated, measured, rhythmical prose.

Part Two of the novel presents Margarita and her pact with the devil. Inspired and guided by her selfless love for the Master, she receives the proposal to participate in the "Great Ball at Satanà's": scheduled for Good Friday at midnight under the aegis of the peripatetic Voland, the ball requires the presence of a Queen of local origin in order to conform with demonic liturgy. In the hope of finding out her lover's whereabouts, she accepts the proposal—thus inverting the terms of the pseudo-intellectuals' compromise with the absolute Evil of dictatorship: whereas *they* sell their souls to an establishment which claims to do the good of humanity, while actually working evil, *she* temporarily rents out her body for the celebration of a principle which, while theoretically evil, actually creates the good (as the novel's motto, drawn from Goethe's *Faust*, emphasizes). Whereas the untalented intellectuals of the MASSOLIT act out of greed, Margarita acts out of generosity: the intention, and not traditional demonological iconography, commands here the moral sign of the action.

After the ball, during which human wickedness is again punished by Voland-Satanà (an informer is solemnly executed and his blood drunk, in a sort of reverse Eucharist inspired by the tradition of occultist black masses), Margarita's zeal is rewarded: the Master is magically materialized on the spot from the insane asylum where he lay oblivious of the world, and the two lovers are reunited and transported together to a never-never land set in the reassuring, crepuscular light of Voland's realm. As for Ponty Pilat, he will be forgiven and will eventually attain the "light" in which Ieshua dwells (*Master*, 480-81). The novel written by the Master is supernaturally reinstated and read "on High": "*He* has read the Master's work".[7]

The novel is then concluded by a final vision of Voland and his retinue disappearing on a wild celestial horseride into the abyss of the cosmos, while the

Master and Margarita comfortably settle in their protected abode. A comic epilogue which purports to explain away the demonic events with mass hallucination is then appended: at the conclusion of the book, we return to the Gogolian *skaz* that dominates the "realistic" contemporary parts.

*

The Moscow string of narration of *The Master and Margarita* is the story of how local historical reality literally denies the material conditions for the survival of the belated historian-humanist—the Master who has dared to write a novel about the crucifixion of man in the totalitarian system of the Roman empire. The two distinct plots in the novel reinforce and reflect each other in a structure *en abyme* which, beyond the components' obvious stylistic differences, emphasizes the common conceptual nucleus representing the ultimate object of Bulgakov's preoccupations. The so-called "double novel" structure was perhaps never more appropriately used than in the present case—the case of a novel about the devil, the double of man *par excellence*.

The unifying element of the composition is Voland: the "mysterious stranger" knows the Master's text by heart, and quotes its full first chapter to the baffled members of the MASSOLIT who just declared in public their atheism. In *The Master and Margarita* the devil is the *perpetuum mobile* which activates all the internal references between the two planes of the novel. He connects the parallel levels and allows the readers to glide from each of them to the next. He is present incognito in the Ershalaim section; and in the modern voyage to Moscow he certainly outbids and outclasses the evil of man, thereby justly punishing it. Finally, in his movement between epochs Voland literally creates the space for the evocation of the ideal Utopia—the epoch of the Romantic humanism of the early nineteenth century, culturally influenced by Goethe and artistically dominated by the ironic genius of Pushkin. Such a "third level" of Utopia, the lovers' "Eternal Home" distinguished by the "Venetian windows" and the vine (*Master*, 482), is entirely his creation. In the midst of the novel's complex orchestration of themes, epochs, and ciphered literary allusions, there arguably are but two constant features: the grotesque comic of the Riders of the Apocalypse who (a novelty in the genre) accompany Voland—and the devil's own irony toward human assumptions and presumptions. The two effects converge toward the creation of a polyphonic discourse relativizing the soundness, the solidity, the ultimate *reality* of human "reality".

The contrast between the farcical and the serious moments of the novel is striking; and Voland, the ultimate Stranger, revels in the conflict by regularly making a display of the grand contempt he harbors for man's pettiness. To the MASSOLIT writer Berlioz, after having predicted the latter's death, and not long before calmly witnessing it, he says:

> Yes, the human being is mortal, but that would still be a half disgrace ["polbedy"]. The bad thing is that sometimes he's suddenly mortal, that's the trick [...]
>
> (*Master*, 21)

When Sokov (Mr. "de Juices"), the director of the buffet in the Moscow Variety Theater, comes to him to complain about the disappearance of the magic money created during the previous night's show, Voland forces him into the following tragicomic exchange:

> — No, no, no! Not one word more! I'll never take into my mouth anything from your buffet! My most esteemed, yesterday I walked past your bar, and I still can forget neither the sturgeon nor the *brynza* cheese! My dear! *Brynza* is not green, someone must have cheated you [...] It is customary that it be white. And what about the tea? [...] No, my dearest, that's not the way! [...]
> — The sturgeon that was sent was of second freshness — declared the buffet manager.
> — My little dove, that's rubbish!
> — What is rubbish?
> — The second freshness—that's what's rubbish! Freshness, there's only one—the first one, and it's also the last one. And if the sturgeon is of second freshness, then that means that it's rotten [...]
>
> (*Master*, 259-60)

The irony of the situation consists here in the fact that the devil, traditionally held to be "the father of lies", *en passant* opens a philologically impeccable trapdoor affording the reader a brief glimpse into the labyrinthine perversion of the Russian language "demonically" operated by the dictatorial system through its *second freshness* recycling of human Logos for its own purposes of political repression.

When Sokov is finally allowed to present his case and complains that the ten-rouble bills used by many theater-goers to pay for snacks later turned into paper shreds, Voland at first avoids the question in an ironically hypocritical tone, expressing perplexity at the idea that there may be "such crooks" in Moscow. But then the ineffable devil carries the irony a few steps further and into a quite different domain:

> — [...] You must be a poor person? [...] How much do you have in savings?
> The question was asked in a participating tone, but nonetheless one cannot but admit that such a question is an indelicate one. The buffet manager stopped short.
> — Two hundred and forty-nine thousand roubles in five savings banks — echoed a cracked voice from the next room — and at home, under the floor, two hundred gold ten-rouble coins.
> The buffet manager was as if glued to his stool.
> — Well, of course, that's not a big sum — condescendingly said Voland to his guest — even though, actually, to tell you the truth, you don't need even that amount. When will you die?
> (*Master*, 262-63)

When the same mysterious voice announces when and where this will occur—in nine months' time in a Moscow hospital—Voland "reflectively" proceeds to divide the available sum by the number of months Sokov has left to live, and advises him to live it up as much as he can afford to, while he still can.

Another example of Voland's picaresque mockery of the human establishment is a scene, freely inspired by the Philemon and Baucis episode at the end of *Faust II*, in which Bulgakov parodically deals with demonic arson. On Saturday at sunset, shortly before leaving Moscow, Voland observes the city from the terrace of "one of the most beautiful constructions of Moscow, built about one hundred and fifty years ago".[8] He there receives orders "from above" regarding the Master's and Margarita's final destiny. Then his servant Korovev and the cat Begemot suddenly appear: the

MASSOLIT restaurant, lodged in the Griboedov House, has just burned to its foundations—and the two staunchly claim to have been defending it against the flames. Voland pretends to care for the salvage of the building; in actual fact, however, he knows better. Tongue in cheek, he accuses his cooperators. They justify themselves:

> — I was helping the Fire Department, Messir — answered Korovev, pointing at his ripped trousers.
> — Ah, if that is the case, then, of course, it will be necessary to erect a new building.
> — It will be built, Messir — responded Korovev, — I dare to assure you of this.
> — Well then, it remains to be hoped that it will be better than the previous one — observed Voland.

The two buffoons (who—as in the whole novel—have been lying all along) comment:

> — So it will be, Messir! — said Korovev.
> — Believe me, — added the cat, — I am a formal prophet.
>
> (*Master*, 455)

Clearly, the new Griboedov will be just as corrupt and un-"Griboedovian" as the old one;[9] and the devil knows this full well. Voland, the devil, is once more the relativizer of human evil. In the "foreigner"'s visit to Moscow, the distopia of human perversion at long last finds its match: the devil is here the outsider who *makes strange* the world and emphasizes the distortions which hypocrisy and habit have automatized.

Bakhtin has convincingly analyzed the function of the Outsider in the development of the novel as a genre. At first, he writes,

> [t]he *rogue*, the *clown* and the *fool* create around themselves their own special little world, their own chronotope [...] Essential to these three figures is a distinctive feature that is as well a privilege—the right to be "other" in this world [...]
> These figures are laughed at by others, and themselves as well. Their laughter bears the stamp of the public square where the folk gathers. They re-establish the public nature of the human figure [...]

> *The novelist stands in need of some essential formal and generic mask that could serve to define the position from which he views life, as well as the position from which he makes that life public.*
> (Bakhtin 1981, 159-61; emphasis added)

Bakhtin's characterization can help us better grasp the causes and implications of the disconcerting mixture of styles (i.e., the polyglossia) in Voland's voice: tragic and comic at the same time—in one word, grotesque-uncanny. This is the deep-level reason underlying what has been called the carnivalization operating in *The Master and Margarita*.[10]

Later on in the history of the novel, the Outsider whose glance relativizes the world takes the well-known traits of the *pícaro*. In Bakhtin's words,

> The next stage in the transformation of the rogue, clown and fool occurs when they are introduced into the content of the novel as major protagonists [...]
> [T]he major protagonist is almost always the bearer of the authorial point of view [...]
> In one form or another [...] all the aspects we have analyzed appear in the *picaresque novel*.
> (Bakhtin 1981, 163)

It is clear how much Bulgakov's Voland, by opposing and destroying much less divine theodicy than the castle of human lies, becomes the textual bearer of the author's desire for a less perverse world. In *The Master and Margarita*, the devil is the *pícaro*—so to speak, the "unholy fool"—who lays bare and unmasks the defects of the Soviet version of mankind.

> [...] *The author needs the fool*: by his very incomprehending presence he makes strange the world of social conventionality. By representing stupidity, the novel teaches prose intelligence, prose wisdom. Regarding fools or regarding the world through the eyes of a fool, the novelist's eye is taught a sort of prose vision, the vision of a world confused by conventions of pathos and by falsity.
> (Bakhtin 1981, 404; emphasis added)

Voland is the potentiation of such fools, in charge of redressing wrongs. His stature has grown so much that it has overshadowed the human protagonists of the novel: he has become a gigantic, omnipotent *universal pícaro*. His ontological status only barely falls short of being that of an exterminating angel in the Lord's service.11

In fact, in his endeavor to fulfill the Lord's plans as they are transmitted to him by Levy-Matvey, the disciple of Ga-Notsri, Voland does not even remotely intend to thwart Margarita's and her Master's desires. The epigraph from Goethe's *Faust*: "I am a part of that force which would / Do *evil* evermore, and yet creates the good" (vv. 1335-36) must then be read with a certain circumspection.12 But why should this be surprising when dealing with that which is, by definition, Other? The Other is always slightly displaced in relation to where we would expect to find it. Bulgakov's allusions in the novel are "almost, but not quite" exact quotes: there is always a margin of irony between text and sub-text. As Siniavsky brilliantly put it in his book dealing with "us in the shadow of Gogol" (or: us, dealing *with* the Shadow *in* Gogol): "All is *wrong and out of place*—right there is where the devil is hiding" ("Vsë ne tak i ne to—tut-to i skryvaetsya chort") (Terts/Siniavsky 1975, 530; emphasis added).

Bulgakov's Voland insurges against the distopia of the Stalin epoch; and he dispenses the yearned-for "Schubertian" idyll to the worshippers of an innocent past. How "evil" is he ultimately? To what extent does he advocate actually criminal acts in order to promote the Lord's designs? What is the nature of his relationship with the forces above him—forces which, in *The Master and Margarita*, are subject to a radical silence? The mythical-prophetic novel does not answer these questions univocally; and Voland, the image of the wrong-and-out-of-place, the incarnate neither-nor, disappears with his ambiguous retinue in the silence that surrounds the text, taking Bulgakov's secret with him into the abyss "without cliffs, without mountain top, without moonlit path"—without the dawn promised to the Master and Margarita.

*

The Master and Margarita is endowed with a dimension that transcends irony: there, the grave visage of Voland's absolutizing role appears.13 The one element of *The*

Master and Margarita which does *not* undergo carnivalization is the final Utopia granted to the lovers—the eternal refuge to which they are led by Voland. And Voland himself, as earnest Mentor, operates parody without being subject to it.

There are two stages of Utopia which are addressed in the novel. There is a regressive one, consisting in the mere reinstatement of the two lovers in the basement in which they had spent their own "golden age" (yet another allusion to the early nineteenth century)—and a progressive one, located in the mythical, undefinable *locus* of "Peace" which, according to God's messenger Levy Matvey, lies somewhere between the historical world and the world of "Light".

The first of the two Utopias is activated at the end of the Great Ball at Satanà's, when, as a reward for having played hostess at the Muscovite Sabbat, Margarita is allowed to formulate a desire. This desire is kept secret (*Master*, 364). The Master, however, is not willing to actively concur: he says that he "no longer wishes for anything in life", except for seeing Margarita. Nothing around him interests him; he has been broken ("menya slomali"), and he wants to return to the basement. He has even come to hate his own novel: he has suffered too much because of it. He completely renounces life and would be content to vegetate along, begging ("nishchestvovat'") in order to survive. Even though he is attached to Margarita, he still thinks it would be best for her to abandon him before it is too late: "Leave me, or you will be doomed with me" (364-70).

When, in accordance with the Master's *reduction of desire*, the two lovers are finally returned to the basement, everything appears to be just as it used to—but it is not. In spite of Voland's omnipotence, Utopia cannot be made retroactive, because the Master no longer believes in its effectiveness. There can be no question of soliciting utopian images from such a crushed human being—or, as Margarita calls the Master, "a being of little faith, unhappy" ("maloverny, neschastny"). Utopia fails here by default of the drive meant to support and sustain it: the loss of life due to the investment of past desire is irretrievable.

Accordingly, those who, *in excelsis*, decide the destinies of the humans, have a different kind of Utopia in store for the historian-writer and his beloved. Through

Levy Matvey, the Supreme Authority tells Voland on the terrace high above Moscow:

> — *He* has read the Master's work [...] and asks you to take the Master with you and to reward him with peace [...]
> He has not deserved light, he has deserved peace.
>
> (*Master*, 453)

The words "he has not deserved light, he has deserved peace" have justifiably stimulated a considerable amount of speculation. Why should there be a distinction between the two principles? And, even if the notion of a "two-tier Utopia" (perennial Limbo? temporary Purgatory before Paradise?) were self-evident, why has the Master's striving only earned him the lesser of the two recompenses?

During the final ride through the air in "Forgiveness and Eternal Refuge" (Ch. 32), Voland tells the Master:

> — That which I offer to you both, and that for which Yeshua also asked for you—is better still! [...]
> Then Voland waived his hand in the direction of Ershalaim, and it became dark.
> — And there too, — Voland pointed behind them, — what can you do in the little basement? — The sun, fragmented in the glass, went out. — To what purpose? — Voland continued convincingly and softly. — Oh three times romantic master, really do you not want to go for walks during the day with your friend under the cherry trees, which are now starting their first bloom, and listen in the evenings to music by Schubert? Really will you not find it pleasant to write, in candle light, with a goose feather? Really do you not want to sit, like Faust, in front of a retort in the hope that you will manage to create a new Homunkulus? Go there, go there! There is already waiting for you a house with an old servant, the candles are already burning, and they will soon go out, because you will promptly meet the dawn. Follow this path, master, this one! Farewell, it is time for me to go!
>
> (*Master*, 481-82)

The third historical level of the novel, the golden period of Romanticism, to which the narration has constantly made oblique, ciphered references, returns here in its full form; it reveals itself as the ultimate utopian support for desire, interposed symmetrically between Ershalaim and Moscow. All references accumulated in this final section, whether literary, social or technological (from the cherry orchard to the goose feather, from the "old servant" to the wrong-and-out-of-place ironic confusion of Wagner with Faust) point to a utopian foregrounding of the period of Russian late eighteenth-early nineteenth century's Romantic humanism.

This, however, is precisely the problematic point in Bulgakov's novel. Such a Utopia can only be realized as a result of the pact contracted with the devil.14 There must be something inadequate in the Master's (and indirectly Margarita's) existential choice if the final Utopia they are granted explicitly remains in the sphere of the demonic and has no access to the "light" to which even Ponty Pilat is finally admitted.

The novel, then, denounces the Master's *passivity* toward the pursuit of the humanist ideal, whose militancy is not sufficient to sustain his actions past the miraculous end of his vicissitudes. The Master ceases to have faith in Light (Utopia) in times of suffering and distress; he no longer believes in the meaningfulness of witnessing for man. He gives a negative answer to Hölderlin's question about the sense of *Dichten* (writing, creating): *Dichten* is, for him, impossible in times of anguish. Accordingly, he is only rewarded according to his faith: he only receives a non-negative, demonic version of Utopia. The Master's retreat from *poiêsis* entails a final destiny that is the opposite of the one imagined by Goethe: "*less* light". It is then only consistent that the novel perform the lovers' apotheosis within the lunar, rather than within the solar sphere.

The contrast figure to the Master is Ieshua. Ieshua is the ultimate witness. He thinks nothing of dying to uphold his own view of a pacifist Utopia:

> — And now tell me [asks Ponty Pilat], why do you use all the time the words "good people"? Do you call everyone that, by any chance?
> — Everyone, — answered the prisoner; — there are no evil people on Earth.
>
> (*Master*, 37)

The further course of the dialogue between Ieshua Ga-Notsri and Pilat merely reinforces the recklessness with which the accused stresses his transcendental views—

in spite of Ponty Pilat's partly commonsense, partly truly sympathetic remarks. Hence, it has been justly pointed out that the Master and Ieshua, certain common features notwithstanding (essentially the persecution, the "crucifixion" they undergo), are remarkably different and in some ways even opposite characters (Gasparov 1979, 244-45; Proffer 1984, 554).

Ieshua Ga-Notsri is the humanist of the first historical level, who believes in his Utopia, in his "kingdom of Truth" ("tsarstvo istiny", 42) and who acts for it to the very end. The Master is the humanist of the third historical level, who believes in the past Utopia of the second one and who would like to see it reproduced, but does not (or not any longer) have the courage to materially struggle on for its realization. Stagnation in a basement is his only alternative; and even when Margarita daringly strikes a pact with the devil and obtains supernatural support, he still only uses such support for an anamnesis of the past. Since he desires to go back a few months in time, the devil brings him back to the extent of his power—to the first third of the nineteenth century. The Utopia enjoyed by the Master is a Utopia away from the front, away from the struggle; it is a retrospective, rearguard Utopia. "They broke me, I'm sad ['mne skuchno'], and I want to go to the basement" (369): man's desire is here reduced to the immobilization in a half-uterine, half-funereal Hades.

In *The Master and Margarita* desire is undermined and rendered impossible by the impossibility of its practical fufillment; the entire process is blocked before it can take place. This is the world of difference separating Bulgakov's novel from Balzac, from Flaubert—and, of course, from Goethe's *Faust*.

*

The question which Faust proudly asked of Mephisto: "What would you, wretched Devil, offer?" (v. 1675) could be answered in a thousand different ways by Bulgakov's Voland. The two Muscovite lovers lack everything: from material goods to all that is spiritual and social. Above all, they lack freedom: the freedom to write, live, love, defend themselves against their enemies. They lack freedom to the point that even Utopia seems impossible to the Master. This situation implies that the weight of problematization is shifted from desire to the possibility of its fulfillment.

Here an historical perspective on the theme of the pact with the devil becomes indispensable for interpretation. The turning away from the problematization of desire, and toward the problematization of the ways and means of its fulfillment, cannot but in many respects suggest a reverting to pre-nineteenth-century tradition. The awareness of the diachronic dimension of the genre can thus help us put in perspective and explain the striking incompatibility of Bulgakov's novel with a work such as Goethe's *Faust*, to which, at first glance, it would seem to be heavily indebted.[15]

It has been customary to examine *The Master and Margarita* and *Faust* as two isolated specimens outside the historical development of the literature of the demonic. In so doing, the specificity of each of them (and of any other similar work) as a phenomenon belonging to a continuous chain of development has been lost. Instead, the complete context, which has offered the two authors a choice of material for textual re-elaboration, must serve as a background for our understanding; the texts examined must be reinscribed within it. Features that at first sight appear to be diametrically opposed will then reveal themselves as *variants* distributed within a complex system that transcends the limitation of a one-to-one opposition between the Master and Faust. There exists, after all, no absolute canon or norm for the demonic genre in literature, no "center" for its definition—there are only a number of (re)interpretations on the periphery, in the texts: Goethe's philosophico-allegorical poem was itself a novelty, one of the turning points in a diachronic succession. *Faust* was but a historical phase in the genre, dialectically tied to its predecessors, and by no means its supra-temporal model. As for Goethe's successors, Bulgakov was neither the first nor the best-known writer to reverse some of Goethe's innovations.

The point of Bulgakov's major innovation with respect not only to Goethe but to the whole genre must be identified in the combination of the *problematization of fulfillment* with an unprecedented *salvation* (i.e., moral justification) of the hero. *The Master and Margarita* conserves the pre-modern focalization on the exchange of services, but creatively combines it with the Goethean *absolution*. Such is the area where the story of Margarita and her lover truly crosses genders / genres. This feature is even more important than the (doubtless relevant) ones indicated by the critics—namely, that we witness here a woman striking the deal; that there is never any question of a soul's salvation being at stake; that the service provided by the human comes before the one assured by the devil; that there is complete vagueness as to the kind of return the human is to expect; that the "pact" is really engaged in on behalf and for the benefit of someone else, etc. While important, all these discrete facts are, in historical perspective, individually less essential than the discrete leap in the genre which, as a whole, they ultimately contribute to produce.

Medieval Christian texts foregrounded desire in order to condemn its demonic fulfillment; they problematized the relationship between desire and faith. The very process of expanding the self to cover the world was the target of the attacks launched by the Protestant Faustbook. There, desire was evil, and the desiring self was condemned to eternal punishment. Later, Klinger's work sketched a partially different state of affairs: certain forms of desire were laudable, others were not—the epitome of guilt being human *hybris*, the "noble arrogance" consisting in the claim to be able to judge the universe and improve upon it. In the long run, Klinger's Faust was also condemned—but, typically, found in his own punishment yet another triumphal occasion for heroism.

Goethe's work was then consistent in reversing *both* moral signs. Goethe inverted the judgment to be passed upon human desire—which became for him unconditionally "good" as a whole, even when its *Streben* implied evil collateral consequences—[16] *and also* granted access to salvation to the desiring human being. The German Romantics' complaints about the "Catholic smack" of Gretchen's apotheosis failed to recognize the internal coherence of Goethe's conception; and the misadventures they incurred in attempting to produce a Romantic counter-Faust of a stature comparable to the all too "classical" one may have more than a little to do with inadequate reflection on the necessity of a balanced relation between the function of desire in the demonic work and the moral judgment to be passed on the human's association with the devil.

A number of ways out of these aporias were envisaged. By endowing man with exclusively commendable, moral desires—and, accordingly, condemning the devil alone—Nerval's Faustian *opus* perhaps suggests the most linear one. As for Balzac, he suspends all transcendental notions, and has desire sanctioned in a purely physical-thermodynamic way. In Balzac's view, there no longer are a punishing God or the intercession of a Gretchen: for him, whether desire is "good" or "evil" is simply a non-applicable question, and the second law of thermodynamics is the only judging authority. Finally, Flaubert's work applies a fundamentally "traditional" notion of desire: desire as tempting, but guilty transgression. In his work on Saint Antoine, Flaubert envisages a sort of titanic *transfiguration without God*—the apotheosis of a self united with the Absolute without the mediation of embarrassing intercessors. In order to match a positively charged desire with a final absolution deprived of the ultimate Absolver, Flaubert has to strain the subject to the point of disintegration. Accordingly, his man-of-desire moves from the Goethean personal *Erlösung* to Antoine's de-personized *Auflösung*, and shifts (in Baudelaire's terminology) from the centralization to the vaporization of the self.

Within these general coordinates, *The Master and Margarita* should be viewed as a work returning to a traditional—i.e., pre-modern—relation of the self with desire. In Bulgakov's text, desire is a given; only its realization is problematic. This is not significantly different from the striving of Rutebeuf's or Gautier de Coinci's Theophilus. And when Theophilus recites: "Tolue m'a ma seignorie" (Gautier de Coinci 1955, 62; v. 199), one cannot but hear the echo of the crushed Master's complaint: "When people have been as completely spoliated as I and you have, they seek salvation with the Force Beyond!" (*Master*, 461). The radical break with the problematization of desire typical of the early nineteenth century is thus the bridge that links the Master with times far preceding the Goethean *novelty* and *exception*.

On the other hand—and this *is* the obvious difference opposing the Master to Theophilus—in Bulgakov's demonic novel the heroes are innocent; accordingly, salvation is maintained. On this, Bulgakov not only conserves and subsumes Goethe's development, but in fact goes farther by one, final step: he makes Voland, the medieval cavalier, a direct agent of God. At this point, the reversal vis-à-vis the traditional structure (typical of, for example, Spieß's chapbook) comes into full light: the desire prompting the human to the pact is no longer sinful, but humane; the pact with the devil is also good, and it deserves remuneration. Punishment is only deserved, and promptly incurred, by human obtuseness, which is commanded by "desires" of a base and grotesque type. The desire of the truly humane part of man (not only spiritual, but material as well) deserves the alliance of the Highest—and the help of a whole band of variegated *mal'âk Jahwe*.[17]

With respect to the literary proto-history of the genre, in *The Master and Margarita* the transmutation of values is an accomplished fact. In modern Moscow, the inversion of the moral sign runs full circle and leads to a valorizing image of the Other. At the same time, however, the complexity of the interplay of subtexts and the reshuffling of the foregrounded elements show us that such a reversal paradoxically takes place within a narrative structure that sends the reader back to a pre-modern view of desire. And such a return to the origins strikes us as even more complete when we realize that, in a remarkably parallel move, even the devil image activated by Bulgakov is a pre-Christian, Biblical one. In *The Master and Margarita* the conflicting pulls toward tradition and re-accentuation create a complex cipher which, more perhaps than in the case of any other novel, is to be read in the polyphony existing between the *analogy with* and the *difference from* the similar—with and from the whole literary *corpus* which, crossing literary and cultural traditions, revolves around the demonic contract as a subtext.

*

It is said that in 1926, upon completing the novel *The White Guard*, Bulgakov claimed that the figure of his mother had given him the impelling force to write it; to which he then added: "According to my plans, the figure of my father is to be the starting point for another work that I have in mind" (quot. in Proffer 1984, 525). He may have then been consciously thinking of the "scholarly research on religious and historical subjects" (*ibid.*) to which his father, who had died when the writer was sixteen, had devoted himself at the Kiev Theological Academy around the turn of the century. More probably, however, at the beginning of the nightmarish reign of Stalin—the "mysterious stranger"-dictator bizarrely claiming to be "the father of peoples"—Bulgakov was subconsciously imagining the compensatory, omnipotent protection of an Other Father, fantasmatically recuperating the absence of the real one. It is likely that we owe it to the figure of the absent scholar if the writer was fascinated by the protective Mentor, the demonic "Father toward whom is felt admiration". Metamorphosed, he became the black-clad cavalier, the ironic-severe Voland, in charge of guaranteeing "eternal refuge" to all humane desire legitimately coming from the children-figures of the Master and Margarita—the only *truly* "most humane among human beings".[18]

Things, however, may be more complex still, and Voland may at the same time be also a prefiguration of that other "eternal refuge" promised to man beyond the principle of pleasure—namely, death. The conclusion of the novel stresses this component of Voland when, with agonizing intensity, the deadly diseased author writes:

> Gods, Gods! How sad the evening earth! How mysterious the mists over the bogs! Whoever has wandered in these mists, whoever suffered deeply before death, whoever flew over this earth burdened beyond human strength knows it. The weary one knows it. And he leaves without regret the mists of the earth, its swamps and rivers, and yields himself with an easy heart to the hands of death, knowing that it alone can bring [him peace] ["uspokoit"].
> (*Master*, 476; transl. Ginsburg 1967, 383)

The end of *The Master and Margarita* is overdetermined, and its Other accommodates both contradictory functions: the father's protection *in* life, the transcendental protection *of* death. As the most complex and complete literary devil of the twentieth century and perhaps the staunchest defender of human-humane desire to ever appear on the literary scene, Bulgakov's Voland is the most appropriate devil-figure with which to conclude and by which to remember our own ride through the air over the land of desire.

III
Bêtise and Others

Bulgakov's posthumously published novel on the "grand canular de Satan" reminds us that the Master and Margarita—*and* the exterminating angel Voland—have countless enemies. Who are these? They are the mass of brutish individuals revelling in greed, blindness, conformism. They are the countless ones (whether belonging to the Soviet party's or to other bourgeoisies) to whom Goethe's Mephisto referred when he claimed that human beings are no more advanced today than they used to be in the times of superstition: "The Evil One is gone, the evil ones remained". If Flaubert had believed in the existence of the devil, he would have probably defined the omnipotence of human *bêtise* as "demonic" ("demonic" only globally, of course, since its isolated manifestations would never have qualified for him as sufficiently evil to aspire to Satanic distinction). In sum: it seems to be a rashly optimistic assumption to establish, as Bulgakov does, that the "true" devil would be siding for intelligent, humane desire. What if it sided with the Moscow bureaucracy—or any of its equivalent avatars generously scattered across the world? The novel of the paternal-protective Voland is still the compensatory fantasy of an optimist.[19]

Clearly, the massification and banalization undergone by the devil in recent years has spurred a definite reticence, if not an outright self-censorship, on the part of literary authors who are tempted to handle themes demonic. I am not aware of any considerable anthropomorphic epiphany of the Other in literature after Voland's dazzling incursion. Could this be an effect of perspective—the well-known false impression that, because as we approach our own times we have fewer phenomena available for observation, history somehow "slows down"?

More likely, the devil's anthropomorphic figure will resume its substantial contribution to literature when—and if—humanity will again need it *as a device* to economically express the goals that animate it, or the fears which haunt it. For the moment, neither seems to be urgently the case: Hell seems to be closed for Practical Reason—and pacts involving the sale of one's "soul" do not necessarily require devils to be contracted. The post-modern world has perhaps become too diversified and elusive even for such a complex notion as that of the Other.

I think, however, that we should still attach some semantically negative meaning to the notion of the demonic. If we did not, what *other* term could we use to designate the "other", actually evil phenomena of which we do have empirical experience in our psychic and material universe? For, Ponty Pilat is right, and Ga-Notsri is deluded: not all people are *dobrye lyudi*—not all people are good. And the inevitable question returns: why has the anthropomorphic demonic disappeared from reality and literature alike? Into what cracks, into what margins of reality has the Other nested, exerting on the world the most effective action—by sheer absence?

Flaubert's strikingly modern, and post-modern, answer appears in the *Voyage en enfer* which he wrote at the wise age of thirteen: "C'est que le monde, c'est l'enfer". The only terrestrial omnipotence is set in motion by human *bêtise*—a demonism not excited by greatness, but created by default. For Flaubert, hell is the dwelling of *a humanity spiritually turned sub-human*. The final answer to the contemporary dispersal of the devil-pact tradition should be sought in this direction.

As another author who was active during the years of Flaubert's adolescence well saw: the devil is laughable—which means that it is ever-present and all-powerful. In Gogol

> [...] The devil is something that is begun and is left unfinished, but purports to be without beginning or end. The devil is the noumenal median of being, the denial of all heights and depths—eternal planarity, eternal banality [*poshlost'*]. The sole subject of Gogol's art is the devil in just this sense, that is, the devil as the manifestation of "man's immortal banality", as seen beneath the specifics of place and time—historical, national, governmental, social; the manifestation of absolute, eternal, universal evil—banality *sub specie æternitatis*.

> Everyone can perceive evil in great violations of the moral law, in rare and unusual misdeeds, in the staggering climaxes of tragedies. Gogol was the first to detect invisible evil, most terrible and enduring, not in tragedy, but in the absence of everything tragic; not in power, but in impotence; not in insane extremes, but in all-too-sensible moderation; not in acuity and profundity, but in inanity and planarity, in the banality of all human feelings and thoughts; not in the greatest things, but in the smallest [...]
>
> He was the first to understand that it is the devil who is the smallest thing that exists, and seems big only because we ourselves are small; that he is the weakest thing that exists and seems strong only because we ourselves are weak [...]
>
> Gogol [...] was the first to realize that the self of the devil is not remote, alien, strange, fantastic, but is, rather, a very common, familiar, real and human, all too human self, the self of the crowd.
>
> (Merezhkovsky 1974, 57-59)

In *Fusées* XVII, Baudelaire makes an observation that closely parallels Merezhkovsky's comments on Gogol. Indirectly answering his own question—the question with which I opened the present work: "Se livrer à Satan, qu'est-ce que c'est?"—Baudelaire writes:

> Il ne faut pas croire que le diable ne tente que les hommes de génie. Il méprise sans doute les imbéciles, mais il ne dédaigne pas leur concours. Bien au contraire, il fonde ses grands espoirs sur ceux-là.
>
> (Baudelaire 1961, 1281)

The conclusion is unequivocal: the real servants of the really evil Other are the imbeciles. *Bêtise, poshlost'*,—and others.

All this complicates, rather than simplifies, the task. The devil, the truly evil devil, the Other behind the Others, behind the masquerades of nightmare and literature (shall I call it: the *infinitesimal devil*?) is "too stupid" for refutation.

The devil of *bêtise, poshlost'*, and others, is merely laughable: in today's post-systematic world, the only phenomenon that is and remains essentially "demonic" is human pettiness-stupidity. That means, however—that "the devil" is invincible.

Notes to Chapter Three

[1] Pushkin's aesthetics is governed by the same (pan-Romantic) notion of the necessity to "sing in sorrow" which the episode of Lucien de Rubempré's drinking songs perfectly exemplifies in *Lost Illusions*. (For a Pushkinian parallel, cf. e.g. the *Lied* "Burya mgloyu nebo kroet").

Pushkin, incidentally, by no means limited himself to the "ironic" (in Schlegel's philosophical sense) approach to the problem of the demonic: his "Scene from Faust" (1825) thematizes with Leopardian or Baudelairean intensity the inevitable unhappiness to which existential boredom condemns man; and the poem "Demon" (1823) features a mysterious interior voice slandering the beauty of life and advocating moral nihilism.

[2] In Russell's words: "For Bernanos [...] the struggle between good and evil in the individual soul is the microcosm of the cosmic opposition between God and devil, and human sin is a part of the greater shadow we call evil. Evil is not a mere human category but a real thing whose ultimate characteristics are nothingness and immobility. It is essentially incomprehensible because it has no essence; its heart is the void. This nothingness is a cosmic coldness whose tendrils reach out, penetrating our minds and beckoning us to join it in hell [...] The symptoms of this choice are pride, which separates us from love; lying, which separates us from truth; and despair, which separates us from mercy" (Russell 1986, 276-77).

[3] This motto appears as epigraph on the first page of the manuscript of the novel in the version of 1932. At that time the title was still *Fantastichesky roman*. Cf. Proffer 1984, 524 (photogr. reproduction of manuscript).

[4] The Moscow MASSOLIT is modeled after the historical RAPP, the Association of Proletarian Writers, and after the Association of Soviet Writers, which relayed the former under Stalin and, unchanged in spirit, survives to the day of this writing. An interesting analysis of the activities in which the actual Association typically engaged can be found in Voynovich's *Ivan'kiada* (1976).

[5] Most of these circumstances had an autobiographical source in the historically proven Soviet attitude toward Bulgakov's *The White Guard*.

[6] "Voland" is a term used by Goethe in the *Walpurgisnacht* scene of *Faust I* (v. 4023); it is there applied to Mephistopheles. On the other hand, "voland", "valand", "valant" is one of the most frequent Middle High German names used to designate the (or a) devil. The erudite Bulgakov may as well have found the reference in, for example, J. Grimm's well-known *Deutsche Mythologie*, II, Ch. 33 (essay on "Teufel")—or could have found it directly in the sources.

[7] This detail, too, grotesquely parodies reality, since Levy Matvey's words echo the ones which Stalin himself used in acknowledging receipt of a letter addressed to him by the desperate Bulgakov at the time of his marginalization.

[8] The date brings us back once more to what Bulgakov perceives to be the golden age of Russian culture—the period of Romantic humanism, sparked and influenced by the philosophy and literature of Western Europe.

[9] The pun implicit in Bulgakov's text is tied to the personality of the writer Aleksandr Sergeevich Griboedov (1795-1829), author of the liberal-progressive play

Gore ot uma ("The Disgrace of Being Intelligent"). Bulgakov locates the MASSOLIT in the Griboedov family house in Moscow as an antiphrastic allusion.

For subtextual echoes of the play in *The Master and Margarita*, cf. Gasparov 1978, 207.

[10] Milne 1977, 1-4; Proffer 1984, 531, and 636-37, nn. 9, 10. The carnivalization active in the novel through the figure of Voland is so strong that it irradiates into the domains of all characters: first and foremost, into the Master's as pseudo-Faust and into Margarita's as pseudo-Gretchen. Carnivalization could here be said to appear once more as the indispensable prerequisite for the portrayal of the devil in modernity—in a way, the price to be paid for the passage through the text of a figure of omnipotence. Hence, all tragic themes are here filtered through the lens of opera, music, melodrama: to mention but one striking case, "Excuse, but maybe, by the way, you haven't even heard about *the opera Faust*?"—*Master*, 173 (emphasis added).

[11] A summary of this state of affairs is offered by V. Sergeevich's brilliant statement: "The *unclean spirit* [one of the current Russian denominations for the Other: *nechistaya sila*, C.T.] cleans up left and right" (quot. in Milne 1977, 19).

[12] On the differences between the two works, even, on certain points, their opposition, cf. Gasparov 1978, 241-42; Fieseler 1982, 266; Barratt 1987, 277-78.

[13] Such a dimension develops, as Barratt puts it, in the space "beyond parody" (Barratt 1987, 278).

[14] Gasparov (1978, 243) aptly points out that the Master's refuge is "suspicious"; it lies "in the sphere of Voland".

[15] Upon more careful consideration, the apparent similarities between the two works turn out to be of little import indeed—either completely general ("man may err if need be, but he must not stagnate"—Proffer 1984, 557; Barratt 1987, 291), or, at the opposite extreme, minute and incidental, and debatable at best (Stenbock-Fermor 1969, 312-15, 320-23). The relationship between the two works is not that of a "+/-" use of isolated elements, but rather, that of a *comparable* orchestration and reaccentuation of common themes aimed at altogether *diverging* goals.

[16] More accurately than "good as a whole", one should perhaps describe it as "good enough to deserve, as a whole, the Grace of pardon".

[17] For the notion of *mal'âk Jahwe*, cf. Schärf 1948, 207.

[18] The author's denunciation of the Soviet claim to create the new "humane human being" is clearly *the* general structural theme of the novel—but it circulates more specifically and intensely in the allusions to Mayakovsky, who had coined the well-known definition of Lenin as the "samy chelovechny chelovek" (cf. Gasparov 1978, 205).

[19] L. Milne (1977) subtitles her work on *The Master and Margarita* "a comedy of victory".

Appendix

Gérard de Nerval: The "Beautiful Idiot"

> Bednye lyudi kaprizny:—eto uzh tak ot prirody ustroeno.
>
> Poor folk are whimsical:—that's the way it is, by nature.
>
> Makar Devushkin in Dostoevsky's *Poor Folk*

Nerval's rebellion is not that of the dispossessed son who in vain claims his part of the patrimony; rather, it is the rebellion of the son who refuses direct competition, and who questions the acceptability of the world of money—the world of the fathers. The Balzacian son contests the father by striving to take over his role; the Nervalian one dissociates himself from the role altogether. While the former's revolt is localized and contingent, the latter's is generalized, and attacks the very foundations of the world administered and commanded by the paternal principle. The conflicts formulated by Balzac in terms of energy are in Nerval expressed in ethical terms as a question of moral compromise with the demonic evil of a repulsive world. If in Balzac's universe, as for the protagonist of Goethe's ballad "The treasure digger", few (and justly sublime) are the exceptions to the maxim "Poverty is the greatest plague, / Riches are the supreme good",[1] for Nerval gold represents everything that is base and corrupt—or, to use knowingly significant qualifiers, everything that is paternal and demonic.

Gérard de Nerval (whose father, as is well known, was not named de Nerval, but Labrunie: the symbolic substitution is, in this respect, illuminating)[2] constantly establishes the moral universe of his heroes on the basis of the multiple identity Gold = Corruption = Father(s) = Devil. For Nerval, poverty is a sign of spiritual nobility; it is the narrative equivalent of the "de" which Gérard fantasmatically attached to his own pseudonym. Balzac and Nerval represent two extreme attitudes in their handling of the conflict that opposed the "Sons" of the July Monarchy to their historical and intellectual fathers.

Whether through identification or through rejection, both Nerval and Balzac associate the father figure with the uncanny phenomenon of the proliferation of wealth which was typical of the Paris of those years. The difference separating Balzac's hypnotization with money from Nerval's almost physical repulsion for it is a surface-level phenomenon disguising a deeper common element—namely, the connection which they both establish between the proliferation of wealth and the paternal sphere. It is as though both extreme "wings" of the younger generation identified the figure of the father with the "Old Witches' Master" of Goethe's ballad "The Apprentice Sorcerer": the father was for them the full-fledged magician who held the power and could be accepted or rejected, but with whom one in any case had to come to terms if one wanted to be initiated into the secrets of "reproduction"—in the broadest sense of the word.

The multiplication of power is the feature which most distinctively qualifies the paternal symbolism of this epoch for identification with the demonic. The apparently miraculous generation of wealth typical of the Parisian years around 1830 was the concrete historical phenomenon founding this pervasive existential feeling; and the industrialization that paralleled it and rendered it possible quite logically partook of the same aura of "evil miracle" characterizing the new times.

A number of peculiar phenomena point to the notion of a complex conflation of the paternal—industrial—financial—demonic realms in the period of Romanticism. Already in Goethe's poem we can find the first traces of it. Faust's rebellion, for example, is coupled with a marked refusal of the technocratic view of science. Faust's science is the science of man: he neither invents nor multiplies objects—his efforts are directed toward improving humanity's tangible living conditions (cf. the land reclamation in Part II, Act V). By contrast, the mad multiplier of Goethe's text is Mephisto, whose invention of paper money at the Emperor's court is the *point de fuite* of at least three major phenomena: the eeriness of industrial production, the demonism of the proliferation of wealth, and the decline and final demise of the imperial (i.e., paternal) authority and credibility.

As Goux convincingly indicates in *Les monnayeurs du langage*, a study devoted to the epoch-making "rupture entre le signe et la chose, qui défait la représentation et inaugure un âge de la dérive des signifiants" (Goux 1984, 9), Mephisto's invention of paper money is the birth certificate of an *inconvertible modernity*:

> Le papier monnaie est le symbole de la tromperie de l'intellect calculant qui perd contact avec le trésor des profondeurs. En termes différents, c'est le symbole de la perte de la dimension symboliste: la conscience instrumentale manipule des jetons conventionnels qui ne gardent plus aucun lien avec les significations de l'inconscient [...]
> Ce qui est méphistophélique, c'est cette coupure, [...] une intelligence purement combinatrice et opératoire *séparée* des significations plus profondes et plus riches où le sens est en état permanent de fusion [...]
> Le papier monnaie est une folie car il ouvre le règne du signe pur. Un signe qui est maintenant détaché de toute réalité: un jeton clivé du trésor. La sphère de la valeur d'échange devient autonome. Et ceci est diabolique.
> (Goux 1984, 210-11)

If banknotes are "lies" concocted by the fathers, then it is only too logical that the latter should, with full right, be joined by Mephisto, the father of lies: among fathers, Mephisto is really among his peers. By the time of Balzac and Nerval, in the Parisian catch-as-catch-can atmosphere of the bourgeois-industrial revolution, the terrain was favorably prepared for such a symbolic conflation of paternity, technology and demonism.

To be sure, while technology is the material instrument used by the bourgeois minority in order to pursue its disquieting "ghastly multiplication", it could, at least in principle, also be the means to a self-assertive emancipation on the part of the younger intellects. Indeed, in the case of Nerval and Balzac, there seems to be a parallel effort to conceive and describe an alternative use for science, no longer subservient to the purposes of the economic establishment. So, for example, in

L'imagier de Harlem Laurent Coster intends to harness mechanical reproduction to the cause of the forces that enlighten humanity; and in *Illusions perdues* the other printer, David Séchard, strives to produce better and cheaper paper, not for his own profit but for the benefit of literacy. In an essentially analogous endeavor, both Raphaël de Valentin and Louis Lambert hope to develop a *Théorie de la volonté* that would crown the sons' efforts to construe an intellectual alternative to the fathers' empirical "pratique de la richesse". However, these are all, as it quickly turns out, also *lost illusions*: either (as in David's case) the paternal world manages to divert the sons' creativity for its own purposes, or the enterprise is interrupted or comes to a sorry end (in the cases of Raphaël and Louis Lambert). In *L'imagier de Harlem*, gratuitous creativity triumphs only at the cost of being refracted through a symbolico-allegorical plane which has more in common with the rarefied final visions of *Aurélia* than with historical reality—and certainly nothing with the Parisian milieu in which Gérard materially lived.

*

Nerval wrote in virtually all literary genres: lyrical poetry, drama, novel, novellas, translations, travel reports, erudite works on the history of religion, as well as poetic autobiography. Finally, he realized with *Aurélia* the modern equivalent of the philosophical poem, on a line with Dante's *Comedy* or Goethe's *Faust*. While it is generally agreed that his dramatic works cannot compare with *Aurélia* itself or the sonnets of the *Chimères* cycle in terms of aesthetic success, it is nonetheless true that Nerval's works for the theatre strike the reader for a reason of a different order: namely, their constant obsession with the theme of the pact with the devil. Equally striking is the omnipresence of the complementary factor of poverty as a motivation: in each of Nerval's demonic dramas or sketches, poverty accompanies the pact-motif with such insistence as to form virtually one theme with it. This feature is, at first sight, all the more surprising because it is so strongly at variance with Nerval's favorite pact story—Goethe's *Faust,* which he partially translated and published in

1828, then repeatedly re-editing it until 1850, just a few years before his death. As Richer put it in describing Nerval's activity as a dramatist, "le sujet de *Faust* [...] était pour lui le seul sujet dramatique, celui où il se retrouvait et qu'il souhaitait amener à un point de perfection" (Richer 1970, 101). One must indeed admit that there is something "demonic" in the very proliferation of Faustian figures, finished or left unfinished, in Nerval's *œuvre*; it is almost as though Goethe's multiplicative devil, upon being attacked, took its revenge by applying to its own identity the same principle of deliberate inflation for which it had come under fire in the first place.

Of all these projects, the only demonic text which attained full development was *L'imagier de Harlem*. Written in great haste toward the end of 1850 and co-signed, along with Gérard, by his friend Méry and an otherwise unknown Lopez, this work met with an ephemeral success on the stage in January 1851 (Nerval 1967, V). Some of the other texts, such as *L'alchimiste,* while starting from similar situations, in the course of the events turn away from the demonic plot and return to the traditional articulation of the *vaudeville* and the bourgeois comedy. Others, finally, preserved their original inspiration, but remained at the stage of fragments.[3]

Among the many, the work which it is most fruitful to examine in detail is probably Gérard's short *Faust* fragment. There is a twofold justification for this choice: on one hand, a great number of the fragment's key passages are repeated practically verbatim in the *ébauche* of *Nicolas Flamel* and thus show a textual permeability clearly indicating the points of persistence in Nerval's imaginary universe; on the other hand, the peculiar innocence with which the Goethean inspiration is exhibited in Nerval's *Faust* is a promising circumstance for the possibility of detecting the essence of Nerval's own view of the pact-theme, which must necessarily be situated in the points of variance from the model. It is striking that Nerval's own *Faust* has found little echo in criticism, if any, in spite of the widely recognized role of Nerval as (among other things) the most influential nineteenth-century translator of Goethe's masterpiece.

Nerval's *Faust* fragment is a story of poverty and temptation. Just as David Séchard in Balzac's *Illusions perdues,* Faust appears here as a young inventor who has ruined himself in the pursuit of the discovery of printing. He has submitted his recent invention to the Frankfurt Senate, in the hope of being rewarded for it.[4] He needs a certain sum in order to win not so much the heart of his Marguerite (who has already given it to him), but rather, the family's formal permission to marry her: "Sa mère a mis à mon union avec elle la condition d'une fortune honnête, et il a bien fallu qu'elle se soumît comme moi à cet ordre cruel" (Nerval 1965, III, 358-59; henceforward *Faust*). We easily recognize the established convergence between money and sexuality: being deprived of money symbolically equals exclusion from sexuality, i.e. equals castration.

The opposition that structures the text is the one between Faust as an idealistic researcher and the world of the Frankfurt senators, marked by the notions of productivity and usefulness. The senators accumulate, whereas Faust squanders. This *topos*, which is far from being uncommon in Romanticism, is here pursued with an intensity equalled perhaps only in de Vigny's *Chatterton* (the poet and the inventor both being, in the Romantics' view, "artists"). The contrast between fathers and son is here so intense that it is even theatricalized in an actual judgment—the judgment which the Senate has to pass over Faust's invention. Here, the revealing free play of fantasy comes on stage directly in the text, and the Romantic hero becomes the sacrificial lamb (in René Girard's sense) for the well-being and the peace of conscience of capitalism.

The polarity between Faust as "homme généreux" and the greedy pragmatism of the world of the fathers is further stressed by Faust's adjutant Scheffer, when he says:

> [...] voici ce qu'il fallait faire: au lieu de présenter votre invention comme glorieuse et pouvant faire le bonheur des hommes, il fallait la faire envisager comme une opération lucrative, une mine d'or ouverte aux premiers qui l'exploiteraient, il fallait y intéresser les membres les plus influents, en leur offrant une forte part dans les bénéfices; alors, leur générosité n'aurait eu rien à vous refuser [...]
>
> (*Faust*, 359)

Faust, however, voices his opposition against all ideological compromise with the corrupt world embodied by the Frankfurt establishment. Commercializing his invention by sharing it with the "most influential members" among the Senators would, for all moral purposes, rank Faust as one of them. As Faust puts it, "cette fortune, cette gloire, à laquelle je veux atteindre, me doit arriver pure et sans reproche. Si les hommes de talent se pliaient moins d'ordinaire à une si honteuse conduite, les hommes puissants ne les mettraient pas dans la nécessité de l'employer" (*Faust*, 359).

The apparition of the Frankfurt *bourgmestre* puts the two economic systems in direct confrontation. Symbolically, here the father figure appears face to face with the son to explain him that his invention is none other than "un enfantillage": it will, he claims, merely obtain by the use of a machine what has always been done by scribes; it will ruin the copyists' guild; and, above all, it will make it more difficult, for powerful people like the *bourgmestre* himself, to ... silence his interlocutors once they have become learned and educated. (This argument, of course, contradicts his first one). In conclusion, his philosophy is simple: "Laissons le monde comme il est, mon bon ami [...] ": such is the highest and most urgent of his preoccupations (*Faust*, 361).

The clear ideological contrast is illustrated by the burgomaster in his eulogy of a "useful" invention as an alternative to Faust's "whimsical" one. The invention in question is a telling one: gunpowder. The burgomaster's argument is that guns and gunpowder have an essential function in the world of the political establishment, whereas printing does not. The phallic symbology evoked by firearms is completely consistent with the paradigms set up by Nerval in his contrasting the son's and the father's worlds. Accordingly, Faust so much agrees on the reality of the moral incompatibility between the two inventions that he declares that he would rather "kill himself" than heed the advice and join, by a deadly invention, the destructive world of the fathers.[5]

The subsequent passage reinforces the identification between burgomaster and father figure. In advising Faust to come to grips with "le solide, le positif", the burgomaster mentions an important question being debated in the City council: " [...] c'est [...] de savoir qui doit passer le premier du Doyen, ou du président: ceci est d'un intérêt général. Voyez, faites des recherches historiques, composez là-dessus quelques mémoires, et venez me trouver [...] " (*Faust*, 363). As Freud indicated in *The Family Romance of the Neurotics*, the child's fantasizing (i.e., in his own way, "researching") about the true identity of the father is a common phenomenon: "His sense that his own affection is not being fully reciprocated then finds a vent in the idea [...] of being a step-child or an adopted child" (Freud *GW* VII, 230; *SE* IX, 238).

Gérard changed his last name to make it symbolically correspond to his mother's; we also know that toward the end of his life he wrote letters to his friends speculating about his own descent from various Roman and German emperors. As Sébillotte put it,

> [...] s'appeler "Nerval" c'était revendiquer exclusivement ses origines maternelles, les seules acceptables, et dénier au Dr. Labrunie une paternité dont il ne voulait rien recevoir. Cependant, comme il lui était impossible de supprimer ce père [...], il est amené par un besoin de compensation à anoblir aussi la ligne paternelle. Il place donc à la base de l'arbre paternel les cimiers éclatants des trois seigneurs Labrunie ou Brunyer de la Brunie, chevaliers d'Othon, empereur d'Allemagne [...]
> On retrouve là l'ébauche du mythe de la seconde naissance qui se serait peut-être développé si Nerval n'avait été aussi fortement attaché à la mère qui lui manquait.
>
> (Sébillotte 1948, 251)

In the *Faust* fragment, Gérard's refusal of identification *with* the father is posited in the most evident terms by his insisting on the theme of the identification *of* the father. In the fragment we find these preoccupations disguised under a thin varnish, when the burgomaster condescendingly defends "les recherches historiques" as that which is most proper, sound and desirable in the intellectual world of the fathers, and thus most befitting for a youth who claims to have absorbed their values and intends to find *his* place—in *their* world.

Predictably, Gérard's Faust rejects with disdain the proposal: the suggested inquiry into the respective rights of the Dean *vs.* the President of the Senate is viewed by him as a laughable enterprise implying complicity with what appears to him, essentially, as corruptness and cowardice. For him, both candidates are morally insignificant; neither of them can be his true spiritual "father".

*

Until the point discussed so far, Nerval's text is an adaptation—and a radical reworking—of the idea of Faust as a printer originally introduced into literature by Klinger's *Faust* of 1791. However, after the end of the father-son dialogue, Nerval's fragment resolutely enters the gravitational field of Goethe's model.

Feeling rejected by the world, Gérard's Faust despairs and envisions committing suicide by swallowing the contents of a "fiole empoisonnée". As in Goethe, the cup that is to give death is here inherited from the fathers: "Cette coupe est l'unique reste de ce que m'avaient laissé mes pères [...] " (*Faust*, 363-64). In the two contexts, however, the detail acquires entirely different meanings. In Goethe the inheritance is a mass of knowledge which Faust has re-elaborated and re-created, fashioning it after his own needs. Goethe's Faust *has* used his fathers' tools—if only to discover that they cannot wrest the ultimate secrets of Nature from the sealed books of the Universe. He *has* read and studied the inherited texts, if only to find out "[t]hat men have always suffered everywhere, / Though now and then some man lived happily" (Goethe 1971, vv. 661-75; Kaufmann, 115). His impatience comes at the end of a lifelong usage of precisely that intellectual and scientific inheritance; it is by no means identical with the a priori rejection of tradition operated by Nerval's young hero. When Goethe's Faust makes his regretful statement: "What from your fathers you received as heir, / Acquire if you would possess it. / What is not used is but a load to bear; / But if today creates it, we can use and bless it" (Goethe, vv. 682-85; Kaufmann, 115), he is taking a dialectical stand which leaves the door open for a personal re-elaboration of the inherited tradition, scientific or otherwise.

Even more importantly with respect to the relationship between the hero and the world of the fathers, while despair for Goethe's aging Faust is brought about by the rejection inflicted by the Spirit of the Earth ("Peer of the spirit that you comprehend, / Not mine!"—vv. 512-13), i.e. by an eminently super-human entity, the humiliating rebuttal that conjures up thoughts of suicide in Nerval's young inventor has come directly from the only too human world of the fathers—in fact, from the main father-figure itself. We thus see here how the substitution of a "Klingerian" protagonist for the main character radically alters the meaning of further passages in the text even when, at surface level, they more or less literally draw upon Goethe.

The essential point is that for Nerval's Faust (as opposed to Goethe's) the choice of intellectual integrity has implied a radical break with the world of the fathers and caused a progressive impoverishment. The same symbolism operates when we learn that the young hero has had to sell all his cherished books in order to support his own scientific enterprise. This is a way of stating that the practical world of economic efficiency swallows up and surreptitiously appropriates the resources of the young, selfless inventor(s) who illustrate the nobility of the son-figure.[6]

When the attraction of the world and the thought of Marguerite's love persuade Nerval's destitute Faust not to commit suicide after all—that is the moment for the devil to appear. The paraphrases from Goethe now become numerous and extended; the difference in emphasis lies in the fact that the theme of poverty acts here as a major extenuating circumstance. Nerval's Faust needs an ally, if he is to pursue his struggle against the injustice he suffers in the world of the fathers.

No textual similarity can obscure the fact that both in Klinger's and in Goethe's texts the *contract* signed between Faust and the devil is in actual fact *a bet* (specifically: in Klinger, a bet for or against the hypothesis of the intrinsic goodness of mankind; in Goethe, for or against the possibility of Faust ever finding fulfillment in a fixed form of desire). *No such bet exists* in Nerval's fragment—nor could it, since the contract is completely transformed: Faust is here deeply repelled by the demonic, and, unlike his Goethean counterpart, has by no means exhausted the possibilities of "moral" thought. He does, however, need tactical support; and no one in the world is ready to give him credit, except for Mephistopheles. Nerval's Faust resorts to Mephistopheles only as a last resource, for lack of a better guarantor.

For Gérard the devil, and the devil's gold, are deprived of all metaphysical function: we are very far from the "part of that force which would / Do evil evermore, and yet creates the good" of Goethe's *Faust*. One single omission is here more decisive in one direction than many lines of paraphrase in the opposite one. To Goethe's whole complex page of metaphysical definition of the devil as a cosmic force, there correspond in Nerval the dry, matter-of-fact lines: "Quel est votre nom?" — "Méphistophélès" (*Faust*, 366). This happens hardly because Nerval could think of nothing more original. Simply, in his imaginary universe the rebellious son, having been deprived of his due in the fathers' world, needs no more than mere money in order to survive and to marry his Marguerite. Here the son already holds the moral truth; his devil is only the incarnation of a bag of gold. Goethe's and Klinger's Fausts would have been horrified at this prospect—because their starting points were radically different.

But at this point in the plot, in an unexpected development, the alliance between Faust and the devil of riches is suddenly questioned. To his horror, Faust discovers that there is an intimate intertwining of interests between the devil and the abhorred world of political and economic power:

> *Méphistophélès*: Ne va pas t'effrayer encore; remercie plutôt notre roi [Lucifer] de l'honneur qu'il daigne te faire, et moi-même d'avoir accepté l'ambassade; car un démon tel que moi, un ministre infernal, ne devrait être adressé qu'à des princes ou à des ministres de la terre.
> *Faust*: Et si vous les avez tous gagnés, et que je sois encore le plus distingué de ce qui vous reste à séduire dans ce monde.
>
> (*Faust*, 366)

This exchange—which *does not appear* in Goethe (and whose contrast value is therefore all the more evident)—clearly shows what the devil's main defect is in Nerval's view: he turns out to be a good friend and ally of the powerful people of the Earth, the same ones whose political establishment Faust purported to struggle against. The devil is here, then, the partner of murky deals with the fathers, with whom Faust wanted to avoid all compromise.

When, immediately afterwards, the devil embarks upon an explanation of why his appearance is modern and bourgeois, lacking the traditional medieval attributes, Nerval's procedure in paraphrasing Goethe is again revealing. Nerval takes here a passage from "Witch's kitchen" and expands it to include the two following notions, absent from Goethe's text: "Mais ne t'étonne pas que je t'apparaisse *si bourgeoisement* [...] [Les diables] sont venus à se déguiser si bien que *la société en est remplie* sans s'en douter [...] " (*Faust*, 367; Goethe 1971, vv. 2495-2501; emphasis added). What in Goethe functions as a justification for Mephisto's bourgeois dress is in Nerval reformulated in such a way as to foreground precisely the obverse: the demonism of bourgeois society. Whereas the first perspective is just slightly less than comical, the latter is definitely sinister. Nerval's view implies the notion that money, whether it comes from sharing a genial invention with greedy exploiters, or whether it is assured by a pact with the devil, always originates in the pool of corruption, the "moral Hell", which is the world of the fathers.

This is the reason why in Nerval the devil can have such a highly suspect role. Far from being an ally (or an at least potentially constructive force, as in Goethe), the devil is for Nerval a friend of the fathers and an enemy of the liberation of mankind—both ontogenetically and philogenetically. Such is the deep-rooted justification for Gérard's abhorrence toward the devil, for his describing "l'alliance de l'Enfer" as "le plus horrible de tous les sacrifices qu'un mortel puisse faire" (Nerval 1967, V, 368). How is it possible, Gérard implicitly asks, to revolt against the fathers, if one is to do so by resorting to the alliance with a *double* of the hated figure?

According to the psychoanalytical categories established by Jones in *On the Nightmare*, it could be said that in moving from Goethe's *Faust* to Nerval's Faust-fragment we shift from an at least partial identification "Devil = Son who defies the Father" to an absolute identity "Devil = Father toward whom is felt hostility" (Jones 1951, 166, 173). Nerval's situation closely corresponds to the one described by Jones of "paternal arbitrariness, savage cruelty, unjustness, petty tyranny and general unreasonableness that disfigured the Yahweh of the Old Testament [...] inherited to the full by the Christian devil" (Jones 1951, 173-74). Money, devil and father are for Nerval symbolic equivalents. As a consequence, the pact with the devil can be assumed only in the most extreme circumstances, out of despair, when all—including Marguerite—is lost already. Nerval's Faust only gives in to signing the pact when he realizes that the deprecated "fortune injuste", "injustice du Ciel", "ingratitude des hommes" condemn him to being a slave in the world of the fathers regardless of what he does.[7] His pact is signed begrudgingly, both morally and existentially: such is the radical novelty introduced by Nerval in the demonic text thanks to a subtle game of mixed, modified, and transposed quotes.[8]

At this point in the Faust-fragment, one may legitimately wonder as to the possible presence and function within the Nervalian universe of that other opportunity which the devil traditionally offers to man as a barter for his soul: namely, the chance to womanize at will. As Mephistopheles suggests to Faust just after the pact scene and shortly before the text breaks off: "je puis te donner à choisir entre Hélène, Cléopatre, Aspasie, et toutes les beautés les plus renommées de l'Antiquité" (*Faust*, 370). But logic functions in the inventor's mind better than it does in the tempter's: if he has accepted the devil's help, he has done so only in order to obtain, by supernatural intervention, the access to sexuality which he was denied by the castrating world of the fathers. He already knows Marguerite, who, by being "his own", renders it dispensable to have recourse to the ghosts / women provided by the devil. And, if the devil is the deceiving, treacherous ally who merely doubles the father figure in an only apparent diversification, it must follow that the phantoms whom it can materialize also are but further hypostases of one and the same abhorred paternal principle. Here, Nerval's argument is that sexuality must be asserted *against* the father, if it is to have any value at all.

In Nerval the male world of the father-devil can produce no feminine emanation; Faust must resort to an alternative protective entity. This is the reason why the first exchange between Faust and Méphistophélès after the stipulation of the pact takes a deceivingly anticlimactic form: "*Méphistophélès*: [...] Par où commençons-nous? Je suis à tes ordres". — "*Faust*: Allons voir Marguerite!" (*Faust*, 370). Jones aptly describes the psychoanalytical meaning of our hero's impulsive response:

> The most powerful refuge of the threatened human being [...] was to call on the Virgin Mary for help. Indeed, so universal was this that the whole matter largely resolved itself into a standing fight between the devil and the Holy Mother [...]

It is surely impossible to overlook the analogy between this situation and that of the child running to his mother for protection against an ill-tempered father, with the consequent marital bickering.

(Jones 1951, 176-77)

*

The second act of the fragment does not go beyond a mere half page in print, and it is impossible to speculate on what would have been the protective role of the Eternal Feminine in the struggle (not unlike the one to be found in *Aurélia*) which opposes Nerval's hero to the father-devil figure. All we can say is that no feminine figures appear in the fragment, and that only *L'imagier de Harlem*, whatever its formal shortcomings, will adequately develop Nerval's theme of predilection—the salvation from the evil principle operated by and through femininity. In Gérard's Faust-fragment the reader is left suspended in a somber atmosphere in which the protagonist's desires are castrated, wherever he turns, by a series of interchangeable, threatening entities: money, a mechanized and corrupt world, the fathers—the devil.

Biographically, such an extended, multiple psychological equation had the well-known parallel feature: Gérard's radical, self-destructive incapability of dealing with money.[9] A self-punishing impulse also predominated in Gérard's attitude toward his artistic possessions: he made it a habit of treating with absolute carelessness all he owned—be it in terms of energy, productive interests, or manuscripts. Many of his works, which were at various stages of development, have thus been lost, distributed among friends and acquaintances who could not, or did not want to, ensure their preservation (Nerval 1967, V, v-vi).

Short of being able to kill the father figure (and as a punishment for the subconscious desire to do so), the son turns against himself. The symbolic suicide perceivable in Gerard's attitude toward his own production is thus obvious: Gérard must have somehow felt that even admitting literary ownership was but a way to legitimize the principle of paternity. It is hardly surprising, then, that his text on Faust is very concretely and physically a "fragment"—i.e., it consists of a few pages torn out of a larger notebook, which as a whole is now lost (Marie 1955, 229). In an effort to distance himself from the father figure, Nerval strove as much as possible to create "orphan" texts. Accordingly, he compulsively proceeded to disperse his "patri"-mony—financial, vital, *and* artistic.

Théophile Gautier, who was a good friend of Gérard's, wrote that

> [...] l'argent était son moindre souci. Jamais l'amour de l'or, qui cause aujourd'hui tant de fièvres malsaines, ne troubla cette âme pure et vraiment antique. La richesse lui semblait un embarras, et, comme Diogène voyant un jeune berger puiser de l'eau dans sa main, il eût volontiers rejeté sa coupe inutile [...]
> [L]es louis lui causaient une sorte de malaise et semblaient lui brûler les mains; il ne redevenait tranquille qu'à la dernière pièce de cinq francs.
> (Richer ed. 1970, 23-24)

Feeling relieved only when one's money reaches below the five-franc level: this graphically describes Nerval's attitude toward money, and in general toward the world of the devil-father in which money circulates. For Gérard de Nerval, *owning* is something that only "fathers" would do.

*

The Faust-fragment presents us on the textual plane with a peculiar *mise en abyme* of Nerval's symbolic choice of bankruptcy: the text chooses the suicidal strategy of mixing and rewording Klinger and Goethe, up to the extreme point where the game of reaccentuation—a true gambling with the text, an artistic equivalent of his models' great *bets* against the devil—becomes no longer tenable. How could one write a story of a barter with the devil, if the devil has himself become an absolute enemy, the embodiment of the very principle against which the hero has set out to struggle? Faust's silence is here steeped in an ambiguous twilight, in a mirror game of repetitions and subtractions.

On the whole, however, the most striking feature of Nerval's fragment consists perhaps in the highly ironic fact that this "rebellious" text, a text of suicidal revolt against the father-devil's money, is construed by using almost exclusively *texts of the fathers* as building blocks. As Goethe's Faust had proposed in his monologue: "What from your fathers you received as heir, / Acquire if you would possess it [...] " (vv. 682-85, quoted). Nerval takes him at his word; and indeed, the books of tradition are here eagerly set to work. The dialectical process denied *by* Gérard's *Faust* is nonetheless tacitly activated *in* it. In yet another example of Nerval's "demonic" intertextuality, Klinger and Goethe are here—to use the economic metaphors most appropriate for the context—borrowed, plundered by Nerval for his own purposes. The fragment's most fascinating feature consists precisely in having been able to turn the models' words against themselves, as the son turns against his fathers. Paradox of the text: Gérard's Faust fears to be corrupted, "castrated" by contamination with the fathers' gold; and he disappears, he commits symbolic suicide *with* and *in* their words. Such is the ironic nemesis of a text in which words and gold, the tokens of meaning and the tokens of value, are exchanged and confused with each other.

The circle is thus closed. The dialectic of poverty appears in Nerval as a conflict between self-spoliation and compromise with a demonico-paternal world; it appears as a struggle between the self-punishment of poverty and the castrating affluence of corruption. In opposite ways, both rebellion against *and* acceptance of the identification with the fathers prove to be destructive for the self. Whether Nerval was meditating consciously along those lines while translating Goethe's ballad: "Poverty is the greatest plague, / Riches are the supreme good", must remain open to speculation.

*

Part 1, Ch. 11 of *The Idiot* contains Ganya's famous outburst of "scoundrel pride" addressed to Prince Myshkin:

> You're telling me that I'm an unoriginal person. Please take note, dear Prince, that there is nothing more insulting to the human beings of our own time and generation than telling them that they are not original, weak in

character, without special talents, and common persons. You didn't even deign to consider me a *proper scoundrel* [...]

That has infuriated me for a while now; and I want money. Once I've gotten money, mark my words, I will be a *supremely original person*. Money is all the more filthy and repulsive, because it even gives people *talents*—and it will do so until the end of the world.

(Dostoevsky 1960, 153-54; emphasis added)[10]

In different ways, Dostoevsky's Ganya and Balzac's Raphaël de Valentin both "rebel"; but they do not rebel in order to change the structure of power. They rebel in order to assert their right to repeat the same. *Ôte-toi de là que je m'y mette.*

Raphaël's identification with the father role is clearly expressed in his acceptance and approval of the social prestige of money. His dilemma is simply one of procuring enough coins to start his own game, and never one of ascertaining how (or whether in the first place) the fathers' world, the world of money-making, can be assumed without *ipso facto* forfeiting one's soul to the "demonic". Gavrila Ardalionovich Ivolgin, for his part, at least has a lucidity adequate to his ambitions: he knows that there always is a pact with the devil within reach—and with brave pride proceeds to envisage his own as a lesser humiliation than the misery he was born into.

The alternative stands under everyone's eyes: the poverty of *the Nervalian idiot*. Nerval's son-figures refuse to identify with the father-role: there is no possibility of a compromise between their *beautiful souls* and the world of money which the fathers inhabit. By all worldly standards, they are what Dostoevsky's Makar Devushkin calls "whimsical".

And Raphaël and Ganya are, by all worldly standards, sensible men.

Notes to the Appendix

[1] Nerval translated "The treasure-digger" in his *Poésies allemandes* of 1830 (cf. Dubruck 1965, 97).

[2] Nerval was a pseudonym connected—not only in actual fact, but above all in Gérard's fantasy—with his mother's side of the family. "Nerval" is an anagram of the mother's last name. Cf. Richer 1967, vii.

[3] All in Nerval 1965, III.

[4] The idea that Faust was the inventor of printing is a popular misconception with no historical foundation. Klinger, however, took it up from legend for his own purposes, and Nerval followed Klinger on his point. Cf. Smeed 1975, Ch. 4: "Faust and Fust". There was an obvious political affinity between Klinger and Nerval amply justifying the borrowing.

[5] As Mauron puts it in his *Des métaphores obsédantes au mythe personnel: Introduction à la psychocritique*, "En contraste avec la richesse [des] images féminines, on remarquera [chez Nerval] la pauvreté et la stéréotypie du groupe masculin. Dans l'œuvre romanesque et poétique, il se dessine à peu près ainsi: Nord [...] — [...] diable [...] — empereur — prince — duc — [...] — [...] armes [...] objets phalliques — argent [...]. Mis à part le grand-oncle maternel et ses avatars, rares images d'une instance protectrice, presque toutes ces figures sont chargées d'hostilité. Leur source biographique est, sans conteste, le docteur Labrunie [...]

[L]a structure inconsciente impose la double image de persécution: mauvais père (ou frère ennemi) et fils révolté—surmoi punisseur et pulsion rebelle—Jéhova et Antéros. Les mécanismes sont représentés de façon presque schématique. L'agressivité, aussi violente que refoulée, est enfin retournée contre le moi en auto-accusation mélancolique" (p. 153).

In Nerval's *Faust* we have the rebellious son, the threatening father, and also the principle of a merciless auto-accusation.

[6] Significantly, in *L'imagier de Harlem* such lost books will surface again in the private library of Count de Bloksberg, an incarnation of the devil—who there plays the role of an "evil father", enemy of the son.

[7] The accusations which fatalism levels at destiny are also, at bottom, but a projection on the cosmic plane of an unconscious protest against paternal authority. "Even Fate is, in the last resort, only a later projection of the father" (Freud *GW* XIV, 409; *SE* XXI, 185).

[8] The same feature of a pact imposed rather than chosen returns in an even more extreme form in *L'imagier de Harlem* and doubtless constitutes one of its remarkable traits.

[9] For a few episodes, cf. Marie 1955, 135, and Richer 1970, 39, 296, 301. Baudelaire's life also had similar traits: squandering indeed seems to be a strategy for the acquisition of peculiarly Romantic *lettres de noblesse*—the poet's answer to a castrating "commonsense" and to what Bataille brilliantly calls "la splendeur sans condition des choses matérielles" (Bataille 1967, 45).

10"Vy mne govorite, chto ya chelovek ne original'ny. Zamet'te sebe, mily knyaz', chto net nichego obidnee cheloveku nashego vremeni i plemeni, kak skazat' emu, chto on ne originalen, slab kharakterom, bez osobennykh talantov i chelovek obyknovenny. Vy menya dazhe *khoroshim podletsom* ne udostoili schest' [...]

Eto, batyushka, menya davno uzhe besit, i ya deneg khochu. Nazhiv den'gi, znayte, ya budu *chelovek v vysshey stepeni original'ny*. Den'gi tem vsego podlee i nenavistnee, chto oni dazhe *talanty* dayut. I budut davat' do skonchaniya mira". Emphasis added.

Works Cited

Primary Sources

Alighieri, Dante. 1965. *La Divina Commedia*, ed. F. Chiappelli. Milano: Mursia.
Balzac, Honoré de. 1950. *Melmoth réconcilié. La Comédie humaine*, ed. M. Bouteron, vol. 9. Paris: Gallimard Pléiade.
----------. 1951. *Gobseck; Le père Goriot. La Comédie humaine*, ed. M. Bouteron, vol. 2. Paris: Gallimard Pléiade.
----------. 1966. *Illusions perdues*, ed. P. Citron. Paris: Garnier Flammarion.
----------. 1968. *Splendeurs et misères des courtisanes*, ed. P. Citron. Paris: Garnier Flammarion.
----------. 1979. *La peau de chagrin. La Comédie humaine*, ed. P. Citron, vol. 10. Paris: Gallimard Pléiade.
Baudelaire, Charles. 1961. *Œuvres complètes*, ed. Y.-G. Le Dantec, C. Pichois. Paris: Gallimard Pléiade.
Broch, Hermann. 1976 (1945). *Der Tod des Vergil*. Frankfurt a. M.: Suhrkamp.
----------. 1945. *The Death of Virgil*, transl. J. S. Untermeyer. New York: Pantheon.
Bulgakov, Mikhail Afanas'evich. 1969 (1966). *Master i Margarita*. Frankfurt a. M.: Posev.
----------. 1967. *The Master and Margarita*, transl. M. Ginsburg. New York: Grove.
Byron, George G. N. 1901. *The Works of Lord Byron: Poetry*, ed. E. H. Coleridge. New York: Scribner, vol. 5.
Dostoevsky, Fedor Mikhailovich. 1926-1930. *Polnoe sobranie khudozhestvennykh proizvedeniy*. Moskva, Leningrad: Gosudarstvennoe izdatel'stvo, vols. 7, 9, 10.
----------. 1960. *Idiot*. Moskva: Gosudarstvennoe izdatel'stvo khudozhestvennoy literatury.

----------. N.d. "Bednye lyudi" ("Poor Folk"), *Povesti i rasskazy*. Paris: YMCA, vol. 2, 1-136.
Dürrenmatt, Friedrich. 1962. *Die Physiker: Eine Komödie in zwei Akten*. Zürich: Die Arche.
Espronceda, José de. 1982. *El estudiante de Salamanca. El diablo mundo* (1840). Ed. R. Marrast. Madrid: Castalia.
Flaubert, Gustave. 1964. *Œuvres complètes*. Paris: Seuil Intégrale, vol. 1.
----------. 1965. *L'Éducation sentimentale*, ed. S. de Sacy. Paris: Gallimard folio.
----------. 1967. *La Tentation de Saint Antoine*. Paris: Garnier Flammarion.
----------. 1980. *Correspondance*, ed. J. Bruneau. Paris: Gallimard Pléiade, 2 vols.
----------. 1982. "The Legend of Saint Julian the Hospitable," *Saint / Oedipus: Psychocritical Approaches to Flaubert's Art*, ed. W. J. Berg, M. Grimaud, G. Moskos. Ithaca: Cornell U Press.
Gautier de Coinci. 1955. "Comment Theophilus vint a penitance," *Les miracles de Nostre Dame*, ed. V. F. Koenig. Genève: Droz; Lille: Giard, vol. 1.
Goethe, Johann Wolfgang von. 1961. *Faust*, transl. W. Kaufmann. Garden City, N.Y.: Doubleday.
----------. 1969 (1840). *Faust, Tragédie de Goethe*, transl., ed. Gérard de Nerval. Paris: Garnier.
----------. 1965. *Poetische Werke*. Berlin: Aufbau, vol. 1.
----------. 1971. *Faust I, II*, ed. L. J. Scheithauer. Stuttgart: Reclam.
Gogol', Nikolay Vasilevich. 1969. *Mertvye dushi: Poema* (*Dead Souls*). Moskva: Detskaya literatura.
----------. 1973. *Sochinenii v dvukh tomakh*, ed. N. Stepanov. Moskva: Khudozhestvennaya literatura, vol. 1.
----------. 1985. *The Complete Tales of Nikolai Gogol*, ed. L. Kent. Chicago: U of Chicago Press, 2 vols.
Griboedov, Aleksandr Sergeevich. 1967. "Gore ot uma" ("The Disgrace of Being Intelligent"), *Sochineniya v stikhakh*, ed. I. N. Medvedeva. Leningrad: Sovetskiy pisatel', 63-172.
"Historia vnd Geschicht Doctor Johannis Faustj des Zauberers / Darjnn gantz Aigentlich vnd warhafftig beschriben wirt. sein gantzes Leben vnnd Endt / [. . .] . - Das Faustbuch nach der Wolfenbüttler Handschrift," 1963, ed. H. G. Haile, *Philologische Studien und Quellen*. Berlin: Schmidt, No. 14.
"Historia von D. Johañ Fausten, dem weitbeschreyten Zauberer unnd Schwartzkünstler [. . .] ," 1981 (1587), ed. R. Noll-Wiemann, *Deutsche Volksbücher in Faksimiledrücken*. Hildesheim: Olms, ser. A, No. 13.
Hofmannsthal, Hugo von. 1951. "Ein Brief," *Gesammelte Werke in Einzelausgaben*, ed. H. Steiner. Frankfurt a. M.: Fischer, vol. 6, 7-22.
Kleist, Heinrich von. 1987. *Sämtliche Werke und Briefe*. München: Deutscher Taschenbuch Verlag, vol. 1.
Klinger, Friedrich Maximilian. 1964 (1791). *Fausts Leben, Taten und Höllenfahrt*. Frankfurt a. M.: Insel.
Leopardi, Giacomo. 1956. *Opere*, ed. S. Solmi. Milano: Ricciardi, vol. 1.
----------. 1982. *Operette Morali: Essays and Dialogues*, ed. G. Cecchetti. Berkeley: U C Press.
Mann, Thomas. 1971 (1947). *Doktor Faustus: Das Leben des deutschen Tonsetzers Adrian Leverkühn erzählt von einem Freunde*. Frankfurt a. M.: Fischer.

Montaigne, Michel de. 1962. *Œuvres complètes,* ed. A. Thibaudet, M. Rat. Paris: Gallimard Pléiade.
Musset, Alfred de. 1968. *La Confession d'un enfant du siècle.* Paris: Garnier.
Nerval, Gérard de. 1966. *Œuvres,* ed. H. Lemaitre. Paris: Garnier, vol. 1.
----------. 1965-1967. *Œuvres complémentaires de Gérard de Nerval,* ed. J. Richer. Paris: Lettres Modernes Minard, vols. 3, 5.
Nietzsche, Friedrich. 1980. *Morgenröte: Gedanken über die moralischen Vorurteile.* München: Goldmann Klassiker.
----------. 1981. *Menschliches, Allzumenschliches: Ein Buch für freie Geister.* München: Goldmann Klassiker.
Novalis. 1981. *Werke.* München: Beck.
Pauli, Johannes. 1866. "Schimpf und Ernst," *Bibliothek des literarischen Vereins,* ed. H. Österley. Stuttgart: Literarischer Verein, No. 85.
Pushkin, Aleksandr Sergeevich. 1974. *Sochineniya v trekh tomakh.* Moskva: Khudozhestvennaya literatura, vols. 1, 3.
Rimbaud, Arthur. 1960. *Œuvres.* Paris: Garnier.
Rutebeuf. 1885. "Le miracle de Théophile," *Rustebuef's Gedichte,* ed. A. Kreßner. Wolfenbüttel: Zwissler.
Soulié, Frédéric. 1843. *Les Mémoires du diable.* Paris: Gosselin, vols. 1, 2.
"Ulenspegel." 1952. Ed. W. Krogmann. *Verein für niederdeutsche Sprachforschung.* Neumünster: Wachholtz, No. 11.
Vigny, Alfred de. 1968. *Chatterton.* Paris: Garnier Flammarion.
Voynovich, Vladimir. 1976. *Ivan'kiada: Ili rasskaz o vselenii pisatelya Voynovicha v novuyu kvartiru* [. . .]. Ann Arbor, Mich.: Ardis.

Secondary Sources

Abrams, Meyer Howard. 1971. *Natural Supernaturalism: Tradition and Revolution in Romantic Literature.* New York: Norton.
Adorno, Theodor W. 1974. "Zur Schlußszene des *Faust,*" *Gesammelte Schriften.* Frankfurt a. M.: Suhrkamp, vol. 2, 129-138.
Affron, Charles. 1966. "Patterns of Failure in *La Comédie humaine,*" *Yale Romanic Studies II.* New Haven: Yale U Press, No. 15.
Arnheim, Rudolf. 1971. *Entropy and Art: An Essay on Disorder and Order.* Berkeley: U C Press.
Bakhtin, Mikhail Mikhailovich. 1981. *The Dialogic Imagination.* Austin: U of Texas Press.
Baldensperger, Fernand. 1904. *Goethe en France.* Paris: Hachette.
Barbéris, Pierre. 1970. *Balzac et le mal du siècle: Contributions à une physiologie du monde moderne.* Paris: Gallimard, 2 vols.
Bardèche, Maurice. 1974. *L'œuvre de Flaubert.* Paris: Sept Couleurs.
Barratt, Andrew. 1987. *Between Two Worlds: A Critical Introduction To* The Master and Margarita. Oxford: Clarendon.
Bataille, Georges. 1967. *La notion de dépense* (1933). *La part maudite.* Paris: Editions de Minuit Points.

Bem, Jeanne. 1979. *Désir et savoir dans l'œuvre de Flaubert: Etude de* La Tentation de Saint Antoine. Neuchâtel: La Baconnière.

----------. 1979b. "La fonction des bêtes dans *La Tentation de Saint Antoine*," *Le bestiaire dans la littérature française, Cahiers de l'association internationale des études françaises* 31 (May), 35-44.

Bersani, Leo. 1970. *Balzac To Beckett: Center and Circumference in French Fiction*. New York: Oxford U Press.

Blanchot, Maurice. 1959. *Le livre à venir*. Paris: Gallimard.

Bonwit, Marianne. 1946. "Flaubert et l'impassibilité," diss. U C Berkeley.

Brombert, Victor. 1966. *The Novels of Flaubert: A Study of Themes and Techniques*. Princeton: Princeton U Press.

----------. 1975. *La prison romantique: Essai sur l'imaginaire*. Paris: Corti.

Buck, Stratton. 1966. "Gustave Flaubert," *Twayne World Author Series*. New York: Twayne, No. 3.

Butler, Eliza Marian. 1952. *The Fortunes of Faust*. Cambridge: Cambridge U Press.

Butler, Ronnie. 1983. *Balzac and the French Revolution*. Totowa, N.J.: Barnes and Noble.

Butor, Michel. 1974. "La spirale des sept péchés," *Répertoire IV*. Paris: Editions de Minuit, 209-235.

Danger, Pierre. 1979. "Sainteté et castration dans *La Tentation de Saint Antoine*," *Essais sur Flaubert*, ed. C. Carlut. Paris: Nizet, 185-202.

----------. 1982. "La castration dans *La peau de chagrin*," *L'année balzacienne* Nouvelle Série 3, 227-246.

Dédéyan, Charles. 1954-1967. *Le thème de Faust dans la littérature européenne*. Paris: Lettres Modernes, 4 vols.

DiAmico, Eliseo Frank. 1979. "The Diabolical Pact in Literature," diss. U of Michigan.

Dubruck, Alfred. 1965. "Gérard de Nerval and the German Heritage," *Studies in French Literature*. The Hague: Mouton, No. 4.

Feynman, Richard Phillips, R. B. Leighton and M. Sands. 1963. *The Feynman Lectures on Physics*. Reading, Mass.: Addison-Wesley.

Fieseler, Margret. 1982. "Stilistische und motivische Untersuchungen zu Michail Bulgakovs Romanen *Belaja gvardija* und *Master i Margarita*," *Slavistische Texte und Studien*. Hildesheim: Olms, No. 3.

Foucault, Michel. 1967. "Un 'fantastique' de bibliothèque," *Cahiers de la compagnie Madeleine Renaud—Jean-Louis Barrault* 59 (March), 6-31.

Freud, Sigmund. 1940-1952. *Gesammelte Werke*. London: Imago, 18 vols.

----------. 1953-1965. *Standard Edition of the Complete Psychological Works of S. F.*, transl., ed. J. Strachey. London: Hogarth Press, 24 vols.

Gasparov, Boris M. 1978. "Iz nabliudeniy nad motivnoy strukturoy romana M. A. Bulgakova *Master i Margarita*," *Slavica Hierosolimitana* 3, 198-251.

Girard, René. 1982. *Le bouc émissaire*. Paris: Grasset Biblio Essais.

Gomila, Jacques. 1978. "Desiderio," transl. from French M. V. Malvano, *Enciclopedia*, ed. R. Romano. Torino: Einaudi, vol. 4, 572-599.

Goux, Jean-Joseph. 1984. *Les monnayeurs du langage*. Paris: Galilée.

Grimm, Jakob. 1876 (1844). *Deutsche Mythologie*. Berlin: Dümmler, vol. 2.

Hempel, Wolfgang. 1970. *"Übermuot diu alte ... "*: *Der Superbia-Gedanke und seine Rolle in der deutschen Literatur des Mittelalters*. Bonn: Bouvier.
Isaac, Bonnie. 1983. "'Tous les refrains sont bons': Balzac and Poetry's Lost Illusions," *Modern Language Notes* 98 (May), 728-744.
Jones, Ernest. 1951 (1931). *On the Nightmare*. New York: Liveright.
----------. 1964. *Essays in Applied Psychoanalysis*. New York: International U Press, vol. 2.
Jung, Carl Gustav. 1976. "Symbols of Transformation," transl. R. F. C. Hull, *Bollingen Series*. Princeton: Princeton U Press, No. 20.
Kayser, Wolfgang Johannes. 1957. *Das Groteske: seine Gestaltung in Malerei und Dichtung*. Oldenburg: Stalling.
----------. 1963. *The Grotesque in Art and Literature*, transl. U. Weisstein. Bloomington: Indiana U Press.
Lacan, Jacques. 1966. *Écrits*. Paris: Seuil.
Lalande, André. 1947 (1926). "Désir," *Vocabulaire technique et critique de la philosophie*. Paris: Presses Universitaires de France, 209.
Laplanche, Jean, and J.-B. Pontalis. 1967. "Désir," *Vocabulaire de la psychanalyse*. Paris: Presses Universitaires de France, 120-122.
Lombard, Alfred. 1934. *Flaubert et Saint Antoine*. Paris: Attinger.
Lukàcs, Georg. 1952 (1935). *"Verlorene Illusionen," Balzac und der französische Realismus*. Berlin: Aufbau, 46-65.
----------. 1950. "Balzac: *Lost Illusions*," *Studies in European Realism*, transl. E. Bone. London: Hillway.
Maksimov, Sergey Vasil'evich. N.d. [1908-1913]. "Nechistaya sila—Nevedomaya sila," *Sobranie sochineniy*. S.-Peterburg: Samoobrazovanie, vol. 18.
Marie, Aristide. 1955 (1914). *Gérard de Nerval: Le poète et l'homme*. Paris: Hachette.
Marx, Karl and F. Engels. 1968. "Geld." "Ökonomisch-philosophische Manuskripte aus dem Jahre 1844," *Werke*. Berlin: Dietz, Ergänzungsband 1.
Mauron, Charles. 1963. *Des métaphores obsédantes au mythe personnel: Introduction à la psychocritique*. Paris: Corti.
Mayer, Hans. 1979. "Höllenfahrt des Doktor Faustus," *Doktor Faust und Don Juan*. Frankfurt a. M.: Suhrkamp, 7-53.
Merezhkovsky, Dmitriy. 1974 (1911). "Gogol and the Devil," *Gogol From the Twentieth Century*, ed. R. A. Maguire. Princeton: Princeton U Press, 55-102.
Milne, Lesley. 1977. "*The Master and Margarita*: A Comedy of Victory," *Birmingham Slavonic Monographs*. Birmingham: Dept. of Russian Language and Literature, U of Birmingham, No. 3.
Milner, Max. 1960. *Le diable dans la littérature française de Cazotte à Baudelaire: 1772-1861*. Paris: Corti, 2 vols.
Moretti, Franco. 1983. *Signs Taken For Wonders: Essays in the Sociology of Literary Forms*. London: Verso Editions—NLB.
Mukarovsky, Jan. 1964. "Standard Language and Poetic Language," *A Prague School Reader on Esthetics, Literary Structure, and Style*, ed. P. L. Garvin. Washington, D.C.: Georgetown U Press, 17-30.
Nadeau, Maurice. 1969. *Gustave Flaubert écrivain*. Paris: Les Lettres Nouvelles.

Pantke, Alfred. 1936. "Gustave Flauberts *Tentation de Saint Antoine*: Ein Vergleich der drei Fassungen," diss. Leipzig.
Proffer, Ellendea. 1984. *Bulgakov: Life and Work*. Ann Arbor: Ardis.
Rancour-Laferrière, Daniel. 1978. "The Identity of Gogol''s *Vij*," *Harvard Ukrainian Studies* 2 (June), 211-234.
Reboussin, Marcel. 1972. *Le drame spirituel de Flaubert*. Paris: Nizet.
Reik, Theodor. 1912. *Flaubert und seine* Versuchung des heiligen Antonius: *Ein Beitrag zur Künstlerpsychologie*. Minden (Westfalen): Bruns.
Richer, Jean. 1967. "Un opéra fabuleux," *Œuvres complémentaires de Gérard de Nerval*, ed. J. R.. Paris: Lettres Modernes Minard, vol. 5, vii-xxx.
----------. 1970 (1963). *Nerval: Expérience et création*. Paris: Hachette.
----------, ed. 1970. "Nerval par les témoins de sa vie," *Nouvelle bibliothèque nervalienne: Etudes et documents*. Paris: Lettres Modernes Minard, No. 2.
Ritter, Joachim. 1971. "Begehren, *appetitus naturalis*," "Begehren, Begierde," *Historisches Wörterbuch der Philosophie*. Basel: Schwabe, vol. 1, 776-780.
Robert, Marthe. 1982. *En haine du roman*. Paris: Balland.
Rodríguez-Hernández, Raúl. 1987. "El imperio del Mal / El Mal del imperialismo: Julio Cortázar y la utopía de la Nueva Nicaragua," *International Conference on the Expressions of Evil in Literature, Philosophy and the Visual Arts*. Atlanta, Ga., 11/8th/1987.
Rudwin, Maximilian. 1931. *The Devil in Legend and Literature*. Chicago: Open Court.
Russell, Jeffrey Burton. 1986. *Mephistopheles: The Devil in the Modern World*. Ithaca: Cornell U Press.
Sartre, Jean-Paul. 1971. *L'Idiot de la famille: Gustave Flaubert de 1821 à 1857*. Paris: Gallimard, vols 1, 2.
Schärf, Riwkah. 1948. "Die Gestalt des Satans im Alten Testament," *Symbolik des Geistes: Studien über psychische Phänomenologie*, ed. C. G. Jung. Zürich: Rascher, 153-319.
Sébillotte, L. H. 1948. *Le secret de Gérard de Nerval*. Paris: Corti.
Séginger, Gisèle. 1984. "Le mysticisme dans *La Tentation de Saint Antoine*: La relation sujet-objet," *Etudes de critique et d'histoire littéraire*. Paris: Archives des Lettres Modernes, No. 215.
Seznec, Jean. 1943. "Saint Antoine et les monstres: Essai sur les sources et la signification du fantastique de Flaubert," *PMLA* 58 (March-September), 195-222.
----------. 1949. "Nouvelles études sur *La Tentation de Saint Antoine*," *Studies of the Warburg Institute*. London: Warburg Institute, U of London, No. 18.
Smeed, John William. 1975. *Faust in Literature*. London: Oxford U Press.
Staël-Holstein, Germaine Necker de. 1968. "Faust," *De l'Allemagne*. Paris: Garnier Flammarion, vol. 1, 343-367.
Stenbock-Fermor, Elisabeth. 1969. "Bulgakov's *The Master and Margarita* and Goethe's *Faust*," *The Slavic and East European Journal* 13 (Fall), 309-325.
Terts, Abram (Siniavsky, Andrey). 1975. *V teni Gogolya*. London: Collins, Overseas Publications Interchange.

Thibaudet, Albert. 1935. *Gustave Flaubert*. Paris: Gallimard.
Tynyanov, Yuriy. 1969 (1921). "Dostoevsky i Gogol': K teorii parodii," *Texte der russischen Formalisten*, ed. J. Striedter. München: Fink, vol. 1, 300-371.
Unwin, Timothy. 1979. "Flaubert's first *Tentation de Saint Antoine*," *Essays in French Literature* 16 (November), 17-42.
Vodichka, Felix. 1964. "The History of the Echo of Literary Works," *A Prague School Reader on Esthetics, Literary Structure, and Style*, ed. P. L. Garvin. Washington, D.C.: Georgetown U Press, 71-81.

Index

to authors and titles

(All titles are listed in alphabetical order under their respective authors' entry; anonymous works appear under the title).

Abrams, 27.
Adorno, 26.
Affron, 72.
Arnheim, 47, 48, 49, 50, 65, 67.
Bakhtin, 29n, 78, 143,144.
Baldensperger, 30n, 77.
Balzac, 4, **31-76**, 121, 122, 131, 149, 152, 161, 162, 163.
    La Comédie humaine, 31, 32, 33, 34, 36, 38, 56, 60, 61, 65, 70, 72.
        Gobseck, 60, 61.
        Illusions perdues, 32, 34, 35, 36, 55, 56, 74n, 122, 137, 158n, 164, 165.
        Lost Illusions, v. *Illusions perdues.*
        Louis Lambert, 68, 164.
        Le lys dans la vallée, 71.
        Melmoth réconcilié, 37.
        La peau de chagrin, 28, 30n, **36-76**, 121, 122, 131, 164, 177.
        Le père Goriot, 33-35, 37, 72.
        La recherche de l'absolu, 33.
        Splendeurs et misères des courtisanes, 36, 69.
Barbéris, 55, 56.
Bardèche, 127n.
Barratt, 159n.
Bataille
    La notion de dépense, 41, 42, 43, 45, 46, 50, 52, 56, 57, 58, 59, 67, 75n, 178n.
    La part maudite, 74n.
Baudelaire, v, 26, 152, 157, 158n, 178n.
Bem, 1, 86, 92, 97, 102, 106, 107, 108, 114, 126n, 127n, 128n.
Bernanos, 131, 132, 133, 134.
Bersani, 66, 74n.
Blanchot, 2.
Bonwit, 109.

Broch, 115, 116, 117.
Brombert, 71, 103, 104, 121, 127n.
Buck, 127n.
Bulgakov, 9, **136-59**.
    The Fantastic Novel (Fantasticheskij roman), 158n.
    The Master and Margarita (Master i Margarita), 4, 28, 71, 122, **136-59**.
    The White Guard (Belaya Gvardiya), 153, 158n.
Butler, E. M., 30n.
Butler, R., 52.
Butor, 126n.
Byron
    Cain, 77, 80, 81, 82, 92, 99, 100, 103, 123, 126n.
Danger, 59, 75n, 88, 127n.
Dante
    Divine Comedy, 36, 53, 164.
Dédéyan, 10, 29n, 30n.
DiAmico, 9, 10, 30n.
Dostoevsky, 131, 132, 134.
    The Brothers Karamazov (Brat'ya Karamazovy), 131, 132.
    The Demons (Besy), 131.
    The Idiot (Idiot), 176, 177.
    Poor Folk (Bednye Lyudi), 74n, 75n, 161, 177.
Dubruck, 178n.
Dürrenmatt, 23.
Espronceda, 135.
Euclid, 92.
Eulenspiegel, 15.
Faustbook, *Faust* chapbook, *v.* Spieß; Wolfenbüttel manuscript.
Feynman, 74n.
Fichte, 129.
Fieseler, 159n.
Flaubert, 4, 73, **77-128**, 130, 131, 149, 155, 156.
    Agonies, 136.
    Correspondance, 79, 121.
    La danse des morts, 124.
    L'Éducation sentimentale, 73, 120.
    La Grande Dame, 89.
    La légende de Saint Julien l'Hospitalier, 80, 127n.
    Madame Bovary, 73, 109, 122, 123, 126n.
    Mémoires d'un fou, 89, 110, 111, 128n.
    Un parfum à sentir, 89.
    Salammbô, 123.
    Smarh, 85, 99, 100, 101, 123, 124, 126n.
    La Tentation de Saint Antoine, 28, 73, **77-128**, 130, 131, 152.
    Voyage en enfer, 99, 124, 156.
Foucault, 128n.
Freud
    Beyond the Pleasure Principle (Jenseits des Lustprinzips), 47, 49, 50, 51, 74n, 118.
    Dostoevsky and Parricide (Dostojewski und die Vatertötung), 74n, 178n.
    The Family Romance of the Neurotics (Der Familienroman der Neurotiker), 168.
    From the History of an Infantile Neurosis (Aus der Geschichte einer infantilen Neurose) ["Wolf-Man" case], 110, 113.
    The Interpretation of Dreams (Die Traumdeutung), 5.
    Psycho-Analytic Notes on an Autobiographical Account of a Case of Paranoia (Psychoanalytische Bemerkungen über einen autobiographisch beschriebenen Fall von Paranoia) [Schreber case], 128n.
    The Theme of the Three Caskets (Das Motiv der Kästchenwahl), 126n.
    The Uncanny (Das Unheimliche), 83, 107.
Friedrich, *v.* Ritter.
Gasparov, 149, 159n.
Gautier, 55, 175.
Gautier de Coinci
    "Comment Theophilus vint a penitance" (*Les miracles de Nostre Dame*), 9, **10-12**, 152.

Girard, 75n, 166.
Goethe, 148.
    Ballads: "The Apprentice Sorcerer" ("Der Zauberlehrling"), 162; "The Treasure-Digger" ("Der Schatzgräber"), 161, 176.
    Faust, 4, 5, 8, 10, **15-28**, 33, 37, 51, 52, 67, 68, 69, 75n, 76n, 77, 79, 99, 100, 103, 104, 105, 106, 124, 125, 127n, 129, 134, 136, 139, 142, 145, 148, 149, 150, 151, 152, 153, 155, 158n, 162, 163, 164, 165, 169, 170, 171, 172, 175, 176.
"Goethezeit", 140.
Gogol, 3, 138, 140, 145, 156, 157.
    Dead Souls (*Mertvye dushi*), 36.
    The Viy (*Viy*), 104, 128n.
Gomila, 29n.
Goncourt, 116, 118.
Goux, 76n, 163.
Griboedov, 143, 158n, 159n.
Grimm, 158n.
Guizot, 55.
Hegel, 129.
Hempel, 30n, 90.
Hölderlin, 117, 136, 148.
Hoffmann, 37.
Hofmannsthal, 109.
Hugo, 52.
    La fin de Satan, 124.
    Notre-Dame de Paris, 29n.
Isaac, 35, 51.
Jeunes-France, 55.
Jones, 5, 81, 82, 93, 94, 98, 107, 113, 126n, 127n, 172, 173, 174.
Jung, 29n.
Kant, 1, 131.
Kayser, 107, 108, 115.
Kleist, 97.
Klinger, 4, 127n, 134, 151, 169, 170, 171, 175, 176, 178n.
Lacan, 2, 29n.
Lalande, 29n.
Laplanche-Pontalis, 29n.
Lenin, 159n.
Leopardi, 158n.
    "Dialogo di Malambruno e Farfarello" (*Operette Morali*), 30n.

Lewis, 29n.
Lombard, 127n.
Lopez, 165.
Lukàcs, 55, 56, 92.
Maksimov, 29n.
Mann, 9, 134.
    Doktor Faustus, 131, 132, 133.
Marie, 175, 178n.
Marx, 20, 46.
Mauron, 178n.
Mayakovsky, 159n.
Mayer, 14, 29n, 30n.
Merezhkovsky, 3, 157.
Méry, 165.
Milne, 159n.
Milner, 31, 69.
Montaigne, 7, 79.
Moore, 71.
Moretti, 32,35.
Mukarovsky, 14, 29n, 78.
Musset, 54.
Nadeau, 87, 116, 127n.
Nerval, 4, 82, 83, 102, 123, 127n, 128n, 131, **161-79**.
    L'alchimiste, 165.
    Aurélia, 164, 174.
    Les Chimères, 164.
    Faustian fragments, 5, 122, 152, **161-79**.
    L'imagier de Harlem, 5, 164, 165, 174, 178n.
    Poésies allemandes, 178n.
    Translations from Goethe, 28, 127n.
Nietzsche, 30n, 45, 83, 91.
Novalis, 117, 129.
Occam, 122.
Pantke, 126n.
Pauli, 15.
Proffer, 149, 154, 158n, 159n.
Pushkin, 131, 137, 140, 158n.
Rabelais, 15, 71, 103.
Rancour-Laferrière, 128n.
Reboussin, 106.
Reik, 91, 103, 105, 108, 119, 127n, 128n.
Richer, 82, 165, 175, 178n.
Rimbaud, 130.

Ritter, 29n.
Robert, 126n, 128n.
Rodríguez-Hernández, 29n.
Rudwin, 10.
Russell, 132, 158n.
Rutebeuf
    Le Miracle de Theophile, 9, 10, **13-14**, 152.
Sand, 29n.
Sartre, 102, 126n.
Schärf, 159n.
Schelling, 129.
Schlegel, 131, 158n.
Schönpflug, *v.* Ritter.
Sébillotte, 168.
Séginger, 127n, 128n.
Sergeevich, 159n.
Seznec, 108, 109, 113.
Shelley, 29n.
Siniavsky, *v.* Terts/Siniavsky.

Smeed, 126n, 178n.
Soulié
    Mémoires du diable, 74n, 100.
Spieß, 4, 9, **14-15**, 32, 64, 83, 103, 127n, 151, 153.
Staël, 79.
Stalin, 137, 154, 158n.
Stenbock-Fermor, 159n.
Stendhal, 30n, 55, 71, 75n, 122.
Terts/Siniavsky, 145.
Theophilus, 4, 152; *v.* also Gautier de Coinci; Rutebeuf.
Thibaudet, 104, 127n.
Tynyanov, 126n.
Unwin, 109, 127n.
Vigny, 166.
Vodichka, 77, 78.
Voynovich, 158n.
Wolfenbüttel manuscript, 98, 99.
Wolfram von Eschenbach, 14.